WORSHIP THE KING!

MESSAGES OF HOPE AND INSPIRATION FROM GOD'S WORD

DAVID RENISON

WESTBOW
PRESS®
A DIVISION OF THOMAS NELSON
& ZONDERVAN

WestBow Press books may be ordered through booksellers or by contacting:

WestBow Press
A Division of Thomas Nelson & Zondervan
1663 Liberty Drive
Bloomington, IN 47403
www.westbowpress.com
844-714-3454

ISBN: 978-1-6642-8801-0 (sc)
ISBN: 978-1-6642-8802-7 (e)

Library of Congress Control Number: 2022923881

Print information available on the last page.

WestBow Press rev. date: 01/17/2023

Dedication

To my parents,
Jerry and Christine Renison
You led me to the Cross of Calvary

Contents

INTRODUCTION

The Christian experience is a journey of faith. What is this way of trusting? It is that we find the world of the unseen more convincing than this one. In the uncertainties of life, there is certainty in what God has promised: "Which hope we have as an anchor of the soul, sure and steadfast… even Jesus" (Heb. 6:13-20). Let us hold fast the profession of our hope without wavering, for He is faithful that promised (Heb. 10:23). He is with us to accomplish His perfect will in our imperfect lives. When trouble comes, our confidence in God never remains the same. It either diminishes or deepens. Why? Because our faith has been challenged. We want to figure things out and understand the reasoning behind everything that happens. But there are so many things we cannot understand. And when we suffer, any intellectual response seems inadequate. In times of difficulty, we need more than logic. We need hope. Jesus Christ is that hope! I understand deep grief. The intense pain of losing my dear wife, Marjorie, cannot be said. But God is healing my broken heart and turning precious memories into treasures more valuable than anything I will ever own. Do not stumble at the mysteries of life where there is no explanation. Instead, find comfort in the knowledge that you are a child of God, living by faith with heaven in view (Rom. 1:17). Jesus taught us to live one day at a time (Matt. 6:11), and if we want peace, we must give up the need to understand. Trusting God in all things is essential to a victorious life in Jesus. Do you want direction or an explanation? Live with a desire to have a deeper, more meaningful walk with the Lord Jesus Christ.

To Whom Shall We Go?

In John's Gospel, we read that many who had been following Jesus did not accept a specific teaching - and they left Him. The Bible says they "went back and walked with Him no more." Jesus then turned to the twelve apostles and asked, "Will ye also go away?" Simon Peter answered, "Lord, to whom shall we go? thou hast the words of eternal life" (John 6:65-69). Peter declared that Jesus was the unparalleled Master of their lives, and there was no one else. This is the testimony of those who walk faithfully with the Lord. It is the response of Spirit-filled believers, even when the teachings of Christ disrupt their preferences, traditions, or personal opinion. On that day, when others focused on what they could not accept, the apostles chose to focus on what they knew and believed. And, with surrendered hearts, they remained with Christ. Today is no different.

Speaking of His cousin and spiritual forerunner, Jesus said, "Blessed is he, whosoever shall not be offended in me" (Matt. 11:6). Taking offense is a great dilemma in today's society. It is a mindset that can also make its way into the church. There will come a time in our service to the Lord when we can blame God and others for our displeasure. Even in our local assembly ministry, the enemy is at work. At the start, our enthusiasm and motivation are pleasing to God. But over time, serving others can become to us an obligation, a mere duty apart from the love in which we began. We become "weary in well doing" (Gal. 6:9). Chances are, someone will say or do something to hurt our pride. Disillusioned and self-absorbed, we become convinced that no one appreciates our work any longer (Gal. 6:9–10). We are bitter in spirit at the way things are going, so we pull back from our responsibilities and church attendance. Then, finding ourselves alone and without the joy of the Lord, it is easy to lash out at those around us or clench a fist at God for not intervening on our behalf. One of two things will happen. We will shake ourselves and repent or miss God's blessing altogether. Scripture warns us: "Beware lest ye... fall from your own steadfastness" (2 Peter 3:17).

A storm may have broken out in your life. It may have been a storm of doubt, confusion, trouble, worry, or sudden loss. It is wind so severe that it has driven you away from Christ instead of nearer to Him. A storm that leads one person to Jesus Christ will drive another away (Acts 27:9–12). Why? Because, at the time, the latter could not see the reason, the meaning, nor the righteousness of it. And so, everything in God they once embraced slips away; everything, including Christ. They begin to wonder if the things they have lived for in Christ are real. They are afraid to let anybody in. Then comes a depression that causes them to make unwise decisions. They lose the joy they once had in God. When difficulties come, fear begins to express itself. The winds of temptation blow, the current of worldly tradition runs strong, and the force of old habits will increase. We will inevitably part company with the Lord if we have no sustaining faith. What is this drift? It is the decline of belief, doctrine, and practice of biblical principles that we once valued most.

The cares of life have a way of gradually loosening us from our moorings, and little by little, we are affected by adverse forces. But we have a faithful friend in Jesus, and we can find peace with Him by our side! The Bible tells us to continue in those things we have learned, to observe the teachings in which we have His assurances (2 Tim. 3:14). There are no words so profound as those in the Bible. They warn us of hell, and they welcome us to heaven. We cannot allow His Word to slip away nor treat the "pearl of great price" irresponsibly. If there were no sure and steadfast anchor for us anywhere, life would be hopeless (1 Cor. 15:19). Only Jesus Christ abides. He is the same yesterday, today, and forever (Heb. 13:8). He is our unchanging friend and Savior! Let us hold fast the profession of our hope without wavering, for He is faithful that promised (Heb. 10:23). Never let a sermon be preached without some profit. Meditate on what you have heard—conference with others (Luke 24:13-15). Pray. Read the Bible. We hold firm through prayer and obedience to the Word by the power of the Holy Spirit. The sufficiency of Christ is this: "And ye are complete in him... buried with him... risen with him through the faith of the operation of God, who hath raised him (Jesus) from the dead" (Col. 2:8–23). The Psalmist said, "My soul, wait thou only upon God; for my expectation is from him. He only is my rock and salvation... I shall not be moved" (Psalm 82:5–6). Jesus Christ is our hope (1 Tim. 1:1), a steadfast and secure anchor (Heb. 6:19–20). When life gets hard, lean into the mercies of God to find help in times of need (Heb. 4:16).

The following words were discovered on the wall of a cellar in a Jewish concentration camp during the Second World War: "I believe in the sun, even when it is not shining. And I believe in love, even when there is no one there. And I believe in God, even when He is silent." Jesus Christ is the strong and trustworthy anchor of our souls. Even when the harshest winds of adversity blow, our Lord is "both sure and steadfast." Corrie ten Boom (1892–1983), a godly woman who received recognition for her efforts to hide Jews from arrest during the Nazi occupation of the Netherlands, said, "To realize the worth of the anchor, we need to feel the stress of the storm." The answer to the question "Why?" is found at the center of the prophet Habakkuk's book, "The just shall live by faith" (2:4). Relying on God is not the natural disposition of our heart, and it is an act of faith. If we lean into His grace, it will not be by accident but by choice (Rom. 12:1–2).

I love the words of the 1708 hymn written by Isaac Watts. He paraphrased the 90th Psalm: "O God, our help in ages past, our hope for years to come, our shelter from the stormy blast, and our eternal home. O God, our help in ages past, our hope for years to come, be thou our guide while life shall last, and our eternal home." The Psalmist declared, "Lord, thou hast been our dwelling place in all generations. Before the mountains were brought forth, or ever thou hadst formed the earth and the world, even from everlasting to everlasting, thou art God" (Psalm 90:1–2). In 1882 Priscilla Jane Owens wrote, "Will your anchor hold in the storms of life when the clouds unfold their wings of strife? When the strong tides lift, and the cables strain, will your anchor drift, or firm remain?" Christian friend, we have an anchor of the soul, sure and steadfast. And with unshakable trust, we look forward to the day when we will be in the heavenly presence of God. Jesus Christ is more than our dwelling place in this life. He is our anchor. He has bought for us unlimited access to the eternal holy of holies. To whom shall we go? Only to Jesus Christ! He is our unfailing and everlasting hope for all eternity!

Even Now, O Lord

Learning from John's Gospel, chapter eleven: As soon as Martha heard that Jesus was approaching the village, she went to meet Him. Knowing His compassion and great power and seeing the miraculous wonders He had performed, Martha understood that Jesus could have prevented her brother's death. She could not help herself; she was on her feet, rushing to meet her friend. The thought that had burned in her heart was already on her lips. Martha said to Jesus, "Lord, if only you had been here, my brother would not have died." She was not given an explanation or why He did not come sooner. She had sat alone, hurting in silence because she felt like the One who could make everything right had abandoned her. Perhaps she wondered if she had angered or offended Jesus. Maybe He was punishing her for something she had done. Maybe He was too busy. Perhaps He did not care. Maybe He was not powerful enough for this crisis. In the dark of night, it is easy to surrender to Satan's lies. Martha could not see what the Lord was doing in the situation. Sometimes it just feels that God is far from where we are. Yes, we see glimpses of Him, giving us cause to believe. But we are human, and we want to know everything that is happening. Grief is a winding road with no predictable course. The best thing we can do is travel the rugged pathway with Christ. When our souls are tempted to despair over the lot we have been given, we can cling to the truth that the Lord has something better for us. He has not forgotten us nor abandoned us. Things will not always be as they are. The road will level out, and the Christian journey will be enjoyable as before. When His time has come, He will walk the long road to where we are. And answering our cry, He will bring joy to our hearts - and glory to Himself!

Even after hearing of His friend's death, Jesus abode two days in the same place. God has an excellent plan for us, but He only reveals it one step at a time. Martha's life was turned upside down with sorrow, and it seemed all hope was gone. But she said something to Jesus that was amazing. She said, "But even now, I know that whatever you ask from God, He will give you." She says, "I am not certain what it is you can do now, Jesus. But I am convinced you can do something to improve everything." Immediately, Jesus comforts Martha by telling her Lazarus will rise again. He tells her exactly what he plans to do. Martha misunderstands the statement, thinking the Lord refers to the resurrection at the end of time (Matt. 24:30-31). And although she misses the direct meaning, her response is good. She expresses hope through theology. Martha holds to the Jewish belief in the resurrection of the dead that will occur on the last day (Daniel 12:1–2; John 5:28–29). She put her theology to work with a confident faith that even now, Jesus, the resurrection and the life, can always do something. Indeed, he is the Light that conquers the darkness. God starts with the impossible – not the possible. He starts with zero – and then creates something extraordinary!

Recall the story of Mary Magdalene as she made her way to the tomb of Jesus (John 20:11-18). She was overcome by sadness and emotion. Jesus was precious to her in life, and now she loved him in death. Everything was out of context. Yes, she was a follower of Jesus, but now she had no direction. Her heart was broken, and she was sure she would never be happy again. But there stood a man she thought was the gardener… that is until He called her name. And, when she heard her name, she immediately recognized the voice of the One who made her life worth living. With great joy, she answered, "Master!" He was more than a friend to her. He was everything! Our Lord is often closest to us when we feel the most alone. When Jesus spoke, he conveyed many things to her. "I am here. I am alive. I still know you; you are my friend, and I still love you." Many are making their way through the struggles of life – yet continuing to walk with the Lord. How wonderful to know that God is "nigh unto them that are of a broken heart; and saveth such as be of a contrite spirit" (Ps. 34:18).

There is no comparison for raising a man who has been dead for four days. While Martha was crying in agony over the loss of her brother, her tears moved Jesus, and He began to weep. He is not crying over the death of Lazarus, for He knows what He will do. He is not crying because the situation is hopeless. He knows that his friend will walk out of the tomb in a short time. He is weeping because He is a caring God. He has compassion for the suffering and weeps over sin's calamity. He cries because we cannot see what He can see. He weeps because sin interrupted everything He had planned for us in creation (Gen. 1-2). But there is a safe place with the Lord where we do not need to have all the answers. It is the haven of faith where we press into Him despite the circumstance. God will do wonderful things in our lives, but we must not jump to our assumption of how He will intervene. The Lord did not ask Martha if she was sad or disappointed. He asked her how her faith was. These are His words, "I am the resurrection, and the life: he that believeth in me, though he were dead, yet shall he live: And whosoever liveth and believeth in me shall never die. Believest thou this?" Notice her answer, "Yea, Lord: I believe that thou art the Christ, the Son of God, which should come into the world" (John 11:27). She believed Jesus was who He said He was. She was convinced He could do what He said He could do. What a great answer. What an incredible revelation of who Jesus is!

Are there situations in your life that you need to say, "Even now, I believe God can do some impressive things for me?" Do you feel like only a miracle could help? God still does the impressive. He does the improbable. Indeed, He does the impossible! Throughout the Bible, we read how God stepped in and helped his people. He will do the same for us today. First, Jesus gave Martha a promise. Then He drew attention to Himself. Lastly, He called upon Martha to confess her faith and to act on that faith. To know Jesus is to know resurrection and life. To have Jesus is to have resurrection and life (Phil. 3:7-11). Whether or not Jesus had spared her brother, Martha would have worshipped Him. She loved Jesus because of who He was, not what He did for her. Mary's worship was revealed when she poured a perfume bottle with a present value of $35,000 on His feet (John 12:1-3). The Lord is always glorified when we give Him our best!

Are you convinced even now that God can do all things? Do you believe that He is real and that He is in control? Jesus could have healed Lazarus without even coming to Bethany. But He chose to resurrect him the way He did for the benefit of those who saw it. He asked the people to remove the stone, for He wanted them to be a part of the miracle. They were hesitant - and they had good reason. A man had been dead for several days, and his body was decaying. Yet they answered the call and moved the stone away. Are we so distraught and fearful that we cannot act when He tells us to bear it? Are we going to allow human reasoning to hinder God's work? Or do we trust Him enough to put our hands on the rock? There is no middle ground. There is only fear or trust. We are not guaranteed anything, but we are loved enough to be part of the most extraordinary story ever written. That the Creator whose words marked out the universe would allow us to enter into His plan is profound. It is humbling. Even Martha hesitated to be part of what He was doing. Why? Because she didn't understand what was about to happen. But with a combination of faith and action, she was allowed to see the glory of God! However excellent or dreadful, everything in our lives is an opportunity to bring glory to Jesus Christ. Allow the Lord to bless you with the grace to believe that what lies ahead will glorify Him.

God still does the impossible today. People can change their behavior, but only God can change hearts. What have you been told is impossible in your life? Can you say with Martha, "Even now?" What would you have God do? Even now, He can do the impossible. Today, which of your friends and family will begin a relationship with God that will impact their eternity? Regardless of how often they have rejected the gospel message, can you believe God for them? Can you pray, "Jesus, their history is not good regarding spiritual matters. They have not acknowledged their need for You and rejected Your gospel. But Lord, you are faithful, and you have a plan for each of us. Even now, O Lord, even now - you have the power to do what I cannot do! You are righteous in all your ways. You said if I call upon You in truth, You will hear my cry and satisfy my desire (Ps. 145). You are not willing that any should perish (2 Peter 3:9), but that all would come to repentance. Therefore, I pray fervently for my friends and my family."

Remember the repentant thief hanging on a cross next to Jesus? He who called upon God in the hour of his deepest despair received eternal life in a flash of time. This man did not have a history of righteous living to reinforce his faith. Nor did he have the prospect of turning from a life of crime to prove his repentant heart. Yet salvation came to him when he said in his heart, "Even now, O Lord, Thy will be done in me!" Hold on to God's promises. There are brighter days ahead. Isaiah 40:31: "But they that wait upon the Lord shall renew their strength." Romans 12:12: "Rejoicing in hope; patient in tribulation; continuing instant in prayer." Lamentations 3:25: "The Lord is good unto them that wait for him, to the soul that seeketh him." Psalm 27:14: "Wait on the Lord; be of good courage, and he shall strengthen thine heart." Micah 7:7: "Therefore I will look unto the Lord; I will wait for the God of my salvation; my God will hear me." It is a divine exchange when we offer Him our hurt, and He offers us His healing (Matt. 11:28-30). He truly is the hope of all who seek; the help of all who find!

We all face circumstances that seem as if they will never get better. We don't see how things will improve. The odds are against us. Too often, we settle where we are, accepting that better things were not meant to be. Has it ever seemed like God showed up too late? You prayed and believed, but the problem was still there. Let us pray this way, "Heavenly Father, the medical report doesn't look good, but I believe even now You can heal me. My business is hanging by a thread, but even now, You can prosper me. My marriage looks like it's over, but even now, You can restore the relationship. God, You can turn my child around. Dear Lord, I have struggled with this addiction for years, but you can set me free even now. Master, I am bold enough to believe that even now, despite how long it has been, what I have been told, or what I feel, I know You have the final say. You control the universe, and nothing is too hard for You. I may not see a way out, Lord, but I know You will make a way." When the Israelites came to the Red Sea, they had nowhere to go. Pharaoh and his army were quickly closing in. It looked like they would easily be captured and returned as slaves. But Moses did not panic or complain. He understood the 'even now' principle: "God, it looks impossible, but I know even now you can deliver us" (Ex. 14). Abraham and Sarah received a promise that would defy the laws of nature (Gen. 21): "But God, I believe even now You can give us this baby. Despite how old we are and what reason is telling us, You will do the miraculous."

Jesus asked of Lazarus, "Where have you laid him?" They said unto him, "Lord, come and see." Has something died in your life? Is there something you have given up on? The heavens may have seemed silent for a time. But even now, God can resurrect dead dreams. Charles Spurgeon said, "It is when we are at our wits' end that he delights in helping us. When our hopes seem to be buried, that is when God can give a resurrection."

Just before Lazarus was raised from the dead, Jesus said if we believe, we will see the glory of God (John 11:40). Martha saw that glory. And by faith, so shall we. God's timing, while sometimes perplexing, is always best. Many Jews who had come to mourn with Martha witnessed what Jesus did. They saw the miracle. And in their seeing, they believed in Him. Just as Jesus gave physical life to His friend that day, He gave spiritual life to many new believers. The two-day wait had set the stage for a harvest of souls. There is a lesson here. We must patiently allow God to work things out for His purpose. And, according to His timing. He is always working for something much bigger and better than we can imagine. Jesus will show up and do something so incredible that we and others looking on will know it was His work alone. "Even now, O Lord, You can do all things. Even now, heavenly Father, may You be glorified!"

The Deity of Jesus

Our text is found in John 1:1-4. Verse one declares, "In the beginning was the Word (speaking of Jesus), and the Word was with God, and the Word was God." Jesus' identity has been confused, denied, and wrongly portrayed by many through the years. But Scripture teaches that Jesus is God. When Jesus came to the coasts of Cesarea Philippi, he asked his disciples, saying, "Whom do men say that I, the Son of man, am?" The varied responses He received in Matthew 16:13-16 still happen today. Some will say that Jesus is merely a prophet, an honorable man, or a good moral teacher. But believing in the deity of Jesus is essential to our being saved from the wrath of God (Rev. 20:11-15). The apostle Paul said, "Believe on the Lord Jesus Christ, and you shall be saved" (Acts. 16:31). Then, in his first letter to the Corinthians (15:1-4), Paul declares the gospel by which we are saved; how that Christ died for our sins, that he was buried, and that He rose again the third day according to the scriptures. We must believe in the all-sufficiency of Christ as Savior. Apostle Peter preached this message: "Neither is there salvation in any other: for there is none other name under heaven given among men, whereby we must be saved" (Acts 4:12). The supreme nature of God in Christ is foundational to Christianity. If Jesus is not God and Christ is not risen, our faith is meaningless (1 Cor. 15:14).

After Jesus' disciples told Him the speculations others were making about His identity, He asked a piercing question: "But whom say ye that I am?" Simon Peter answered, "Thou art the Christ, the Son of the living God." The word Christ means "the anointed One." And in identifying Jesus as the Christ, Peter was declaring the Messiah as God incarnate who came to be the Savior of the world. The Bible reveals Christ as the eternal God who took on human flesh so that He might redeem fallen humanity.

Jesus did not begin His life in Bethlehem's manger. He has existed from eternity past and will never cease to exist (Col. 1:16, Rev. 1:8). Every attribute of sovereignty and deity can be ascribed to Jesus Christ. He is omniscient (all-knowing), omnipotent (all-powerful), and His eternality is revealed in both the Old and New Testaments (Micah 5:2, Isa. 9:6, John 8:58, Heb. 7:3).

Of the sufficiency of Jesus, the Holy Spirit led Apostle Paul to write, "For in him dwelleth all the fullness of the Godhead bodily" (Col. 2:9). This is a mystery that we cannot intellectually understand, and I have grown weary of those who say they can. There are many things we cannot comprehend (Rom. 11:33-34); not the least of which is how God manifests Himself to us (John 14:23-26, 2 Cor. 13:14). Nevertheless, Bible truths are inevitable; and they are eternal (Ps. 119:160). My prayer is that we place as much emphasis on 30 and 31 of Mark 12 as we do on verse 29. A resolution of the people does not socially determine the doctrine of the Deity of Christ. As there are inherent physical laws, so there are inherent Biblical laws. Folks could vote unanimously to suspend the law of gravity for one hour, but no one in their right mind would jump off the roof to test it. We live by faith (2 Cor. 5:7). How do you explain a man who had once been hungry (Mark 11:12), then fed thousands with a little boy's tiny lunch (John 6), and later proclaimed, "I am the bread of life?" Who does this? How does a man who was carried in a boat stand to take control of (Mark 5:35-41) - and even walk on - the very sea on which his vessel sailed? How can a man tell a person He is the water of everlasting life (John 4:10-14) and later says, "I thirst" (John 19:28) even as he is dying? How can we understand a man like that? How do we define a man who raised himself from the dead, walked through walls, and ascended into heaven? The answer is, "We can't." But this we know: He is the image of the invisible God (Col. 1:15)!

Christian friend, our journey is one of faith (2 Cor. 5:7), and we must exchange intellectual knowledge and understanding for the simplicity of believing. Accepting Jesus as a great moral teacher but not taking His claim to be God is something we cannot do. Why? Because a man who was merely human and said the same things Jesus said would not be a moral man at all (John 8:58, 17:1-21). The choice is ours to either disbelieve or to bow at the feet of Jesus and call Him Lord! We who teach and preach the gospel must not think of ourselves as public relations agents sent to establish goodwill between Christ and the world. We must not imagine ourselves commissioned to make Christ acceptable to big business, the press, the world of sports, or modern entertainment. We are not diplomats. We are ambassadors. And our message is not a compromise; it is an ultimatum. Jesus said, "I am the light of the world… if ye believe not that I am he, ye shall die in your sins" (John 8). The physical manifestation of Christ was prophesied seven hundred years before Jesus was born. The Old Testament prophet Isaiah said, "Therefore the Lord himself shall give you a sign; Behold, a virgin shall conceive, and bear a son, and shall call his name Immanuel." His very name means "God with us!"

Someone has said, "The chances of just eight of the three hundred Old Testament prophetical references about Jesus being fulfilled in one person is 1 in 10 to the 17th power." He said, "Imagine the entire state of Texas covered in silver dollars, two feet deep. Only one coin would be marked, and the entire sea of silver dollars would be thoroughly mixed. A blindfolded man would be instructed to travel as far as he wished, but he must pick up the marked coin on his first try." Whether or not this is a good illustration is beyond me. But this I know: Reconciliation with God did not come by man's initiative (2 Pet. 1:21). We have redemption through Christ; for salvation is only of God! In 1 John 4:9-10, we read, "In this was manifested the love of God toward us, because that God sent his only begotten Son into the world, that we might live through him." Jesus is the sacrifice for our sins. His purpose in coming was to seek and save those who are lost (Luke 19:10). And as the substitutionary atonement at Calvary, Jesus freely offers eternal life to all who will turn from feeling secure in the deeds they have done (Isa. 54:6) and trust only in Him (John 14:6, Acts 4:12).

The resurrection of Jesus provided resounding proof of His deity. Not only had He raised others from the dead, but He raised Himself from the dead. Henry Morris said, "The bodily resurrection of Jesus Christ from the dead is the crowning proof of Christianity" (1 Cor. 15:17-19). In John 21:12, we read that, after His resurrection, Jesus made Himself known to the disciples through a miraculous work. Then, in verse 12, He invites them to "Come and dine." How are we answering the invitation? I say this because His call to us should be treated as even more than an invitation. Let me illustrate: Someone once wrote and asked Emily Post, the etiquette expert of another generation, "What is the correct procedure when one is invited to the White House but has a previous engagement?" She replied, "An invitation to dine at the White House is a command, and it automatically cancels any other engagement." So, what do we do when Jesus Christ, God manifest in the flesh, the Creator of all things, the King of kings, the Lord of lords, the Ruler of the universe, and the Savior of souls, invites us to grow in relationship with Him? We must consider well the way we answer when He calls.

Shortly after joining the Navy, the recruit asked his officer for a pass so he could attend a wedding. The officer gave him the pass but informed the young man he would have to be back by 7 p.m. Sunday. "You don't understand, sir," said the recruit. "I'm in the wedding." "No, you don't understand," the officer shot back. "You're in the Navy!" If we have been born again, we are not our own (1 Cor. 6:19-20). The apostle Peter says we are a chosen generation, a royal priesthood, a holy nation, a peculiar people; that we should show forth the praises of Him who called us out of darkness into his marvelous light (1 Peter 2:9). In 2 Timothy 2:3-5, Apostle Paul tells us to endure hardness, as a good soldier of Jesus Christ. We dare not entangle ourselves with the affairs of this life in ways - or to the extent - that would displease the One who has enlisted us into His army. Jesus Christ is not valued at all until He is valued above all. There is no such thing as part-time loyalty to Jesus Christ.

George MacDonald wrote,

I said: Let me walk in the field.
God said: Nay, walk in the town.
I said: There are no flowers there.
He said: No flowers, but a crown.
I cast one look at the fields, then set my face to the town.
He said: My child, do you yield? Will you leave the flowers for the crown? Then into His hand went mine, and into my heart came He; and I walk in a light Divine, the path I had feared to see."

Who is Jesus? This is the most important question we will ever consider. Why? Because He is God's only provision for sin (Rom. 5:8). He is the only way to everlasting life in heaven (John 14:6, Acts 4:12). Jesus is infinitely more than a prophet, a good teacher, or a godly man. He is Messiah (John 1:41). He is King (1 Tim. 6:15) and Priest (Heb. 4:14-16). He is the Savior (Matt. 1:20-21), the Sovereign One (Eph. 1:17-23), the Creator (1 Cor. 8:6), and Sustainer of all things (Heb. 1:1-10). He is our Redeemer (Eph. 1:7). He is the One who deserves our highest honor, loyalty, and praise. We who believe in the atoning blood of Christ and His resurrection are justified by grace; we have been redeemed (Rom. 3:24-25). O, how wonderful it is that our Lord is ready to assume full responsibility for a life that is wholly yielded to Him.

SERVING THROUGH SORROW

When we are sorrowful, we tend to be self-centered. We concentrate on our immediate needs, all appropriate and necessary, but often to the exclusion of caring about others. The key to overcoming our pain is ministering to others in theirs. Joseph was imprisoned without cause, yet he used God's gift to help others who were incarcerated (Gen. 39-41). Ruth ministered, even as she waited for God to change her situation (Ruth 2:17-23). Having drawn water for a stranger's camels, Rebecca was blessed (Gen. 24). The apostle Paul suffered many trials by man's hand, yet he faithfully took the good news of Jesus to the Gentiles (2 Cor. 11:23-28). Too many of us are inclined to keep a safe distance from sorrowful people because we do not know how to help them. Some approach the extra mile with an attitude that makes you wonder if they accidentally missed the previous exit. But if the Holy Spirit leads us, compassion will be a tangible expression of love for someone suffering. A compassionate person recognizes the needs of others and then takes action to help. We who trust in the goodness of God are humbled by the ways He ministers to us in the valley of affliction (Psalm 23). While there, we see things from a unique perspective. When we suffer, the light of Jesus seems to shine brighter than before. Why? Because now we see Him against the backdrop of a darker night. This is the blessing of visiting the low places.

God will sustain our joy through the kindness of people. These are the times when we are reminded that family members and friends are among the most precious of God's gifts. Nothing will heal our emotional pain like trying to ease someone else's heartache. Regardless of our circumstances, we must count the people in our lives among the greatest of God's blessings. And we do this by ministering to them in their time of need. The apostle

Paul said, "Blessed be God... who comforteth us in all our tribulations, that we may be able to comfort them which are in any trouble..." (2 Cor. 1:3-4). Christ never leaves us alone in our sorrow. We cannot leave others alone in theirs. One Sunday morning, a Sunday School teacher noticed a little girl standing outside the room, looking in with great eagerness at the fun the other children were having. She went outside and invited the little girl inside. "No... they'll all laugh at me." "Why do you think that, honey?" "Because I don't have any shoes." Heartbroken at this little girl's poverty and knowing she wanted to join in, the leader tried to convince her that the other kids would not laugh at her. But despite her assurances, the teacher could not persuade the little girl to join in with the other kids. Another teacher came over, one who had a remarkable ability to minister to children in situations like these. She took the little girl aside and spoke with her. Then she left the girl and rejoined the children to begin the next activity. But, before she started, she said, "OK, everyone, before we go any further, I want you all to take your shoes and socks off and place them by the wall. We'll have our fun with bare feet for the rest of today." The little girl who had no shoes beamed, ran over, and joined in with the rest of the group. There is a way to show the love of Christ in every situation. It is up to us to find it.

Only one miracle of Jesus is mentioned in all four Gospels. It was that unforgettable day when thousands were fed by the great multiplying of a small lunch (Matt. 14:15-21). But just hours before, the wicked ruler of that region killed John the Baptist, cousin and forerunner of Jesus. When the Lord heard the terrible news of his friend's death, He wanted to spend some time alone (Matt. 14:13). So, he retreated by ship to a place in the desert where he could mourn. He knew from experience that in the solitude of prayer, lonely places could become sacred places (Luke 5:16; Psalm 107:35). But on that day, our Lord's time in worship was short-lived. Instead of spending the day renewing His spirit, Christ was "moved with compassion" toward the multitudes who sought Him, and He began healing the sick among them. Never doubt Jesus always takes time to minister to those who seek Him!

In the Book of John, we read of a man called Lazarus who died. This man had also been a close friend of Christ. The Bible said that when Jesus heard the sad news, he "groaned in his spirit and was troubled." He mourned with the mourners. Having lost yet another friend, Jesus wept

(John 11:35). Yes, the Lord raised Lazarus to life by divine power, but not without experiencing deep human sorrow. As with the multitudes fed, a divine blessing was again born in distress. How so? John records that many saw the "things Jesus did" (John 11:45). They observed how He reacted during his grief and believed in Him. Such is the blessing of brokenness, for nothing in life is more important than believing in Jesus Christ (Rom. 5:9). Truly, we glorify God by helping others.

Do you feel alone in your grief? Please turn to the needs of those around you, both for your own sake and theirs. This principle of generosity (Luke 6:38) begins with God. He is with us! Indeed, Jesus Christ is our example (Luke 23:34, 43). At the cross, He loved His enemies. Being rich, for our sake, He became poor (2 Cor. 8:9). He gave his robe to those who took His cloak, and He prayed for those who spitefully used Him (Mark 15). In the scene of the foot washing of His disciples, Jesus conferred on them a ministry based on service and humility (John 13:5-17). In the twelfth chapter of Romans, the apostle Paul tells us, "Be kindly affectioned one to another with brotherly love; in honor preferring one another… distributing to the necessity of saints; given to hospitality." Showing kindness is a loan to the Lord, and He will repay the lender (Prov. 19:17). God calls His people to serve people. And when we do, He says our "light will break forth as the morning," and our health "shall spring forth speedily" (Isa. 58:7-8). Having great friends to share life with is a gift like no other. The Roman philosopher Marcus Cicero said, "Friendship improves happiness… by doubling our joys and dividing our grief." Through the years, extraordinary people have walked into my life and said, "I am here for you." And I thank God for them!

There is a verse of Scripture found in the book of Jeremiah, which reads, "For I know the thoughts that I think towards you, saith the Lord, thoughts of peace, and not of evil, to give you an expected end" (Jer. 29:11). This is a wonderful promise of God, and it is a verse of comfort! But in times of difficulty, our tendency is to read into this Scripture something of our own interpretation. Why? Because we want quick relief. We are looking for immediate solutions and our own desired outcome. Nevertheless, we are to trust in God's plan and not be afraid because He does all things for our good. How? According to His purpose (Rom. 8:28). He will reveal His righteousness and His glory (Rom. 5; 9). Do not live outside the will of God. To do so is to live outside the blessing of God. We cannot understand life, nor can we fathom eternity. In our human frailty, we often doubt when we ought to believe. Other times we are certain when there is no ground for certainty. But we are called to simply trust and obey, "for the Lord God is a sun and shield: The Lord will give grace and glory: no good thing will he withhold from them that walk uprightly. O Lord of hosts blessed is the man that trusteth in thee" (Psalm 84:11–12). Are you carrying burdens today? Do you have questions or doubts? Commit them to God. Do not make it complicated. Simply trust Him and obey His Word. In Acts 15:18, we read, "Known unto God are all his works from the beginning of the world." In studying the lives of the faithful men and women of the Bible, we see that each event was prearranged by the divine hand of God. But passing through, they did not always know this for sure. And neither do we. Just as they lived by faith when they did not understand the bigger picture, so can we live this way. God has not changed (Heb. 13:8). What He did for them, He will do for us (Acts 10:34). He will not fail us (Psalm 86:15). His thoughts toward us are peaceable, and He designs our highest good. Jesus taught us to pray "Thy will be done" (Matt. 6) that we might live with a continual expectation that every promise in the Bible will be fulfilled (2 Cor. 1:20). His counsel will stand, and He will accomplish all His purpose (Isa. 44, Prov. 19). Expect the Lord to be as good as His word. If we are in Christ, we have nothing to fear or dread. He has defeated pain and death (1 Cor. 15). One day, God will deliver us from all sorrow. We will stand in the presence of Jesus Christ, justified before God, and made perfect (Col. 1:21–22). This will be our "expected end." And what a glorious time it will be!

Jeremiah served the people of God faithfully, yet through sorrow. The prophet understood that the Lord never leaves His people hopeless. D. L. Moody wrote the following words next to Isaiah 6:8 in his Bible: "I am only one, but I am one. I cannot do everything, but I can do something. What I can do, I ought to do, and what I ought to do, by the grace of God, I will do." The Holy Spirit is calling us to a life of ministry. An 'author unknown' wrote, "Then gently He lifted the vessel of clay; mended and cleansed it and filled it that day. Spoke to it kindly; there's work you must do. Just pour out to others as I pour into you." This is the will of God. In all of our serving, we must remember why we do what we do. God so loved the world that He gave (John 3:16). We perform acts of kindness. For what purpose? That God alone might be glorified in the world. Serving people makes us happy. But more importantly, it pleases God. The writer to the Hebrews declares, "For God is not unrighteous to forget your work and labour of love, which ye have shewed toward his name, in that ye have ministered to the saints, and do minister" (Heb. 6:10). As God's people, we live to receive the applause of heaven!

A story is told of a famous violinist who was to perform at a concert hall of world renown. As he stood before the packed house that night and played his violin, he mesmerized the audience. When he lifted his bow off the string on his final note, the hall erupted with thunderous applause, and he was given a standing ovation. He looked at the crowd for a moment and walked off the stage only to return to render an encore performance. To the amazement of the masses gathered there that night, his encore performance was even more beautiful and flawless than the first. He looked to the audience and left the stage for the second time but was beckoned back by the deafening roar of the multitudes that once again stood to their feet in adulation. He gave yet another encore number, leaving the audience fumbling for words to describe what their eyes and ears had just experienced. This sequence was repeated several times until this virtuoso of virtuosos finished his piece, looked to the audience, nodded his head, and walked off the stage. At the same time, the ferocious cheers could still be heard long after he exited. Reporters pressed outside the violinist's dressing room, waiting to catch a word from the man who had just given the performance of a lifetime. As he emerged from the small room, one reporter asked, "Sir, why did you give so many encore performances? You could have stopped after the first, and everyone would have been amazed." The violinist stopped and replied, "For the very first time in my career, my master, who taught me to play the violin, was in the audience. When I finished my performance, everyone stood except for one person. I played again, and everyone stood to applaud except for him. I continued to play. After the last encore, I looked into the seats and noticed that everyone, including my master, was standing and applauding. I was only then satisfied that I had done an excellent job."

Friend, we serve God by serving others and then look only to Him for approval. I ask myself, "Do the praises of men drive my life, or am I striving to please the Master? Do I try to help others with prayer and care in times of trial? When I sorrow, do I still serve?" Dear Lord, I pray it will be so in my life.

THEY WERE BROUGHT TO JESUS

In the Book of Mark chapter nine, we read where Jesus delivered a young boy from the torment of an evil spirit (v17-27). In the following chapter, He blessed little children who knew almost nothing about life (v13-16). In chapter four of Matthew's Gospel, our Lord healed multitudes suffering from various diseases and delivered those manipulated by Satan's power (v24). The apostle Luke tells of Christ healing the body and soul of a man lying on a bed and in desperate need (5:17-26). In the Gospel of John, we see Peter who, having been given a new name by the Lord, was then called to a lifelong ministry of preaching the gospel of Jesus Christ (1:42). These and others in the Bible who were healed, delivered, and called by the Master had one thing in common. They were brought to Jesus by people who knew they couldn't receive God's blessing any other way. Recently, our church Youth Pastor preached a wonderful message about "they" who brought people to the Lord. The beauty of his message is that, as a teenager, he was brought to Jesus by those who served in the soul-winning outreach of bus ministry. Brother Sal's message is indeed the genesis of this writing.

The apostle Andrew is mentioned only a few times in the New Testament, but we find him bringing people to Christ each time. First, he had the incredible joy of introducing his brother Peter to the Lord (John 1:39-42). Then he introduced a boy with a small lunch (John 6:8-9). In John 12:20-22 he trained a group of devout Greeks who came to worship at the temple. Andrew, a former disciple of John the Baptist, was called to even higher kingdom work by the Lord Himself (Matt. 4:18-20). And we are called to the same. We are not told that Andrew ever preached a sermon. But there would have been no sermons from Peter had it not been for this man's faithful witness. What is it that will move people to Jesus?

It is the gospel of truth shared in love and friendship, illustrated in the life of the one sharing it (Eph. 1:13; 2:10).

Our following Jesus begins with a surrendered heart. When our will is submitted, our feet will follow. Jesus said, "For the Son of man is come to seek and to save that which was lost" (Luke 19:10), and there is no more critical labor of love in the world than introducing others to the Savior. How is it done? Consider how we introduce people to Jesus by looking at how we introduce people to each other. According to social practice, "An introduction is a polite method of starting a conversation and establishing a connection between two people who do not know each other. Introductions explain who the person you are introducing is and what the people you are introducing them to need to know about them. Find an opening. If you want to introduce people to each other, it's important to get the timing right. If you find yourself with two people who do not know each other, try to introduce them as soon as possible. Figure out which person of the two has a higher rank or authority in a social setting. This is important because the person of lesser rank or authority should always be presented to the person of higher rank or authority. Always state the name of the person with a higher rank and present the person of lower rank to them. This makes the person of higher rank stand out as the more important person in the situation. Provide background information to help the people start a conversation and provide a connecting thread that can leave them to talk independently." My heart is stirred when I think of the spiritual application of all of this. Undoubtedly, the most crucial introduction we can make is introducing someone to Jesus Christ.

People will respond when they see a Christian faithfully living the joy and goodness of the Lord. Ask God to show you whom to focus on, then set time aside for them. Present the promises of forgiveness and eternal life (John 1:12; 6:37, 40). Invite them to an act of faith to receive Christ (John 16:24, Matt. 10:32, Rev. 3:5), and the Holy Spirit will work in their hearts. Our job is to lift Jesus (John 12:32), and the Holy Spirit will convict of sin (John 16:8). When Jesus said, "Bring them hither to me" in Matthew 14:13-21, the disciples were soon reminded that Jesus alone could satisfy the needs of the people. Jesus worked through the hands of His disciples. And He does the same today. As followers of Christ, we have a place in His work on earth. When asked what experience led him to accept Christ as

Savior, a young man writes, "A couple of years ago, a friend of mine invited me to his youth group at his church, and even though I was hesitant, God used my being there to finally bring me to a relationship with Him that will last forever. In the end, it seems He brought me to Christ." A teenage girl says, "I'd have to say my parents brought me to Jesus. My dad always read to me from the Bible when I was little. They encouraged me to continue reading the Bible and attending church." Another writes, "I was born in a Christian family, raised by Godly parents. I accepted Jesus as the Lord and Savior of my life when I was about five years of age. My dad led me to Christ." A man of later years, this story, "For me, it was my old pastor. I don't know if I'd be a Christian today if it hadn't been for him. I know he didn't make me a Christian, but he made the environment so much easier to become one." The Master calls people through whom He can act and speak (Luke 5:1-11).

Beyond introducing people to Jesus for the first time, there is the ongoing ministry of discipleship (Matt. 28:19). Discipleship is friendship. It is building a relationship where we, like Jesus, share in someone's future. It is where we help people from where they are to the reality of who Christ is! We invite them to "come and see" if God is who He says he is. In John 1:46-47, the apostle had the wisdom not to argue the vain and foolish prejudice against religion but only to invite. Talking about Jesus is nothing like investigating first-hand the claims of our Lord. Do not let yourself get lost in religious debate. Instead, invite others to come and meet the Christ of Calvary. The reason? Because a relationship with God comes not by achieving but only by accepting. Preconception is always a problem when it comes to Jesus. Misunderstanding is complicated in our society because people operate within their own biases. They think they know who and what Jesus is because they measure truth through their experiences. We who share Christ need to understand the ways people object to Him. In many retail stores, employees are instructed to take customers to find what they are looking for rather than simply giving them verbal directions. This may illustrate what it means to walk alongside people seeking help and wholeness. Our genuine interest in their spiritual welfare and our involvement with them will say, "Let's walk together." Discipleship is a relationship in which we share God's Word, our faith, and our lives. Our role is to plant (Mark 4:26-32). The Holy Spirit's role is to grow the plant

(1 Cor. 3:6-7). Pray and believe that the seeds you sow will one day bear fruit to the glory of God.

It is easy to become so preoccupied with life that we care little about other people. But often, the best times of spiritual growth in our own lives happen when we take a friend to Jesus. The person with paralysis in Mark 2 isn't just an object lesson. He was a seriously broken man forgiven and healed by the Master. And all who saw it glorified God that day. Jesus repeatedly made the point that needy, broken, and desperate people were the very ones for whom he had come and on whom his ministry was focused (Luke 4:18). Never doubt; our way of godly living will help illuminate God's Word in the heart of a friend. Our behavior will reveal the nature of God by making the way of Christ easier to understand. Our actions will make our faith visible to the watching world. The Lord's purpose is accomplished by people who do what they can for someone while relying on the Holy Spirit's power to change their life. We do well to think about the people in our lives who helped us understand the love of Jesus. Who are they in your life? Beyond those who walked the pathways of life with us, many in the body of Christ have influenced us from a distance. That is to say; we saw their faithfulness to God without really knowing much about them.

Charles Plumb, a U.S. Naval Academy graduate, was a jet pilot in Vietnam. After seventy-five combat missions, his plane was destroyed by a surface-to-air missile. Plumb ejected and parachuted into enemy hands. He was captured and spent six years in a communist Vietnamese prison. He survived the ordeal and now lectures on lessons learned from that experience. One day, when Plumb and his wife were sitting in a restaurant, a man at another table came up and said, "You're Plumb! You flew jet fighters in Vietnam from the aircraft carrier Kitty Hawk. You were shot down!" "How in the world did you know that?" asked Plumb. "I packed your parachute," the man replied. Plumb gasped in surprise and gratitude. The man pumped his hand and said, "I guess it worked!" Plumb assured him, "It sure did. If your chute hadn't worked, I wouldn't be here today." Plumb couldn't sleep that night thinking about that man. Plumb says, "I kept wondering what he might have looked like in a Navy uniform: a white hat, a bib in the back, and bell-bottom trousers. I wonder how often I might have seen him and not even said 'Good morning,' 'how are you?'

or anything because, you see, I was a fighter pilot, and he was just a sailor." Plumb thought of the many hours the sailor had spent on a long wooden table in the bowels of the ship, carefully weaving the shrouds and folding the silks of each chute, holding in his hands each time the fate of someone he didn't know. Plumb asks his audience, "Who's packing your parachute?"

Everyone has someone who provides what they need to make it through the day. Mr. Plumb also points out that he needed many parachutes when his plane was shot down over enemy territory. He needed his physical parachute, mental parachute, emotional parachute, and spiritual parachute. He called on all these supports before reaching safety. Sometimes in the daily challenges that life gives us, we miss what is essential. But as we go through this week, this month, and this year, may we recognize the people who pack our parachutes. Ask the Lord to use you. Share your story of how you came to know Christ and what He means to you. How did Jesus bring people to faith in God? Often, He moved them from unbelief to belief in the "Emmaus Road" conversion, a journey where He patiently guided the conversation to Scriptural truths (Luke 24:13-35). And in God's mercy, the moment of faith will come. How we connect with others will have everything to do with our sense of God's purpose for us. Today I join others who have expressed this prayer, "Lord, lead me today to those I need. Lead me to those who need me. And let something I do have eternal consequence." May God use us all to bring someone to Jesus!

A Psalm of Care and Provision

We live in a world filled with fear and uncertainty. Many of us wake up with burdens to bear, and we are concerned about our future. Sometimes life is hard, and our hearts cry out with a deep longing for clarity, direction, and peace. How does God want us to respond to the problems of life? The Bible gives us a practical, God-honoring way to respond to fear and anxiety. The Psalmist says we should trust God as the good and faithful Shepherd. Shepherds are the providers, guides, protectors, and constant companions of sheep. In all life experiences, David understood God's protection and provision. And he tells us to rejoice in God's grace (Psalm 118:24). Speaking of the wellbeing of God's people, the writer said, "He that dwelleth in the secret place of the most High shall abide under the shadow of the Almighty. I will say of the Lord, He is my refuge and my fortress: my God; in him will I trust" (Psalm 91:1-2). In victory and defeat, in strength and weakness, the Psalmist was aware of the Lord's presence. In good times and in times of trouble, God was with David. And He is with us when we turn our hearts toward Him (James 4:8). He will never forsake us (John 14:27).

Perhaps one of the most well-known verses of Scripture is the twenty-third Psalm, beginning with these words: 'The Lord is my Shepherd.' David had been a keeper of sheep, and he understood both the needs of the sheep and the duties of a shepherd. He knew what it was like to care for animals inclined to get scared and wander off. Likewise, we, 'the sheep of His pasture' need continual care (Psalm 100:3). Why? Because we are helpless and often panic driven. Isn't it wonderful that we have the twenty-third Psalm? It is a passage of Scripture that will help us respond perfectly to whatever comes our way! "The Lord is my shepherd; I shall not want.

He maketh me to lie down in green pastures: he leadeth me beside the still waters. He restoreth my soul: he leadeth me in the paths of righteousness for his name's sake. Yea, though I walk through the valley of the shadow of death, I will fear no evil: for thou art with me; thy rod and thy staff they comfort me. Thou preparest a table before me in the presence of mine enemies: thou anointest my head with oil; my cup runneth over. Surely goodness and mercy shall follow me all the days of my life: and I will dwell in the house of the Lord for ever" (Psalm 23).

What a profound illustration of our relationship with God and the confidence we can have in Him! We should have no greater goal than to deepen our relationship with Jesus Christ. How peaceful and rewarding it is to live under the love and care of the Good Shepherd (John 10:11). The words 'I shall not want' (v1) may be the most assuring line in this Psalm. When the Almighty, the sovereign God, the Master of the universe, is the one who takes care of us, what more could we want? Under His care and provision, we lack nothing. When He says to me, "As thy days, so shall thy strength be", I have peace, knowing that there is grace for every phase of life (Deut. 33:24). To 'lie down in green pastures' is symbolic of quiet comfort (v2). The phrase speaks of relaxing in the love of a God who never fails. These are the peaceful times of life when we can rest under Shepherd's watchful eye. Troubled waters signify worry and distress. But the 'still waters' revealed in this psalm is an expression of the quiet existence we find in God; tranquility that we could have never found on our own. Jesus Christ leads us to the waters of refreshment, where we can be free of emotional disturbance. What is this trouble? It is always the need for something more. It's our desire for answers to everything that happens to us. It's our longing for the power to change things. A confused mind will never be satisfied, but a trusting spirit lives in contentment. God is steadfast in His love, and He knows what we need. Have faith in Him. He will provide according to His will and purpose.

Indeed, life can be challenging. Our stories of loss and heartache may look different from the outside, but we grieve the same. Many of us are traveling roads we would never have chosen. Yet, as we learn to trust God in our sorrow, we will understand His sustaining grace. Your green pastures and still waters are closer than you think. Trust. Believe. Rest. Even in your most broken moments, your Lord is near (Phil. 4:4-7). He restores the soul (v3). He heals the brokenhearted and binds all wounds (Psalm 147:3). It is often through hardship that we begin to understand things in a new way. Scriptures that were no more than words on a page begin to have meaning. We start to hear and understand and know the voice of our Shepherd. We hear His call, and we respond. Even in sorrow, we follow His leading. He is with us, and His faithful dealings will bring us into a warm and safe place.

God leads us in the paths of righteousness with loving care (v3). Job was a 'perfect and upright' man who 'feared God and hated evil.' Yet he suffered greatly. And in his suffering, he said of the Lord, "I look for Him, but I cannot find Him. He hides himself and I cannot see Him." Is this how you feel? Job continues, "But He knows the way that I take, and when He has tried me, I shall come forth as pure gold" (Job 23:8-10). Are you being tested and tried? Jesus Christ is all you need in this world - and for eternity (John 4:10). As we walk in the paths of righteousness 'for His name's sake' (v3), God will be glorified. It is important to realize that even in times of distress, we still exist to worship Him with faith and determination (1 Cor. 10:31). Much as we grieve in a time of loss, we know that God will not abandon us. His holy name will not be threatened by any calamity, no matter how severe. The apostle Paul said, "Now unto the King eternal, immortal, invisible, the only wise God, be honor and glory for ever and ever" (1 Tim. 1:17). To 'walk through the valley of the shadow of death' (v4) implies that as we travel the path of life, dangers, risks, and threats will be inevitable.

But with Him by our side, no evil can befall us (Psalm 91:10). No danger can dampen our courage. No peril can last long enough to conquer our spirit. Jesus walks with us in all our ways. His rod provides protection. His staff gives comfort (v4). And both are used to alter our direction. Amid the world's evil influences, the Lord 'prepares a table' for His children (v5). He is the bread. He is the living water (John 6:35). Surely, He is the sustaining nourishment of life, and His provision is a feast that we are willing to share with others! His 'anointing of oil' portrays wellness and care in healing our wounds (v5). Our Shepherd regularly inspects his sheep because he does not want today's wound to become tomorrow's infection. David uses the expression 'my cup runneth over' to help us understand God's love's abounding, overflowing nature (v5). Jesus said, "He that believeth on me, as the scripture hath said, out of his belly shall flow rivers of living water" (John 7:38). God gives mercy and grace. He provides more than we need, and the overflow of his provision is meant to be poured out to others (2 Cor. 9:8). We are invited to 'dwell in the house of the Lord forever' (v6). For the Psalmist, this meant living in His presence for a lifetime (Psalm 91:9). Likewise, we who have desired a relationship with Christ live in the abundance of His grace. We have the assurance of eternal salvation, and one day He will lead us into the everlasting joys of heaven (Jn. 5:24; Rev. 7:14-17). Jesus Christ is the sheepfold where the enemy of the soul is not allowed. He is the only door we may enter and be saved (Jn. 10:7-9). He is the God who cares, loves, and leads us to the safety of His arms. Grace and everlasting salvation are found in Him alone (Acts 4:8-12). If you are going through a difficult time, if life seems to overwhelm you, if your heart is so heavy you can hardly breathe, Christ is with you. He has not left you. He will not leave you (Matt. 28:20). Read His Word. Listen for His voice. He wants to refresh your soul. Through storms and strife, the Master calls to us, "Come unto me, all ye that labor and are heavy laden, and I will give you rest" (Matt. 11:28). Some days, we need a hand. On other days we are called to lend a hand. And may we be pleased to have our Good Shepherd restore our souls so that he can use us in restoring the souls of others. Indeed, my cup runs over. Everything in Your time, O God, for goodness and mercy is with me. Everything in eternity, O Lord, for I shall dwell in Your house forever!

NO OTHER GOSPEL

There is only one gospel message to be preached in all the world - to everyone everywhere (Matt. 28:19). And if it includes an 800 number with a requirement to give money, or if it becomes a theological debate outside the grasp of all people, then it is no longer the gospel. If the message of Jesus Christ is not understood by the rich and famous, the poorest of the poor, those without formal education, or those with great intellect, then something is wrong with how we deliver it. To those without total mental capacity, God extends His grace. But if the "glad tidings of great joy" is not simple enough for a child to understand (Mark 10:14), we have layered it with something never meant to be.

Some will remember the translucent film used as an overlay for maps. This material could also be written on, erased cleanly, and reused. It was perfect for when we needed to make temporary visible markings of our choice. Nowadays, we can place an unlimited variety of overlay images on a digital map to visualize anything we desire. We can select the icons that best suit our needs. For example, a hiker may wish to add newly cut trails unavailable on maps. And when the rendering is complete, he will have a map with images of places he has chosen, whether or not they are perfectly matched with accurate geographical positions. A base map is designed to serve as a stand-alone map. It is not to be layered—likewise, the Gospel of Jesus Christ. The church at Galatia had once believed. They had received God's plan of salvation, but now some taught a perversion of the gospel. In Galatians chapter one, the apostle Paul leaves no room for the notion that some could believe one thing about salvation while others believe something else, and yet all find their way to God. Truth is singular. There are no versions of the truth. Jesus said, "I am the way, the truth, and the life; no man cometh unto the Father, but by me" (John 14:6). Concerning the gospel of salvation, grace and works cannot co-exist. Eternal life is ours through grace, by faith alone, in Christ alone. The Bible says, "Being justified freely by his grace… therefore we conclude that a man is justified by faith without the deeds of the law" (Rom. 3:21-31). Faith is the means of salvation and to change that message is to distort the gospel of Christ.

Religious debate without a Biblical definition and foundation is like playing tennis on a court with too many lines. Fabricated markers confuse. Jesus calls us to be 'fishers of men' (Mark 1:17; Matt. 5:16), but don't get hung up on personal opinion or denominational snags that would waste your time. In Ephesians 2:8-9 the apostle Paul affirmed that salvation is a gift, "For by grace are ye saved through faith; and that not of yourselves; it is the gift of God." In Revelation 22:17, the Holy Spirit and the church extend this invitation, "And whosoever will, let him take the water of life freely." A gift is a gift given willingly to someone without payment, never to be taken back. Do not complicate the simplicity and the wonder of God's love. By faith alone, we receive God's grace extended to us through the atonement of Jesus Christ (1 Pet. 2:21-25). Without a lifetime of honorable deeds to point back to, or a chance to prove that he had moved from a life of crime, the thief hanging next to our Lord understood that through believing and confessing (Rom. 10:4-13), salvation is the work of God from start to finish (Luke 23:39-43). Nothing we do is the basis for God's acceptance; it is only that His righteousness is imputed to us (Rom. 5:19).

God's church refers to believers in Jesus Christ from all times and places (1 Thess. 4:16-17), and personal faith in Christ is the hallmark of Christians everywhere. Jesus is both the foundation (Acts 4:10-12) and the head (Eph. 5:23) of His church (Matt. 16:16-18). We "have redemption through his blood, the forgiveness of sins" (Eph. 1:7). Do not get tripped up by someone's overlay map, no matter their religious pedigree. Rules of men may keep wrongdoing in check for a time, but they do not change hearts. Church standards cannot save us, and morality cannot be legislated. We can insist on trying to live by rulebooks, but everything changes when we are filled with God's power (Gal. 2:19-21; Rom. 6:15-18). The Holy Spirit living on the inside and the desire to obey His leading is what we need. Whether Jesus was talking to a woman caught in adultery (John 8:1-11) or a deceitful little man in a tree (Luke 19:1-10), He was a gatherer of broken people, committed to breaking the rules of self-righteous people (Luke 18:9). He valued relationship, and He was willing to upset religious leaders of the day to reach those who needed His mercy (Matt. 23).

The gospel unto salvation is a simple one. It is a base map without overlays. It is "good tidings of great joy" (Luke 2:10), and joy awaits those who accept it! The gospel Paul preached was the death, burial, and resurrection of Jesus Christ "wherein ye stand; by which also ye are saved… (1 Cor. 15:1-4). The gospel is Jesus Christ, who He is, and what He has done (Mark 8:31; 1 Tim. 3:16). The message is a living and breathing truth. It gives life. It transforms life. It sustains life. The true gospel of God's grace will not appeal to our self-interests but our sense of sin. The gospel of Christ is not a reward for the righteous. It is a gift for the guilty. Romans 2:4 tells us the goodness of God leads us to repentance, a desire to turn from sin and take a new path that pleases Him (2 Cor. 7:9-10). God's grace is so amazing and divine, a love we cannot earn nor return in kind. "Herein is love, not that we loved God, but that he loved us, and sent his Son to be the propitiation for our sins" (1 John 4:10). God loves because He is love. How wonderful it is to receive a gift (John 3:5-21) so precious as the unmerited grace of Jesus Christ!

I Faced a Spiritual Crossroads

Having attended a church building for the first time in my mother's womb and then fellowshipping with a local body of believers for over a half-century after that, I could tell you about what it means to be a Christian. I could tell you much about the Bible, a collection of sixty-six books written hundreds of years by dozens of different authors, all coming together to tell one incredible story about Jesus. I could help you understand the gospel of Christ and tell you how I felt when I received the Holy Spirit into my life as an eleven-year-old boy. I could explain the fundamental doctrines of the Bible and share with you the importance of approaching the throne of God in prayer. These and many other beautiful truths based on Scripture are deeply rooted in my heart. I am so thankful for God's love and leadership. I tell of His great salvation because I am a born-again child of the King! Even so, there was a time when I came to a spiritual crossroads. It was a time when a profound change would take place, a point of decision that would alter the course of my life. The Old Testament patriarch Jacob faced a time when he wrestled with the Lord as he confronted his weaknesses (Gen. 27; 32:24). Know this: time spent with God and reading His Word will expose who we are (James 1:22-25). And when we consider Jacob's character flaws, we realize the favor of God is not because of virtuous deeds. Jacob was left alone. It was a difficult night. But there is no more rewarding endeavor than pursuing God's presence and incredible blessing. Jacob emerged with a new name and identity, filled with a divine purpose!

Some will tell you that closeness to God means knowing all the correct answers. I don't see it this way. I think proximity to God begins the night we toss and turn in bed, searching for answers. Some of the finest heroes of the Bible were long on questions and short on solutions. Wrestling with faith is not a sign of weakness - but evidence of humanity. John the Baptist, Thomas, Gideon, Sarah, and many others in the Bible illustrate this truth. A crossroads is a challenging place to be. It is the nature of the intersection to cause doubt and confusion because there is usually a specific problem or question that needs a resolution. But lonely places can be sacred places (Luke 5:16), and I knew God wanted me to experience a greater understanding of who He is. I had the most apparent impression that God was pushing me beyond my comfort zone, orchestrating something that would forever change me. I did not want to live a routine life that did not wholly align with God's purpose for me. I was facing decisions I had never encountered before. I became dissatisfied with who I was, and I struggled with that. Now you might say, "Oh, that's wonderful, Dave. You should be excited about moving forward with God." And you would be mostly right. But not completely. I was fearful of where a more significant commitment to God might take me. I knew the sun would shine brightly for me once I arrived in my new place. But that day did not come right away. For nearly three years, I walked in a fog. Yes, I read my Bible, and I prayed. Sometimes even more fervently than before. I opened my heart to the Lord. I wept. My wife and I cried together. But it seemed God was far away. Things were changing in me, and I wondered how my children, family, and friends would accept the change. It was a challenging time.

King Solomon wrote these words of wisdom, "Trust in the Lord with all thine heart; and lean not unto thine own understanding. In all thy ways acknowledge him, and he shall direct thy paths" (Prov. 3:5-6). We cannot know if a particular course of action is right for us, and we cannot afford to rely upon our understanding (Prov. 14:12). Only God knows. And He will lead - if we put ourselves in a position to hear and receive. The Psalmist tells us that God will make known the right path and that in His presence, there is fullness of joy (Psalm 16:11). This is what I was looking for: the fullness of God's joy! It is the very nature of God to be a saving God. And once you begin to see the fullness of grace, you will see it everywhere in the Bible. You will wonder, "How did I ever miss this?" You will let go of the rulebook and come to a greater understanding of what Jesus did at Calvary (Luke 23:34). You will experience His love as never before (Psalm 36:7). You will see a God who delights in mercy (Micah 7:18) so much that He gives us a new beginning every morning (Lam. 3:22-23).

And this knowledge will bring you to your knees in thankful humility, saying, "Why me, O Lord? How is it that You love me so much?" I cannot tell you how thankful I am for what God has done in my life. I am forever grateful for extraordinary people, family, and friends, old and new, who have walked with me on this faith journey!

Have you come to a time of decision? Do you desire to see your Redeemer more clearly and worship Him more fully? Are you reaching for the deeper depths and higher heights that Paul spoke of in the third chapter of Ephesians? If so, God will be found, and He will bless you. Our Lord delights in blessing those who are desperate for more of Him! Jesus said, "If any man thirst, let him come unto me and drink" (John 7:37). He said, "I am the light of the world: he that followeth me shall not walk in darkness" (John 8:12). Understand, no journey is the same. There is never a "one size fits all" spiritual growth plan. I was searching for the "riches of the full assurance of understanding" proclaimed in Colossians 2:2-6. And for me, it meant moving from the familiar for the blessing of the unknown. This is always challenging. Your choices may seem unreasonable to some, even fellow believers who are commonly satisfied with the status quo. Prayerfully evaluate the role they are trying to play in your life. Indeed, we cannot ignore godly counsel (Prov. 12:15). But look to "the only wise God our Savior" (Jude 1:25) to change the things that require divine intervention (Rom. 8:26-28).

If the Holy Spirit is leading, you will know it. God will respond when we earnestly desire His will to be accomplished in us. The apostle James said, "The effectual fervent prayer of a righteous man availeth much" (James 5:16). Jesus said, "My sheep hear my voice, and I know them, and they follow me" (John 10:27). Faithfully read your Bible. Express your dependency on God through prayer. Beware the company you keep. Be intentional about spiritual growth. Consider your daily routine and its influences. Change is not about a new religious label, organization, or identity, so avoid people who think it is. It is a matter of the heart. Trust the God who saved you for all eternity! The Bible says, "He which hath begun a good work in you will perform it until the day of Jesus Christ" (Phil. 1:6). This is the confidence we have in approaching God that "if we ask anything according to his will" he will hear and give us that which we desire of Him (1 John 5:14-15). Faith is the beginning of fulfilled promises!

There is a well-known verse of Scripture in the Book of Matthew where Jesus says to us, "Ask, and it shall be given you; seek, and ye shall find; knock, and it will be opened unto you" (Matt. 7:7). God gives good gifts to those who ask of Him (Matt. 7:11). James 1:17 says, "Every good gift and every perfect gift is from above, and cometh down from the Father of lights, with whom is no variableness, neither shadow of turning."

When I consider the relationship, theology, and struggle involved in God's plan for me, I see a purpose. He was preparing me for things to come. He wanted me to live in grace. God knew I would face situations where complete surrender would be essential for emotional and spiritual healing. He saw a blindside of deep sorrow coming where I would have to trade human understanding for peace. God wanted me in a place where I would fully acknowledge His will and trust in His sovereignty. To help illustrate the Holy Spirit's work in me, I authored a booklet titled 'Never This Way Before: My Darkest Road.' Today I join the Psalmist in declaring, "The Lord is my song" (Psalm 118:14). The Song Leader put His song in my heart! And how patient He was while I was learning the music. Jesus Christ meets us where we are and loves us to where we should be. Today I joyfully proclaim the goodness of God, for His presence is the most treasured reality of my life.

GOD'S POWER MADE KNOWN

I have had enough failures to know that nothing has a good ending without God. We are weak and broken, each living with a situation or a wound that we would remove from our lives if it were humanly possible. But some things are beyond our control. The apostle Paul said, "there was given to me a thorn in the flesh, the messenger of Satan to buffet me" (2 Cor. 12:7). Three times, our brother Paul sought the Lord for deliverance from this burden of life. But he never received it. In the passage of Scripture found in 2 Corinthians 12:7-8, we learn that sometimes God allows Satan to be involved in our suffering. You might say, "Well, trouble comes when we don't live right." Bad choices indeed lead to wrong results. But read about a man who was "perfect and upright" in the Book of Job. The Bible says Job "feared God and hated evil." And yet this man suffered at the hand of the very ruler of evil. Go back to the beginning of time (Genesis 1-3). Satan played a vital role in the consequential suffering of sin, even in what began as a perfect and sinless Garden of Eden. Never doubt the enemy's intention for you. His aim is misery and death (John 10:10). But there is power and authority in the Lord's answer to Paul's prayer for deliverance. He said, "My grace is sufficient for thee: for my strength is made perfect in weakness." Notice the apostle's response, "Most gladly, therefore, will I rather glory in my infirmities, that the power of Christ may rest upon me" (2 Cor. 12:9). What a tremendous promise. What an incredible response. What an excellent way to live!

The promise that God's grace is sufficient in suffering is much harder to live than to say. But because I want God's power to be visible in my weakness, I must not stumble at that which cannot be understood, but only trust. As the heavens are higher than the earth, God's ways are higher than mine (Isa. 55:8-9). In a recent Sunday morning message, my pastor said, "One of the markers of a spiritually mature Christian is their response to pain and sorrow." I am reminded of Job's statement of faith even through the pain of horrific tragedy, "Though he slay me, yet will I trust in him... He also shall be my salvation" (Job 13). Satan is not the only one at work here. God is at work. Job's circumstance is not just the work of Satan to destroy. It is the work of God to save. He tries our hearts. He checks our motives (1 Thess. 2:4; Deut. 8:2-3). In the life of Job and also in the life of Paul, even in our lives today, there is a purpose in what happens. Can God trust me to be a victorious witness for Him? I pray He can. In 2 Corinthians 12:8, we learn that it is okay to pray for relief. The Psalmist David often prayed the prayer of the sufferer. He cries, "Save me, O God." Soon he will call, "Deliver me... answer me, O Jehovah." He feels like he is sinking in a miry pit, and then he compares his sorrow to floods of waters threatening to overflow him. The entire burden and theme of Psalm 69 are suffering, and the psalmist longed for relief. As in Psalm 22, there comes the assurance that God hears the cry of the needy and that He will save them. Notice what David did after his prayer of supplication. He worshiped! "I will praise the name of God with a song; and will magnify him with thanksgiving." Then, he tells us to seek God and watch Him work (Psalm 69:30-33). It is the power of God resting upon us. It is cause for praise. The strength of God is cause for praise!

An ancient punch tool is on display in the French Academy of Science. The device, used by a leatherworker, fell from a table one day and put out the eye of the man's young son. Soon, the child became blind in both eyes, and he had to attend a school for the blind. The boy learned to read by handling large, carved wooden blocks at this school. When he grew into adulthood, he thought of a new way for the blind to read that involved punching tiny dots onto paper. Louis Braille devised this new method using the same tool that had blinded him in his youth. When Patricia Houch Sprinkle told that story in Guideposts in 1978, she suggested that there would be a falling awl in each of our lives. She added, "When it strikes, some of us ask, "Why did God allow this to happen?" Others ask, "How will God use it?"

How is it that, through suffering, some will exhibit a sweet spirit many others do not have? I believe it is in their response to the trials of life. Certainly, this is much easier said than done. But Paul surrendered to the pain when he learned it was God's will for his life. And He understood there was a divine purpose in it all. God does not delight in our suffering, but He knows that pride and a mindset of self-sufficiency will destroy us (Prov. 16:18-19). Let God be God in your life! Read Hebrews chapter eleven. By faith, some escaped the sword's edge, and the sword killed some. Some stopped the mouths of lions, and others were sawn asunder. Some were mighty in war, and others suffered chains and imprisonment — these things we do not understand. But the ultimate purpose of God in our weakness is to glorify Himself, for He alone is worthy.

The truth of God's sovereignty is our most precious possession in times of hardship and calamity. God grants Satan a measure of authority on earth. But the devil is like a dog on a leash (Mark 1:21-34). Nothing happens to a Christian that God does not design or lovingly allow for their eternal good. The most profound need we have in adversity is not quick relief. It is the established confidence that God is with us in grace and power. The Bible says peace will be multiplied in us "through the knowledge of God, and of Jesus our Lord" (2 Pet. 1:2). This knowledge comes from faithfully reading His Word. And only when we understand this Scriptural principle will we ask, "How can God be glorified in my weakness?" My pastor has said, "Paul could not have done more for God without the thorn." Why? Because the affliction kept him from glorying in his strength. He humbled himself under the mighty hand of God that he may be exalted in due time (1 Pet. 5:6). Without question, it was through Paul's weakness that God's power was made known to the world! Jesus Christ came to do what you couldn't do for yourself. Let Him be your strength in human weakness. This is the power through which God loves to get things done (1 Cor. 1:19-31).

DON'T LOSE THE WONDER

Little children look forward with anticipation that anything can happen. They have a sense of curiosity and surprise. Their eyes light up. Big grins cover their faces in amazement at new and exciting experiences. And what a joy it is to watch them! Likewise, Christians who have been "converted, and become as little children" (Matt. 18:3) live with expectancy. They do not pray prayers without meaning nor preach without passion. They imagine tremendous and mighty things from God. But in our service for the Lord, it's easy to lose the wonder of it in the work of it. British evangelist "Gipsy" Smith (1860-1947) was asked, "What is the secret of the freshness of your ministry, way into your eighties?" He replied, "I have never lost the wonder." Remind yourself that there is no failure in the One who has power over every circumstance. Expect God to do incredible things. Jesus said, "Let your light so shine before men, that they may see your good works, and glorify your Father which is in heaven" (Matt. 5:16). God's light of salvation is full of glory that is evident in our enthusiasm!

In Psalm 8:3-4 David said, "When I consider thy heavens, the work of thy fingers, the moon, and the stars, which thou hast ordained; what is man, that thou are mindful of him?" In the awesome presence of God, wonder makes us feel smaller. Not insignificant, but smaller. We sense that we are a piece of a greater whole; we have a place and purpose in the world. Every day in Christ can be greeted with anticipation because every day holds new possibilities. Begin each day with prayer and thanksgiving. Share your testimony of God's grace with others. Paul tells us to be "fervent in spirit; serving the Lord" (Rom. 12:11). What does this mean? It means sharing the gospel with boldness and power. It means loving God with our heart, soul, mind, and strength. It means loving our neighbor as ourselves

(Luke 10:27). Through faith in things unseen, we can live the wonder of knowing all things work for our good (Rom. 8:28). The story is told of one of the first three men who went to the moon. He said, "I watched an earth that didn't appear to be larger than a dime, aware that every living thing in existence was on it." He said, "I was impressed with the greatness of the Almighty as never before." And as great as this story is, the wonder of God is found, not so much in what we experience but in how we share it. A young man in a remote village wanted to present a gift to the missionary who served his people. Not just any gift would do; it had to be a rare and valuable shell found many miles away on the seashore. The young man traveled miles over mountains and through dangerous jungles to find and return with the shell. When he presented his gift, the missionary was overcome by its beauty but was also amazed at the treacherous, exhaustive journey — to which the boy replied, "The walk is the best part of the gift!"

We can have some wonderful days walking with Jesus. He died for you and me. He loves us always. His love is constant. His love is perfect. His love is unconditional. Take a moment and let that sink in. Consider the Almighty who spoke all things into existence, the God who "divided the light from the darkness" (Gen. 1:4), the One with authority to create something by simply saying He would. Nine times in the very first chapter of the Bible, we read, "And God said... and it was so." Think about the Creator of a vast universe, yet an incomplete world without each of us (Gen. 1:24-28)! Salvation is the miracle of God to every believer (John 15:13). But sometimes I think we have lost the wonder of knowing Him. We have grown cold to something that ought to leave us speechless. We suppose that "encountering God" only happens in highly miraculous or emotional experiences. The Bible says, "Blessed is he whose transgression is forgiven, whose sin is covered" (Psalm 32:1). When was the last time you revered a righteous and holy God, just knowing you are forgiven with perfect love?

In 1955, George Beverly Shea boarded an ocean liner when the Billy Graham crusades were at the height of worldwide outreach. A fellow passenger started a conversation and asked him about the typical program sequence of a Billy Graham crusade. The renowned gospel singer described how the meetings were conducted. But then, he recalls, "I found myself at a loss for words when I tried to describe the responses that usually accompanied Mr. Graham's invitations to become a Christian." Turning to the other passenger, he exclaimed, "What happens then never becomes commonplace, watching people by the hundreds come forward. Oh, if you could just see the wonder of it all!" As the singer pondered the thought later in the evening, he was inspired to rough out a melody and write the words of a song, "There's the wonder of sunset at evening, the wonder as sunrise I see; but the wonder of wonders that thrills my soul, is the wonder that God loves me."

I recall one of many fishing trips my father and I took to Eagle Lake in Northern California. Dad loved nature. He loved all creation. He loved God. We stayed together for a few days on this particular trip in his camp trailer. And every night, the last thing I heard him say before drifting off to sleep was, "Thank you, Lord, for another good day." My father was aware of God's impressive work in the world. He never lost the wonder of it all. A lady writes, "I don't know what made me look at him. He was just an average boy walking down the street. But as he approached the signpost, he took his arm, wrapped it around the post, and flung his body around and around." She said, "I remember doing that! When did I stop doing that? Why did I stop?" I understand physical limitations. But what happens to us when we stop living this way? Too often, we become so preoccupied with the details of life that our focus shrinks to just trying to get through each day. How would you describe your walk with God in one word? Most of us would use the word wonderful, but is it full of wonder? A tourist guide once accompanied U.S. Astronaut Neil Armstrong through the streets of Jerusalem, pointing out different sites as they went. He mentioned that "these steps here Jesus used to go back and forth to the temple." Neil Armstrong stopped him and said, "Are you telling me that my Savior walked up and down these steps?" "These very ones", the guide assured him. Armstrong said, "I was the first person to walk on the moon, and I've never been as excited as I am now."

One of the most heartfelt stories of God's grace is that of a woman who had a longer conversation with Jesus than any other individual in the Gospel of John. It is the story of a woman born into a race of people traditionally despised by Jews. Furthermore, she was a social outcast, living in shame. But with a thirsty soul, she could glimpse the truth behind the words of Jesus when others, including Jewish scholars, could not. She wanted to know more about Him. And because she did, Jesus declared to her something he had not made public in many circles. He told her he was the Messiah, the Christ! What happens next reveals the wonder of it all. She races off, leaving her water jar behind (another great message) - and proclaiming, "Come, see!" Her story was an enthusiastic testimony of love, redemption, and acceptance. It was her encounter with the Master that led to the salvation of many people that day. Why? Because she lived in the wonder of what had been done for her! The death, burial, and resurrection of Jesus Christ is the most profound and exciting thing that has ever happened on this planet. Truly, this is the "good tidings of great joy" (Luke 2:10-11) unto salvation for everyone who will believe. And we who have accepted Christ as Savior have an exhilarating revelation of who He is. I want my relationship with God to be expectancy rather than expectation. Expectations lead to disappointment and dissatisfaction. Yearning leads to faith and thankfulness. I want to live in God's presence with a sense of amazement at who He is, what He has done, and what He will do. Dear Lord, I pray we never lose the wonder of it all!

THE PRESENCE OF EVIL

The Book of Habakkuk offers insight into why God allows evil and suffering to exist and how we should respond. Habakkuk is the only book of the Bible that is entirely a conversation between God and a person. This book was penned during a dark time in Israel's history, with even darker days ahead. The prophet Habakkuk longed for renewal, but all he could see was the wickedness surrounding him. What we learn in this writing is certainly relevant today. Acts of aggression, natural disasters, hunger, greed, sickness, and disorder plague our world. We are not the first to wrestle with the question, "Why this, God?" John Stott said, "Suffering represents the single greatest challenge to the Christian faith." It has been so in every generation.

The first thing we discover in the story of Habakkuk is that God is longsuffering toward those who ask questions. As perplexing as the problem of evil is, let's take our requests to God rather than contend that there cannot be any answers. The prophet could not understand why he wasn't seeing God's intervention in his day's violence, injustice, and evil. Habakkuk is not only wondering how long, but his words became a strong accusation, "How long shall I cry, and thou wilt not hear?" But even as the prophet poured out his heart, God listened and recorded the conversation for us. The cry of "How long?" is repeated frequently throughout Scripture. In desperation, the Psalmist David called on God, "How long wilt thou forget me, O Lord? Forever? how long wilt thou hide thy face from me… (will there be) sorrow in my heart daily?" But notice that by the end of the psalm, he found consolation. He said, "But I have trusted in thy mercy; my heart shall rejoice in thy salvation" (Ps. 13). That's the answer! Sorrow is a universal and unavoidable part of the human experience for Christians and non-believers. We often ask, "What does my problem say about God?"

But the more humble question is, "What does God say about my problem?" When you question God's goodness and ask why He didn't foresee all of this suffering, take another look at Calvary. He did expect it - and He sacrificed His own Son because of it!

Evil comes as no surprise to our Lord. In John 16:33, godly men were grieved and confused as they were told that the One they loved the most would soon leave them. Jesus told them, "These things I have spoken unto you, that in me ye might have peace." I can only imagine what they thought when everything seemed so wrong. They were about to face the darkest, most troubling time of their lives, yet they heard Christ say, "Don't worry about it. I tell you this to make you feel better." Then, to make matters worse, Jesus continued, "In the world, ye shall have tribulation; but be of good cheer." Notice He did not say "cheer up." He said, "be of good cheer." To cheer up is to try harder. To be of good cheer is a state of being that comes only through the power of the Holy Spirit through prayer and Scripture reading. Finally, these men heard the good news, "I have overcome the world." They had witnessed the victory of Jesus through His life, His death, and His resurrection. Therefore, the Lord was trying to impress upon them that His victory would be theirs. His peace would be their peace. And so, on that day, Christ made a promise to a group of men who would believe the promise; the same promise He makes to all who will believe (Mark 11:22)!

Dr. C. Everett Koop served as Surgeon General of the United States from 1981 to 1989. He tells this story: "The most clearly etched lesson I learned about having a sovereign God who makes no mistakes occurred some years ago when our wonderful twenty-year-old son David was climbing the granite face of Cannon Mountain. A large slab he was scaling loosened and carried him off the face of the cliff with it. David was roped to his companion, and when he came to the end of his tether, he fell inward like a swinging pendulum, smashing his body into the face of the cliff. His companion lowered him to a narrow ledge, quickly secured the rope, then rappelled down to him. David had disrupted his right knee, and he bled to death on that ledge. Our grief was crushing. We didn't know where or how to begin to cope, so I drew my family close and prayed a prayer that only the Holy Spirit could have inspired. I thanked God for taking David to be with Him and then closed by asking Him to let us see a blessing come from a tragedy that hurt us beyond description. When a loved one is taken, the reality of one's faith either sustains and comforts or falls apart if not rooted in a loving God. In the weeks, months, and years that followed, we saw God's hand at work in the aftermath of our loss." He said, "One of the greatest spin-offs was our ability to put behind us the "what ifs" and the "if onlys" concerning David's accident; the common quagmire that can hold us in the continuing inability to recover. In a time of adversity or trouble, the Christian has the opportunity to know God in a special and personal way. In difficult times, we learn to rely completely on the grace and mercy of a loving God. And how wonderful to know that we have a Lord who knows the end from the beginning; a God who has fashioned our lives according to His perfect will!" Dr. Koop said, "God's sovereignty remains my greatest comfort."

There are tangles and twists in life that we can never unravel. But we can trust that God can, for He has a higher perspective and wiser purposes (Isa. 55:8). The Creator said the work of creation in its original design was "very good" (Gen. 1:31). But evil entered the universe through Satan. Sin did not originate with God but through a personal choice in the Garden of Eden. Adam and Eve fell prey to their lustful desires, and they corrupted that which God had perfectly created (Rom. 5:12). In this life, we will never understand why a good God would allow evil to exist, but we know that a better day is coming (Rom. 8:22-23). The truth is that God, in His sovereignty, can use even evil to bring about good. This is what he did for Habakkuk.

Have you ever been in the middle of suffering and thought, "I just can't see the good in this?" Just because we cannot see a reason does not mean one does not exist. Cling to this extraordinary promise for it is made to all believers: "And we know that all things work together for good to them that love God, to them who are the called according to His purpose" (Rom. 8:28). There are times when God seemingly allows wickedness to continue unchecked because He is patient and longsuffering. Right now, He is calling all men to repentance (Acts 17:30), but there will be a time when He will execute His judgment. In chapter 2 of Habakkuk, God assures His prophet that He sees the evil and explicitly mentions greed, injustice, violence, drunkenness, and idolatry. By this, we understand that no sin will ever be committed without God's awareness. We also know that no evil will ever be unaccounted for by God. God will judge every work, whether good or evil (Eccl. 12:14). It may not be on our timetable, but it will happen. The whole theme of Scripture is redemption. Oh, thank God for His marvelous grace! Our Lord understands suffering, and He enters our brokenness. Jesus came to us as a servant, obedient to the cross's death (Phil. 2:7-8). Do not miss this truth: the rugged cross of Calvary and what happened there is God's answer to evil in the world. People often ask, "Why do bad things happen to good people?" Only once this happened – and He volunteered (John 13:15, Heb. 5:7-8). If we are God's child, we will experience pain, but never without hope! Why? Because we "have redemption through his blood, even the forgiveness of sins" (Col. 1:14). Jesus has redeemed us from the curse of the law, being made a curse for us (Gal. 3:13). God gave Habakkuk a picture of the beautiful future that awaited him; the same end that awaits all who have believed in Christ for salvation!

The Book of Revelation speaks of a new heaven and a new earth, a time when God will wipe away all tears from our eyes. And there shall be no more death, neither sorrow nor crying; neither shall there be any more pain (Rev. 21). The Holy Spirit told John to write these things, for they are "true and faithful." The curse of sin will be destroyed when God restores the earth to its original perfection. Habakkuk began his book by accusing God of idly standing by, but he ended by claiming God as his salvation. What changed? Habakkuk's perspective changed! Many things we need help understanding. But know this: to have peace, we must give up the need to understand. Trust God and walk by faith. Job, a man who suffered many terrible hardships, said, "Though he slay me, yet will I trust in him" (Job 13:15). Christian friend, our understanding of God is limited, but we can have joy in our salvation regardless of circumstances. This is a joy that is found in Jesus alone. In the closing verses of his writing, Habakkuk said (paraphrasing) though the devastations of the enemy remain, "yet will I joy in the God of my salvation." Then he said, "The Lord God is my strength." Indeed, Satan rules the earth today (2 Cor. 4:4), but he was disarmed and defeated at the cross (Col. 2:14). Our enemy will not rule forever (Rev. 20:10). And because our Savior has secured the final victory (Isa. 45:22-23), we can live with all confidence through the power of the Holy Ghost (Rom. 15:13). At the same time, we anticipate the "blessed hope and the glorious appearing of the great God and our Savior Jesus Christ (Titus 2:13)!

PARENTING IS FOREVER

For many of us, there was a time in our early years of parenting when we thought, "When my children are grown, then it will be the end of my parenting responsibilities. They will have their lives, and I will have mine. They will remember all the good things I taught them. They will go on to find high-paying jobs, get married, and visit me a few times a year with my grandchildren. My parenting season will be over, and I can do the things I have always dreamed of doing." But it didn't happen exactly that way. These days, we understand that godly parenting is forever! Young mom and dad, there are different seasons of parenting responsibilities, but your heart and mind will be with your children for the rest of your life. No matter where they go or what they do, a part of them will be with you. When they are happy, you will be satisfied. When they suffer, you will suffer. You will still be concerned when you are no longer with them daily. Every day – and many nights. You will worry about their safety and struggles, fears and weaknesses, successes and failures, choices and mistakes. The truth is, you will always be that person who deeply cares about your child's well-being, regardless of their age – or yours.

When we see life happening to our adult children in a challenging way, we want to help them. But how much is way overboard, and how little is not enough? Only God knows the answer. There are a few things we need to understand. First, we must realize that we cannot fix everything for them. I have experienced times of asking God to change something in others, only to have Him say, "Oh yes... but first, let's talk about you." We must release our adult children into the Lord's hands and ask Him to take charge of their lives. Meanwhile, they need us to love them, believe in them, and support them. God has trouble with His children too, yet He is always with them. Only God can make changes that will last. Our job is to pray for His will to be accomplished in them and us. He will hear our prayers and deliver us from our fears concerning them. Truly, our prayers will have power if they align with God's Word. We must stop blaming ourselves every time something terrible happens. Guilt is a killer. All of us see how we could have done things differently. Sometimes we ask ourselves, "How did we go wrong?" Perhaps you regret not having been around enough in their childhood. Or there were events you missed, and you know you should have been there. I certainly understand this one! Maybe you were too strict or too lenient in the area of discipline. There is nothing you can do now to erase it or cause it to seem like it never happened. It would help if you got beyond blaming yourself through the power of the Holy Spirit. To be effective in their lives today, we must confess our mistakes to the Lord – and our children. This will bring the freedom of forgiveness that God has for us. Ask yourself, " Can I do anything about it now?" If so, do it. If not, give it to God and ask Him to redeem the situation. He will heal you in the process. The only way to overcome guilt is to bring every disappointment before the Lord in prayer.

There is only one perfect parent. He is our heavenly Father. And He loves our children more than we do. They were His before ours (Psalm 139:16). They are His gift to us! In the same way, we pray for ourselves; we can also pray for them. Pray that your children will develop a heart for God, His Word, and His ways. Live a godly life before them, and they will be persuaded to say, "Great is Thy faithfulness." Why? Because they will see God's faithfulness working in your life. Tell your children what God has done for you. Let them in on some of your struggles and mistakes when they were children. Communicate to them what God means to you today and how He has answered your prayers. Tell them how He has provided for you. It will strengthen their faith!

The lessons we have learned from our failures and accomplishments can help those following behind. We can impact the younger generation by telling of an unfailing God and sharing our experiences of His unchanging promises. J. P. Morgan, perhaps the most influential banker in history, left this testament to his children: "I commit my soul into the hands of the Savior, in full confidence that having redeemed it and washed it in His most precious blood, He will present it faultless before the throne of my Heavenly Father; and I entrust my children to maintain and defend, at all hazard, and at any cost of personal sacrifice, the blessed doctrine of the complete atonement for sin through the Blood of Jesus Christ, once offered, and through that alone." Beyond the gospel of Jesus Christ, the most incredible legacy we can pass on to our children, grandchildren, and others are integrity, character, and faith. At her father's funeral, Billy Graham's daughter told how her dad taught her to love the Bible. Another daughter told the audience of a colossal mistake she had made, but that, in her father's love, there was "no shame, no blame, just unconditional love." She said, "He showed me what God was like that day." The evangelist's son told those in attendance, "Dad was faithful, available, and teachable."

For many, the question becomes, "How can a relationship damaged by events or conversations from long ago be restored?" Unresolved conflicts should be approached openly and honestly (Eph. 4:15). This is difficult for me. But I know that God can turn it around no matter how dark the situation is. He can fix what is broken and always brings hope (Jer. 29:11)! Reflect on the good things that happened in your relationship and build from there. Stop focusing on what might have been. Ask forgiveness and grant forgiveness (Eph. 4:31–32). Look towards what can be and stop torturing yourself with "what if?" The power that raised Jesus from the dead can also raise a doomed relationship. The steps may be slow, but they need not be without purpose (1 Peter 4:8). William Shakespeare said, "No legacy is so rich as honesty." The Psalmist David takes it to a higher level. He remembers God's promises. He remembers his faith in these promises and reminds his son of them. At the end of the king's last prayer of thanksgiving, he asks God that a willingness to give would forever be alive in the people's hearts. Then, his prayer becomes specific. He asked the Lord "to give unto Solomon my son a perfect heart, to keep thy commandments, testimonies, and statutes" (1 Chron. 29:18–19). What would you pray for if you only had one more to pray? David had come to the end of his days. He did not pray that his son would have a wondrous kingdom, an abundance of riches, or a happy life. He prayed for a full heart, a heart at peace. He was not just praying that Solomon would live right, but that he would treasure the Word of God and know God and live for Him. Children are like arrows to be aimed and released (Psalm 127:3–5). They are not ours to keep but to develop for God's glory - at every age.

It could be that you came to God later in life, or you have grown in your relationship with Jesus Christ (2 Peter 3:18). Do not let the regrets of yesteryear overwhelm you. Many of us have received spiritual insight from the Bible these days that we did not have in our early parenting days. We could not give away that which we did not possess. We could not teach lessons to our children that we had not learned ourselves. But it's never too late to be a better parent. A mother tells her story: "One Sunday, I broke down in tears at a prayer meeting at church and asked what I could do to restore my adult son to me. He had made some chilling decisions, and I was powerless to change him. A dear, older woman hurried across the room, sat down beside me, and slipped her arm around my shoulder. 'Your parenting in the flesh is over,' she said softly. 'It's time to parent him in the Spirit. Pray for your son and trust God to do what you cannot do — and He will.' I was set free that day. Today, twenty years after that life-changing day, my son is a fine, responsible adult who has become one of my dearest friends."

Please join me in a parent's prayer today: "Dear Lord, I thank you for my children and grandchildren and the joy they have brought into my life. There is always room to grow in grace and the knowledge of Jesus (2 Peter 3:18). I realize parenting is a life-long endeavor. Teach me when to act on their behalf and when to wait for You to provide for them. Thank you for holding my children in Your heart. I pray for Your divine guidance in their lives. May they bring honor to your name. And may we all find strength and peace as we abide in You. In Jesus' name, I pray. Amen."

Singing at Midnight

Bruised and bleeding, two missionaries were dragged into the deepest part of a prison. Paul and Silas lay there all afternoon and into the night, hundreds of miles from home. Their backs were open to infection. They were surrounded by darkness, unable to adjust their position (Acts 16:16-34). Midnight for them was very dark. And so, it is at times for us. There is something about the darkness of midnight that heightens our sense of fear and anxiety. It is a time when the pain of loneliness is intensified. But consider this: midnight marks the beginning of a new day where the brightness of morning and the mercies of God are sure to follow (Lam. 3:21-25). How did these men respond to such a terrible condition? And what should our response be in situations like this? Picture the amazing scene. With everything gone wrong, Paul and Silas began to praise God and sing worship songs! But this time, they were not praying silently while quietly humming a tune. Oh, no! They wanted everyone around them to hear the incredible testimony of God's goodness. What happens next? The God to whom they offered worship loved it so much that He delivered them out of bondage that very night. What a miracle! But even more remarkable was the deliverance of the jailor and his household from spiritual bondage. Through worship and praise, new believers were delivered from the power and penalty of sin! Likewise, God's power will be made known in us and the world when we worship Him in spirit and truth.

With a heart surrendered to God, we discover our theology at midnight. We find out the difference between theory and reality. We gain a spiritual perspective as never before, and we arrange the things of importance above those of convenience. We acknowledge the Holy Spirit's leading us from where we are to where He wants us to be. And, while we do not understand the way, we lift our hearts in praise for the leading. How do we react to unwelcome news when it comes our way? When tragedy strikes, life caves in, and our plans are dashed on the jagged rocks of reality, we discover what we believe. A time of testing will never leave us in a neutral state spiritually. We will either emerge bitter or better. The good news is that we choose which it will be. So, how should we respond to such a turn of events? It all depends on our religious beliefs. Remember, we do not learn our theology at midnight. We discover it. And if we genuinely believe in the sovereignty and goodness of God, we will put everything in His hands.

Praise is an outward expression of love that comes from deep in the heart. (John 12:3). I encourage you to raise a song of praise in the night. Put your prayer on the wings of a melody. Very often, words sung will fit where spoken words will not. Why? Because songs echo in our hearts, stirring us to worship. How often have you awakened in the night with a theme running through your mind that doesn't seem to go away? God gave us the Book of Songs for a reason. Singing broadens our communication with God. Singing can help tame stress and lift our spirits. Our mood will improve when we sing. Singing brings people together and creates a sense of unity. Bottom line: singing makes us feel good! Sing to the One who breaks the darkness with a liberating light, for "in him, there is no darkness at all" (1 John 1:5). Sometimes, we need to do more than speak His truth to ourselves. We need to sing it. We often refer to an altar as a place of prayer, where we meet God with spoken words or even silence. But in Psalm 43:4, David speaks of singing upon the altar. He said, "Then will I go unto the altar of God, unto God my exceeding joy: yea, upon the harp will I praise thee, O God my God." In Zephaniah 3:17, we find God singing over His people. There are two important observations in this verse of Scripture. First, singing represents God's joy. Second, God's singing parallels the singing of His people. And for a child of God, this remarkable passage is full of promise!

The Psalmist David was afraid, confused, and alone when he wrote, "Weeping may endure for a night, but joy comes in the morning" (Psalm 30:5). But notice how he ends the song, "Thou hast turned for me my mourning into dancing… and girded me with gladness; to the end that my glory may sing praise to thee, and not be silent. O Lord my God, I will give thanks unto thee for ever." We find comfort in knowing that as surely as the sun rises, our Lord will comfort, heal, save, and restore. In Jesus Christ, we have abundant joy in this life (Psalm 16:11) and the promise of greater satisfaction in the eternal heavens (Rev. 7:14-17). The resurrection of Jesus Christ is that morning of history that gives us the courage to endure the hours of darkness, even the night of death. There is power in praise (Psalm 9:1-3). And there is nothing so great as believers joining together, sharing the beautiful things God has done!

Christian friend, you have seen the glory and provision of God in the brightness of day, and you cannot imagine for a moment that His watchfulness is relaxed in the dark of night. The reason for our deepest hurts will remain unknown, and some of our most challenging questions will be left unanswered (Rom. 11:33-36). But faith lives with unanswered questions (Rom. 1:17), and it will be worth it all when we see Jesus! We are comforted when we bring our cares to the throne of grace and leave them there. Worship is not defined by our surroundings but by God's unchanging character. The remedy for David's despair in Psalm 13:5 was his trust in God's unfailing love. For a believer, the confidence of faith is this, "I have trusted in the mercy of God; I still trust, and I will trust forever." We all can sing in the daylight hours. But if we can still sing in the darkness, the world will hear us differently. The melody in our hearts may be softer, but the tone will be sweeter. And those around us will know the difference. Rest well in Jesus, my friend. Keep singing in the midnight hour. For the Light of the world (John 8:12); the God who commands light to shine out of darkness (2 Cor. 4:6); the One who upholds all things by the word of His power (Heb. 1:3) – He is with us!

ACCORDING TO THY WORD

Years ago, a large financial services company would use this catchphrase in advertising: "When E. F. Hutton talks, people listen." Certainly, when God speaks, we need to listen. Scripture is God-breathed (2 Tim. 3:16). The Bible is God's revelation of Himself to us in written form (2 Peter 1:21), where the entirety of His will and purpose is revealed in commandments, statutes, ordinances, testimonies, and precepts. Nothing is more precious than God's holy Word! It is said that when the famous missionary, Dr. David Livingstone, started his trek across Africa, he had seventy-three books in three packs, weighing 180 pounds. After the party had gone three hundred miles, Livingstone was obliged to throw away some of the books because of the fatigue of those carrying his baggage. As he continued his journey, his library grew less and less until he had only one book—his Bible. The Psalmist David was a man of great wealth and power, yet he treasured the words of God more than anything else. In Psalm 119:9-16, he declares, "Let me not wander from thy commandments… teach me thy statutes… with my lips have I declared thy judgments… I have rejoiced in the way of thy testimonies… I will meditate in thy precepts… I will not forget thy Word." Then, with the Psalmist, may we also "delight in the law of the Lord" (Psalm 1:1-6). The apostle Paul said, "Let the word of Christ dwell in you richly" (Col. 3:16). Jesus said, "Blessed are they that hear the word of God and keep it" (Luke 11:28). The Bible paints a vivid portrait of an Author to be praised.

Consider Mary's response to the message from God in Luke 1:38 when she answered, "Behold the handmaid of the Lord; be it unto me according to thy word." That God had spoken to her was cause for surrender. In John 15:3, Jesus said His words cleanse us. In John 6:63, our Lord said, "the words that I speak unto you, they are spirit, and they are life." The words of God remain forever, and obedience is key to receiving His bountiful mercies (Psalm 119:41). We ask for understanding according to His Word (Psalm 119:169). We are sustained in life according to His Word. God speaking is the most potent force in all creation. His words are the source and foundation of all that exists (Rom. 11:36). No less than nine times in the first chapter of the Bible, we read, "And God said... and it was so." Heroes of the Bible trusted in God's wisdom while laying aside their own. And if our lives are forever changed by divine intervention, it will be because we are receptive to the Spirit's leading through God's holy Word. English clergyman and poet Charles Wesley (1707-1788) wrote the following: "Be it according to thy word, this moment let it be. The life I lose for thee, my Lord, I find again in thee" (Matt. 16:24-28). Our perspective is so limited. How foolish, therefore, to ignore God's instruction. How prideful to follow our imperfect philosophy instead of relying on His wisdom. God said, "So shall my word be that goeth forth out of my mouth: it shall not return unto me void, but it shall accomplish that which I please, and it shall prosper in the thing whereto I sent it" (Isa. 55:11). Every Word of Scripture will indeed be accomplished at God's appointed time. His truth is never invalid, and His promises are not empty.

My relationship with God will never be any more profound than my desire for His Word. I need Him every day. Therefore, I need to read what He says to me every day. If we are careless in Bible reading, we will be careless in Christian living. Jesus said, "Take my yoke upon you, and learn of me" (Matt. 11:29). The instruction, the teaching of the Bible, will sustain us. In Psalm 119, David exalts the Lord, and he wants the reader to consider how the words of God will meet every need of life. At least fourteen times, he develops the idea of life "according to thy word." For example, we read: "Give me life according to thy word" (v25), "strengthen me according to thy word" (v28), "give me understanding according to thy word" (v169), "deliver me according to thy word" (v170). Bible-centeredness is the mark of a Christian. The words of the Lord are pure (Psalm 12:6), and obedience brings beautiful results. In Luke 5:4-6 we read where the disciples, having obeyed the Lord's command, received abundant provision. Abraham lived according to God's Word, and he was blessed above measure (Gen. 22:18). Noah lived in the promise of God's

Word, and he was saved from the penalty of sin (2 Peter 2:5). Living according to the Bible means believing - and it means obedience. It is the way of safety, hope, strength, and wisdom. Jesus Christ is the Word made flesh (John 1:1-18), and He sustains the universe by the power of His command (Heb. 1:3).

In 1914, Ernest Shackleton and a team of explorers set out from England to do something that no one before had accomplished—cross Antarctica from one side to the other across the South Pole. Disaster struck when the team's ship, Endurance, became entrapped in ice and eventually sank after her hull was crushed. Marooned on nearby Elephant Island, there seemed little hope for their survival. In a desperate effort to get help, Shackleton and five others set out in a twenty-foot lifeboat across some of the world's most dangerous and storm-filled waters. It was an eight-hundred-mile journey to South Georgia Island, where help could be found. For fifteen days, the men battled the treacherous seas and massive storms. Using only a compass and a sextant, Frank Worsley (who had captained the Endurance) navigated their course until they safely reached land and found help. Shackleton procured another ship and returned to rescue all of his men. He became a national hero in England for his courage and persistence. All of us are making our way through a turbulent world. We struggle to make wise decisions about an uncertain future. The only way to ensure that we do not go astray is to have a divine source of truth that will guide us through uncertain and complex circumstances. We must rely on God's words over personal opinion. The Bible is without error, and we can trust what we read eternally.

Because the Bible is so readily available to us, we often take it for granted. William McPherson treasured the words of God. He was the superintendent of a stone quarry when a blast severely injured him. He lost his eyesight and both hands in the explosion. So determined was he to read the Bible that he learned to read raised letters with the tip of his tongue. Our nature is to live according to sight. But the reason will fail us. God never fails. His Word is the only lifeline designed to keep us safe through the storms of life. An unknown writer said, "This Book is the mind of God, the state of man, the way of salvation, the doom of sinners, and the happiness of believers. Its doctrines are holy; its precepts are binding; its histories are true, and its decisions are immutable. Read it to be wise, believe it to be safe, and practice it to be holy. It contains light to direct you, food to support you, and comfort to cheer you. It is the traveler's map, the pilgrim's staff, the pilot's compass, the soldier's sword, and the Christian's character. Christ is its grand subject, our good its design, and the glory of God its end. It should fill the memory, rule the heart, and guide the feet. Read it slowly, frequently, and prayerfully. It is a mine of wealth, a paradise of glory, and a river of pleasure." The roots of stability come from being grounded in God's Word. All of Scripture is meant for my learning (Rom. 15:4, Psalm 32:8). Therefore, as I read passages of the Bible, I ask myself, "What are the abiding principles, and how do they apply to me? What is God saying that connects to the realities of my life, and how is He calling me to change?" Today my prayer is found in Psalm 119:25-38, "Lord, give me life according to your Word. Teach me the way of your precepts and establish your Word in me."

HE RESTORES MY SOUL

In the days of my childhood, I felt protected, safe, and secure in the love of God. I knew He was with me. I knew He would never leave me. I could memorize the twenty-third Psalm, and I received strength from seeing my parents and other believers resting in green pastures under the careful eye of the Shepherd. But as I watched the varied ways in which people responded to pain and suffering, I learned that only those who are born into Christ (Rom. 10:9-13) could experience the peace that is promised in the Bible (John 14:27). These were the people who concluded that their journey of life was part of a larger plan. They responded with eternity's values in view. The overwhelming nature of the things we face will make us weary. With the passing of years, we often find life's journey to be a series of difficult stretches with an incline that grows steeper still. Trials are complex, and loneliness is real. We all become exhausted physically, emotionally, and spiritually. But climbing the high hills with jagged rocks that lay before us, may we pause and remember the One who restores our innermost being. Physical bodies may be restored with rest, medication, and exercise. A tired brain may recover with an extended vacation. But what about the restoration of our souls? Oh, friend, this takes a work of God. This kind of restoration requires a divine intervention by the Prince of Peace!

Even now, you may be experiencing grief or disappointment. Are you weary? Does hope seem far away? When your closest friends ask you how you are doing, what do you say? Do you default to the safe answer, "Oh, I'm fine," while trying to avoid the painful subject before you burst into tears? I understand. But you will not survive the fires of sorrow by cloaking yourself in the armor of self-protection. Only God can rebuild the shattered pieces of your heart, and He will often use your friends. Let them in. Faithful friends are a blessing from God. Once during Queen Victoria's reign, she heard that the wife of a common laborer had lost her baby. Having experienced deep sorrow herself, she felt moved to express her sympathy. So, she called on the bereaved woman one day and spent some time with her. After she left, the neighbors asked what the queen had said. "Nothing," replied the grieving mother. "She put her hands on mine, and we silently wept together." God cares about you and will give you the strength to live another day. He brings the light of the morning after a night of weeping (Psalm 30:5). Our Lord notices when we become wounded, and He loves us enough to apply His tender mercy with a gentle touch. Let the Holy Spirit work in you. His way is best, and He turns our sorrow into joy (Psalm 30:5, John 16:20). God revives our spirit through singing and fellowship with other people. He restores our souls so that we may rest peacefully, knowing He is in control. Our Lord draws near to heal our broken hearts, and then He offers a garment of praise for the spirit of heaviness (Isa. 61:1-5). With hearts fully surrendered, God will revive us with new hope and purpose!

A mother and her four-year-old daughter were preparing to retire for the night. The child was afraid of the dark, and her mother was going through something that made her fearful. The child caught a glimpse of the moon outside the window when the light was out. "Mother," she asked, "is the moon God's light?" "Yes," said her mother. The next question was, "Will God put out His light and go to sleep?" The mother replied, "No, my child, God never goes to sleep." Then, out of the simplicity of a child's faith, the little girl reassured her mother, "Well, as long as God is awake, there's no sense in both of us staying awake." What does it mean that our souls are restored? Certainly, I understand the Biblical doctrine of restoration that through faith in the sacrificial atonement of Jesus, we can be restored to the perfect relationship with God that existed before the fall of humanity (Rom. 6:1-14). And I am so thankful! But the text I have chosen on restoration is a psalm of quiet trust. Psalm 23 is a song of gratitude to a loving God in a painful world. It is a message of comfort, hope, guidance, and joy. We can become so familiar with specific passages of Scripture that we no longer meditate on them as we should. We pass over them, thinking we have understood all there is to understand. But there is always more. The Word of God does not change (Psalm 33:11, 119:89). But our circumstances change, and the twenty-third Psalm is a passage so familiar that we may need to hear it again. David's great confidence in God's care and protection caused him to rest. Jesus said, "I am the bread of life: he that cometh to me shall never hunger; and he that believeth on me shall never thirst" (John 6:35). Our Lord provides nourishment that cannot be found elsewhere. His Word, His finished work at Calvary, His triumphant resurrection, and His indwelling Spirit will revive our hearts! Trusting in the promises of the Bible, we find strength in our minds, emotions, and will. Jesus came not only to offer eternal heaven to those who believe in Him (John 3:16). He came to give healing, renewal, and wholeness in this life. In this world, God puts our tears into His bottle (Psalm 56:8). In the next life, He will wipe them away forever (Rev. 21:4).

In the mid-1960s, a violent uprising occurred in the newly independent African nation called the Belgian Congo. Many people, including dozens of missionaries, were brutalized and murdered. Dr. Helen Roseveare offered her medical skills, saying she wanted to serve Christ no matter where and the cost. While serving there, she saw some of her colleagues shot through the temple and dropped into an open grave. She and other young women were brutalized at the hands of the rebel troops. Later she wrote a letter about that incredibly challenging time, "The phrase God gave me years ago, during the 1964 rebellion in Congo, in the night of my own greatest need, was this: 'Can you thank Me for trusting you with this experience, even if I never tell you why?'" Dr. Roseveare was able to say "yes" to that question. We have no right to demand an of God explanation, and he has every right to ask of us genuine consecration.

My soul is restored through communion with God and studying His Word. Peace will come when I place each day into God's hands. He cares, and He is sovereign in the details of life. Martin Luther noticed a bird quietly settling for the night one evening, and he exclaimed, "That little fellow preaches faith to us all! When darkness comes, he tucks his head under his wing and sleeps, leaving God to think for him." Reading the Bible reminds me that I depend on God for what happens next. Prayer gives life by stirring my thoughts and guiding my actions. You may ask, "Do passages of the Bible bring you comfort every time?" With joy, I can say, "Most of the time, they do." But there are times when it is difficult for me to move from the reality of a desperate situation to the hope of a promise, even when God made it. And yet, I want to live in faith - with my heart and hands wide open. I know His grace is sufficient (2 Cor. 12:9). I know His strength is made perfect in my weakness and having a verse of Scripture to lean on is what I need when navigating through a new season of life. I do not doubt that the good Shepherd who gave His life for me (John 10:11) will restore my soul!

Will you join me in prayer? Dear Lord, I thank you that you make all things new. In Matthew 5, you said, "Blessed are the poor in spirit: for theirs is the kingdom of heaven." You said those who mourn would be comforted. In Isaiah 61, you said you would give your people beauty for ashes. You promised a garment of praise for a spirit of heaviness. And you said these things that you may be glorified. So, I want you to be celebrated in the world through me. I have been called according to your purpose (Rom. 8:28), and I put my trust in you. I claim your promises of hope and renewal. Make my life a testimony of your faithfulness. I ask you to turn despair into rejoicing, according to your will and purpose, wherever it is needed. I ask these things in Jesus' name. Amen.

THE TESTING OF OUR FAITH

By faith, we are convinced of the things in Scripture that we cannot see, and we have unwavering confidence that God will fulfill His promises (Heb. 11:1). Now, where there is faith, it will be tested. In Hebrews chapter eleven, the writer speaks of many who lived with an assurance of something for which there was no tangible proof. And the faith of every individual recorded in this passage was tested. It is easy to read about these particular people of faith and fail to appreciate the element of surprise. Why? Because we know how the story ends. They did not. Those who are named in Scripture were not superheroes. They did not know if they would live, die, sink, or swim. But they knew God was with them. Therefore, they embraced the uncertainty. They didn't need an explanation for everything. They knew God had a plan. The apostle Peter says when we are "tried by fire," our faith becomes more precious than gold, "found unto praise and honor and glory at the appearing of Jesus Christ" (1 Pet. 1:6-7).

We are prone to skepticism and doubt when our world is rocked by unexpected events that throw us off balance. But as an anchor to a storm-tossed sea, faith is valuable. It produces steadfastness, character, and hope. So often we want to control the experiences of life. But to follow Christ is to surrender to His lordship. How wonderful it is to follow His leading! When we understand what it means to be a child of God, saved for all eternity and looking for eternal rest in heaven, we will find incomprehensible peace (Phil. 4:7). By fully trusting in the sovereignty of God, we become strong disciples who live by faith no matter what happens (2 Cor. 5:7). Most comforting of all, we know that God will never allow us to be tested beyond what we can handle (1 Cor. 10:13). His grace is sufficient! So perfect is God's strength in our weakness that Jesus tells us to rejoice in persecution, for "great is your reward in heaven" (2 Cor. 12:9, Matt. 5:12). Our brother James says a trust that is anchored in Scripture will be rewarded with a crown of life (James 1:2-12).

After we have received the grace of God by faith in the sacrifice of Jesus, the entire Christian life is lived out on the foundation of faith (Rom. 1:17, Gal. 2:20). Faith is the fuel of Christian living (2 Cor. 5:7). Jesus said, "In the world ye shall have tribulation: but be of good cheer; I have overcome the world" (John 16:33). Faith lives with unanswered questions. We are not only empowered by the Holy Spirit to endure but also to find joy in the journey. God will test our faith to humble us and to prove us; to know what is in our hearts and see if we will keep His commandments (Deut. 8:2). So, the next time you are "tried by fire," ask yourself, "What lesson am I supposed to learn?" The Psalmist David said, "Judge me, O Lord, according to my righteousness, and according to mine integrity that is in me" (Ps. 7:8). God loves us dearly. He wants us to grow in grace and the knowledge of Jesus Christ (2 Pet. 3:18). Spiritual maturity is not about what we do. It is what God does in us. King Solomon tells us that fire will test the purity of silver and gold. Still, the Lord evaluates the heart (Prov. 17:3). The Hebrew word translated as "test" in the Old Testament means to "examine, investigate, prove, scrutinize." The Greek word translated as "test" in the New Testament means to "prove, examine and, by implication, to approve." The same word is used for testing and approving. Therefore, passing a test of God's design is a joyous occasion because we emerge approved (1 Thess. 2:4).

Life is hard, and difficulty is certain. But as we walk with God, He promises to get us through even the darkest storms. George Mueller, a man known for trusting God in desperate circumstances, said, "God delights to increase the faith of His children. I say - and say it deliberately - trials, obstacles, difficulties, and sometimes defeats are the food of faith. We should take them from God's hands as evidence of His love and care for us in developing more and more that faith He is seeking to strengthen in us." The Old Testament patriarch Joseph never lost faith because his trust in God was not contingent upon his circumstances (Gen. 37-50). Oswald Chambers said, "Faith for my deliverance is not faith in God. Faith means, whether visibly delivered or not, I will stick to my belief that God is love." He said, "There are some things only learned in a fiery furnace."

Samuel Brengle was a man of profound faith who boldly preached the gospel. He was also a commissioner in the Salvation Army many years ago. As he passed by a saloon, a man threw a brick at his head. The aim was good, and Brengle nearly died. As it was, he spent eighteen months in recovery. During that time, he wrote a little book entitled Helps to Holiness. Thousands of copies were published. After he could preach again, people would often thank him for the book. He would respond, "If there had been no little brick, there had been no little book." His wife saved the brick, and she had Joseph's view of life engraved on it: "But as for you, ye thought evil against me; but God meant it unto good, to bring to pass, as it is this day, to save much people alive" (Gen. 50:20). Something that resembles gold is afraid of fire, but gold is not. If our faith is worth anything, it will prevail over life's disappointments.

Everyone will face challenging events that put confidence to the test. God knows who we are and wants us to know as well. He wants us to be confident in His ability to provide everything we need. David and Angie Maxwell married on June 2, 1990, in Columbus, Mississippi, and later welcomed their son, Reese, and their daughter, Kadie, to complete their family of four. Life was moving at an average pace, but things suddenly changed in 2016. Angie began having a difficult time with headaches, and it was hard for her to remember things. A CT scan in June of 2016 showed a tumor in the right hemisphere of Angie's brain. The couple was told that the cancer was aggressive and would need immediate treatment. "We lost everything in Hurricane Katrina when we were living on the Gulf Coast, and we didn't expect that we would ever be given anything worse than that. We were wrong," says David. But their faith never wavered. Even in the most difficult times, Angie would say, "God's got this." Reese recalls, "Even when mom was getting her head shaved, she wanted to raise money for missions. Part of the reason we could jump into our faith so easily was that mom's faith was so strong." During the two-and-a-half-year journey of Angie's sickness and following her death, this family had many challenging conversations with God that often involved anger and tears. David says, "The key is to stay honest with your feelings. God hears you." He says he will never understand why Angie was chosen to bear the pain and suffering of a brain tumor, but she always used it as an opportunity to lead someone to Christ. Even when God chose not to heal Angie physically, the family remained true to their firm belief that this life is only temporary, and they are all just moments behind her in eternity.

There are times in life when the clock stops and the action freezes. In those moments, we know that as a result of what we are experiencing, things will never be the same again. I do not understand why God took my wife when He did. Sometimes I feel helpless. Other times, overwhelmed. And when I don't know what to pray, I look up and meditate. I find strength in what the Psalmist said, "Give ear to my words, O Lord, consider my meditation. Hearken unto the voice of my cry, my King, and my God; for unto thee will I pray" (Ps. 5:1-2). Psalm 5:3 reveals how David started his day, "My voice shalt thou hear in the morning, O Lord; in the morning will I direct my prayer unto thee and will look up." When our world turns dark, the most faith-filled thing we can do is come to God honestly. Sometimes we come with open hands of surrender. Other times, with clenched fists. But know this: our questions will not sink our faith. Job and David repeatedly questioned God but were not condemned (Job 7, Psalm 10). Jacob was a man who encountered fear and anxiety, and he struggled with God in the process (Gen. 32:24-32). Sound familiar? The prophet Habakkuk was overwhelmed by the dark circumstances around him, and it seemed God was nowhere to be found. But his faith was intact. Doubt is not the enemy of faith. Unbelief is. And somewhere in Habakkuk's confusion and uncertainty, he believed God held the answers to life's problems. At the center of this prophet's book lies a believer's confidence, "The just shall live by faith" (Hab. 2:4). God is to be respected, but He is not fragile. He is sovereign. He knows our concerns before we make them known (Matt. 6:8) and invites us to seek grace in times of need (Heb. 4:14-16).

Corrie ten Boom (1892-1983) was a Dutch watchmaker, Christian writer, and public speaker. During the Second World War, she and her family helped many Jewish people escape the Nazi army by hiding them in her home. They were caught. She was arrested and sent to a concentration camp. Corrie wrote a biography that recounts the story of her family's efforts and how she found and shared hope in God while imprisoned. Afterward, when speaking to audiences about her horrific experiences, Corrie often looked down while talking. She was not reading notes. She wasn't even praying. She was working on a piece of needlepoint. After sharing the doubt, anger, and pain she experienced, Corrie would reveal the needlework. She would hold up the backside of the piece to show a jumble of threads with no discernible pattern and say, "This is how we see our lives." Then she would turn the needlepoint over to reveal the design of beautiful colors on the other side and conclude by saying, "This is how God views your life, and someday you will have the privilege of seeing it from His point of view."

Hebrews 10:23 says, "Let us hold fast the profession of our hope without wavering; for he is faithful that promised." God's plan is always best, faith endures, trials reveal the depth of our faith, and God rewards our loyalty. Charles Spurgeon said, "Believe this book of God, every letter of it, or else reject it. There is no logical standing place between the two. Be satisfied with nothing less than a faith that swims in the depths of divine revelation. A faith that paddles about the water's edge is poor at best. It is little better than a dry-land faith and is not good for much."

A television program preceding the 1988 Winter Olympics featured blind skiers being trained for slalom skiing, as impossible as that sounds. Paired with sighted skiers, the blind skiers were taught how to make right and left turns on the flats. When that was mastered, they were taken to the slope, where their sighted partners skied beside them, shouting, "Left!" and "Right!" As they obeyed the commands, they could negotiate the course and cross the finish line depending solely on the sighted skiers' word. It was either complete trust or catastrophe—a vivid picture of the Christian life. As believers, we should expect that God will test us, and we should pray that we will respond correctly. Testing ascribes the quality of creation to its creator. The testing of our faith is all for God's glory, not ours. Nothing arrests the attention of God like faith. In Luke 7:1-10 we read of our Lord's astonishment at the Roman commander's humility, awareness, and understanding of God's authority. This remarkable man received from God because he believed Him without hesitation!

What is the refuge from the storms of life? The Psalmist declares, "God is our refuge and strength, a very present help in trouble" (Ps. 46:1). From beginning to end, having complete confidence in God is the most wonderful way to live! We must be humble enough to let God call the shots and brave enough to follow where He leads.

JESUS CHRIST LIVES

During the feast of Passover, the message of Jesus to his disciples was clear. He spoke of a new commandment for all believers. Love would be the new standard (John 13:34-35), and Christ said His love in us expressed to others would mark us as His followers (John 17:26). The next day at Calvary, our Lord would prove this incredible love to the whole world. Then, three days later, He raised Himself to life! In John 11:25, Jesus said, "I am the resurrection and the life." Today, we testify of the resurrection because of historical and biblical evidence, and the power of the risen Christ has transformed our lives (Rom. 6:5-14). As a young man, D. L. Moody was suddenly called upon to preach a funeral sermon. He hunted through the four Gospels to find one of Christ's funeral sermons, but he searched in vain. He found that Christ broke up every funeral He ever attended. Death could not exist where He was. When the dead heard His voice, they sprang to life!

The atoning, death, burial, and resurrection of Jesus Christ are central to the Christian faith (1 Cor. 15:1-4), and Resurrection Day is the celebration of the accomplished Gospel. Absent the resurrection, Christianity becomes mere philosophy on balance with all other creeds and religious teachings. Without a living Savior, our belief in God's saving grace is destroyed. The apostle Paul said, "If Christ be not risen, then is our preaching vain, and your faith is also vain" [useless and worthless] (1 Cor. 15:14). But because Jesus lives, we who believe in Him can be assured of His return to earth and the certainty of our place in the reality of heaven (Titus 2:11-13). The resurrection of Christ is the most significant and meaningful event in the history of the world! Before Mary Magdalene met Jesus, she was enslaved by demonic powers. But our Lord liberated her from the forces that kept her spirit bound. Having been delivered, no doubt Mary said to herself and others, "I love Jesus for what He did for me, and I will follow Him wherever he goes." Certainly, this was evidenced by her lifestyle. When Jesus hung on the cross, Mary stood nearby with his mother. When they took his body down from the cross, she was there. When they placed him in the tomb, she was sitting against the sepulcher, watching it all happen (Matt. 27:50-61). Mary's gratitude to Jesus was for a lifetime. To Mary, the resurrection meant freedom from spiritual bondage. She had been delivered from the penalty of sin and the hand of Satan. Likewise, our hope is found in the gift of eternal life that brings us out of the valley of darkness and despair. Life everlasting begins now for all who, by faith, will receive God's grace (Eph. 2:8). Today, we worship the risen Christ, and a glorious future in heaven awaits beyond the grave!

Resurrection power will influence every aspect of our lives. We are saved by an eternal love that will not let us go. When Christ saves us, death will not have the last word, for Jesus has conquered the grave (Rev. 1:18). And because He arose, we too shall rise! Never doubt. There will always be a new morning for you in Jesus Christ! Having been forgiven for failing the Lord (Matt. 26:69-75), the apostle Peter later writes in a triumphant note, "Blessed be the God and Father of our Lord Jesus Christ, which according to his abundant mercy hath begotten us again unto a lively hope by the resurrection of Jesus Christ from the dead" (1 Pet. 1:3). What redemption! Failure is always an event and never a destiny for a child of God. The resurrection is essential to everyday life (Rom. 6:23), for in Him we live and move and have our being (Acts. 17:28). The risen Christ empowers us to walk in victorious faith and obedience (1 Pet. 1:3-5). This is not behavior modification. It is the living, transforming power of the Holy Spirit. It is not wishful thinking but the sure and confident expectation that our future is in His hands. The good news of the empty tomb is that Jesus is the Lord of our days and the Promise of our tomorrows. He is coming again in power and glory (1 Pet. 1:3-9). Christian friend, there is certainty and security in the promise (1 Thess. 4:13-18). Our Savior lives, and the final work of redemption has been accomplished. We no longer fear death. In the second epistle to the Corinthians, we are told what lies ahead for those who have been born again (John 1:12). Paul tells us that we have nothing to fear, that no matter how we die or when or where we have a promise from God that death itself cannot break. Death is not evaporation or annihilation but a glorious transition. Nothing – not even death - can separate us from the love of God in Christ Jesus (Rom. 8).

Scripture was fulfilled in the resurrection of Christ, for He conquered death and hell. Jesus said, "I am the way, the truth, and the life: no man cometh unto the Father, but by me." He was delivered for our offenses and raised again for our justification (Rom. 4:25). For Mary, the resurrection meant forgiveness and righteous living. For Peter, the resurrection meant forgiveness and a second chance. God's strength is made perfect in our weakness (2 Cor. 12:9). This is our testimony in the world. A miraculous entrance and supernatural exit evidence the life of Jesus. Christmas is the promise. Easter is the proof. The ultimate victory has come. Jesus has risen. The Lord is risen indeed! He is the Almighty God (Isa. 9:6), exercising His salvation in the world through the ministry of the Church (Matt. 28:18). He is in the community of his people. "Lo, I am with you alway, even unto the end of the world" (v20). What is the heart of faith? It is that Christ says to us, "All power is mine" (Phil. 2:10). "I am with you to make all things right" (James 1:12). "Do not fear… I live and you will live also" (John 14:19-27). Jesus Christ is not only the promise of our future. He is today's blessed reality through the indwelling of the Holy Spirit. This is our joy on Resurrection Day. Indeed, this is our joy every day. Jesus Christ lives!

WORSHIP THE KING

With all that is happening today, there is a bigger picture. God is aware of it all, and He is in control. News reports and fear, the enemy of your soul and your circumstance, all would lead you to believe otherwise. We need a fresh perspective. In 1 Samuel 30:6, we read that David was "greatly distressed,"… but he encouraged himself in the Lord his God." Pause for a moment and look up. There sits the King on His throne, the all-powerful God; He who "upholds all things by the word of his power" (Heb. 1:3). Trust in the Almighty who reigns forever; the One to whom the angels bow, crying "Holy, holy, holy… the whole earth is full of his glory" (Isa. 6:3). His eyes "are in every place" and nothing is hidden from Him (Prov. 15:3). He is the Lord of glory, the all-knowing Master of the universe. Nothing surprises Him. What you are experiencing right now is not a mystery to God (1 John 3:20). Jesus Christ has overcome the world (1 John 4:4), and "we are more than conquerors through him that loved us" (Rom. 8:35-37). Our perspective is limited, but His view is eternal from the throne of heaven. He sees everything and cares for us (Gen. 16:13; 1 Pet. 5:6-7). We cannot see around the corners. But because He can, we can trust in His guidance, provision, and sovereignty. The Psalmist said, "The Lord is my light and my salvation; whom shall I fear? The Lord is the strength of my life; of whom shall I be afraid?" (Psalm 27:1). This is not to say we will never be afraid, for in another song David declares, "What time I am afraid, I will trust in thee" (Psalm 56:3). But in both passages, trust is vital. A terrible circumstance may not be resolved instantly, but we can experience inner peace beyond explanation (John 14:27). Look up. Look to the sky! See the face of God shining even brighter against the backdrop of the world's darkest night. Open your Bible and see the truth about who God is. Be reminded of His majesty. Worship the King, for He is worthy!

Nearly 100,000 years is the time it would take for light, traveling at 186,000 miles per second, to get from one edge of our galaxy to the other. Then, there are another 350 billion galaxies! The little stars, having a radius of about six miles, can spin six hundred times per second. There is a volcano on Mars three times the size of Mount Everest. The Sun's core releases energy equivalent to one hundred billion nuclear bombs per second. A car ride to the nearest star at 70 miles per hour would last over 356 billion years. How many stars are there in the universe? The number is unimaginable, but scientists will say it's about ten times the number of cups of water in all the oceans of Earth. And, to think that God has a name for each (Psalm 147:4)! I can almost hear Him say, "You're fascinated by what I made? You should see me!" I listen to Him say, "I am with you. I will not leave you. Do not put limitations on me" (Isa. 41:10–20; 55:8-9). God has no rival. He is subject to no other power, and He reigns supreme (Rev. 1:8). Heaven is His throne, and the Earth is His footstool (Acts 7:49). He is robed with majesty, and His throne is established forever (Psalm 92:8). He is Almighty on the throne. All will bow before Him whose grandeur no one can surpass (Rom. 14:11). His majesty is displayed with lightning and thunderous voices going out from the throne proclaiming His holiness (Rev. 4:5). He is God Almighty. He always has been, is now, and forever will be (Psalm 90:1–2). Dominion and glory are His. His authority is everlasting, a kingdom that will never pass away nor be destroyed (Dan. 7:14). All authority in heaven and Earth belongs to Him (Rev. 4). None can fully describe the attributes of God, the manner of His existence or manifestation. His power to create, to produce something out of nothing, is beyond human understanding. The foundation of the Earth and the heavens are the works of His hands (Heb. 1:10).

He is the Creator and sustainer of the universe (Gen. 1). He owes His existence to no one. God is not subject to, altered, or aged by time. He is eternal (Psalm 90:2). In Him, there is height and depth that human intellect cannot measure. God is infinite. There is no limit to His being; therefore, He cannot be compressed into any definition. In His hand is the soul of every living thing and the breath of all humanity (Job 12:10). God's work is majestic in the creation, and His love is made manifest in redemption (1 John 4:9-10). He has all authority to free people from the curse of sin. The power of God will save us for eternity. He is the power unto the salvation of all who believe in Jesus Christ (1 Cor. 1:30). He is love. He is truth. He is life (John 14:6). His grace will change how we live, and by faith, we have the assurance of an eternal home in heaven (Acts 11:16–18). Jesus said, "I go to prepare a place for you…" (John 14:2). If God makes a promise, on what grounds do we doubt its fulfillment? God is not a man that He should lie; neither the son of man that He should repent. Hath he said, and shall he not do it? Or hath he spoken, and shall he not make it good? (Num. 23:19). He will accomplish His purpose! Everything we need is found in Almighty God (2 Peter 1:3–8).

In Him, our salvation, defense, and security are complete. His way is perfect. David said, "Thine, O Lord, is the greatness, and the power, and the glory, and the victory, and the majesty: for all that is in the heaven and in the Earth is thine; thine is the kingdom, O Lord, and thou art exalted as head above all. Both riches and honour come of thee, and thou reignest over all; and in thine hand is power and might; and in thine hand it is to make great, and to give strength unto all" (1 Chron. 29:11–12). Mary said of the Son of God yet in her womb, "My soul doth magnify the Lord… holy is his name" (Luke 1). God is not subject to human limitations. He appeared to Moses in the burning bush, Job in the whirlwind, and Adam in the cool of the day. In the New Testament, God was made flesh and dwelt among us. We beheld his glory, the glory as of the only begotten of the Father, full of grace and truth; God's only begotten Son, Jesus Christ (John 1:1–18). God is revealed in Jesus Christ our Lord! The holiness of God appears in the sanctifying work of the Holy Spirit in our hearts as we fully surrender to His lordship (1 Cor. 6:11). I want to visualize His majesty every day. I want to become enthralled in the throne room of heaven. I want to see the splendor and greatness of the Almighty. Bowing before God in humble gratitude, I will join the apostle Paul and declare, "Now unto the King eternal, immortal, invisible, the only wise God, be honor and glory for ever and ever. Amen" (1 Tim. 1:17).

God's people need hope now more than ever. We all want to know that everything will be okay, but hope can be difficult to find when life is caving, and all hell is against us. So, what does this mean? It means we must find God amid the chaos and uncertainty of the times. We need to be able to say as David did, "I have set the Lord always before me: because he is at my right hand, I shall not be moved" (Psalm 16:8). This means hope must be more than a concept — it must be a reality for us. The good news is that hope is alive! Jesus Christ is hope for the hopeless (Matt. 9:18-26). He mends broken hearts (Psalm 147:3). He is our strength and confidence, our Rock and refuge in times of trouble (Psalm 18:2). Christ never pretended life would be easy. Still, He has already overcome the enemy at Calvary (Rev. 1:18). God provides His Word as a faithful anchor for us when the storms of life come. The Bible declares, "Be anxious for nothing, but in everything by prayer and supplication, with thanksgiving, let your requests be made known to God; and the peace of God, which surpasses all understanding, will guard your hearts and minds through Christ Jesus" (Phil. 4:6-7). In these days of turmoil, may we ask the Lord to give us a new perspective! We are His workmanship, His children, and the love of His life (1 John 3:16). "Now the God of hope fill you with all joy and peace in believing, that ye may abound in hope, through the power of the Holy Ghost" (Rom. 15:13). Oh that we would look heavenward today and worship the King!

USE MY LIFE, DEAR LORD

I enjoy reading about people who have blessed others by surrendering their heartache to the Lord. The stories of how these songs came to us are amazing.

Henry Wadsworth Longfellow had fallen into a depression in 1861 when his second wife, Frances, died. She had been sealing envelopes with hot wax when a flame caught her clothes on fire. She died the next day. Henry, burned severely as well, was too sick to attend her funeral. The death marked a turning point in his life. On Friday, December 25, 1863, Longfellow—as a 57-year-old widowed father of six children, the oldest of which had been nearly paralyzed as his country fought a war against itself – sought to capture the conflict in his own heart and the world of injustice and violence he observed around him. Then, as he hears the Christmas bells ringing in Cambridge and the singing of "peace on earth" the theme of his poem eventually leads him from bleak despair to a confident knowledge that God is alive and that righteousness shall prevail. There is hope for all who sing, 'I Heard the Bells on Christmas Day.'

On December 29, 1876, Philip and Lucy Bliss traveled through Ohio on the Pacific Express train to an engagement in Chicago. At the crossing of a trestle, the bridge collapsed. All seven carriages fell into the icy ravine below. Mr. Bliss survived the fall and escaped from the wreck, but the carriages caught fire, and he returned to try to rescue his wife. Although he was advised against it, Bliss returned to the fire, saying: "If I cannot save her, I will perish with her." The young couple did not survive. Ninety-two of the 159 passengers died on that day of tragedy. Most of the cargo was burned, but a few remains were retrieved from the accident site. Found in his trunk, which somehow survived the crash and fire, was a manuscript bearing the lyrics of the only well-known Bliss gospel song for which he did not write a tune. The lyrics found were titled 'My Redeemer.' Soon after, the lyrics were set to the music of Philip Bliss' best-known hymn, 'I Will Sing of My Redeemer.'

Dr. R. A. Torrey, Moody Bible Institute's second president, told the following story. "I received a letter from a father who told me of a son causing him and his family a great deal of trouble. The father felt that attendance at Moody would help. I sympathized, but I had to deny his request. After many letters of pleading his cause, I finally gave in with the stipulation that the rebellious teen must see me each day and make every effort to abide by the rules of the Institute. Finally, after many months of counseling, the prayers of the boy's father were answered." That young man was William R. Newell. Newell became a minister and later returned to Moody Bible Institute as a teacher. One day in 1895, Newell sat in his classroom during a planning period. He began to pen a word picture as a poem describing his testimony. He wrote the words on the back of a used envelope. After composing the poem, Newell paid a visit to Daniel Towner, the Music Director at Moody. Towner went to a vacant piano room, sat down, and started writing a tune for his friend's lyrics. An hour later, the music was finished, and the two friends sat by a piano, singing the new creation together. Newell's testimony turned song reminds us of all Christ did for us – entitled 'At Calvary.'

When Charles Wesley was converted, he had been ill in bed for some time, and the fear of death had often come into his mind. On Sunday, May 21, 1738, his brother John and some friends sang a hymn. After they went out, he prayed alone for some time. In his journal, we read: "I was composing myself to sleep in quietness and peace when I heard one come in and say, In the name of Jesus of Nazareth, arise, and believe, and thou shalt be healed of all thine infirmities. The words struck me in the heart. I lay musing and trembling. With a strange palpitation of heart, I said - yet feared to say, "I believe, I believe!" These memories he has woven into that wonderful third verse of a hymn: 'Jesus! the name that charms our fears That bids our sorrows cease; 'Tis music in the sinner's ears, 'Tis life, and health, and peace.' This stanza and five others form the words to the great song, 'Oh For a Thousand Tongues to Sing.'

It was December 1772 in Olney, England. John Newton began writing a hymn at forty-seven that would grow increasingly popular over the next 350 years. Newton grew up with both his mother and father. However, his mother died while his father was away at sea. Newton began his career searching the African coast for slaves to capture and sell for profit. On one journey, Newton and his crew encountered a storm that swept some of his men overboard and left others with the likelihood of drowning. With both hands fastened onto the boat wheel, Newton cried to God, saying, "Lord, have mercy on us." After eleven hours of steering, the remainder of the crew found safety with the calming of the storm. From then on, Newton dated March 21 as a day of humiliation, prayer, and praise. God changed him from a man who was an advocate for the slave trade to a man actively working towards abolishing it. In later years, Newton began to suffer the loss of his memory. Although his thoughts were limited, Newton said he could remember two things, "That I am a great sinner, and that Christ is a great Savior." With this conviction of newly found life that he found only in Christ, Newton penned the words to a song that has touched many lives – 'Amazing Grace.'

Charlotte Elliott of Brighton, England, was an embittered woman. Her health was broken, and her disability had hardened her. "If God loved me," she muttered, "He would not have treated me this way." Hoping to help her, a Swiss minister, Dr. Cesar Malan, visited the Elliott home on May 9, 1822. Over dinner, Charlotte lost her temper and railed against God and her family in a violent outburst. Her embarrassed family left the room, and Dr. Malan was alone. "You are tired of yourself, aren't you?" he asked. "You are holding on to your hate and anger because you have nothing else to cling to." "What is your cure?" asked Charlotte. He answered, "The faith you are trying to despise." As they talked, Charlotte softened. "If I wanted to become a Christian and to share the peace and joy you possess," she finally asked, "what would I do?" "You would give yourself to God just as you are now, with your fighting and fears, hates and loves, pride and shame." Charlotte did come just as she was, and her heart was changed that day. Years later, she wrote a song that has been used by many as the call to an altar of repentance and forgiveness, 'Just As I Am.'

Henry Francis Lyte was orphaned. Despite his poverty, he attended college and later served in full-time ministry. The death of one of his friends brought about a profound change in him as he was called to his bedside to offer solace and comfort. But he discovered he had little to offer by way of consolation. Through the prayerful search for God's Word, he came to a firmer faith in Christ. Later he said, "I was greatly affected by the whole matter and brought to look at life and its issues with a different eye than before, and I began to study my Bible and preach in another manner than I had previously done." Having long suffered from a lung disorder that turned into tuberculosis, he preached his last sermon with difficulty at fifty-four. Not long before passing from this life, Lyte took a long walk in prayer along the coast of Italy, then retired to his room. An hour later, he emerged with a written copy of 'Abide With Me.'

Joseph Scriven was a devoted member of the Plymouth Brethren Church who sincerely desired to help those genuinely destitute. His parents had enough financial means to afford an excellent educational opportunity for their son. He enrolled in Trinity College in Dublin, where he graduated with a bachelor's degree. He fell in love with a young lady eager to spend her life with him. However, the day before their wedding, she fell from her horse while crossing a bridge over the River Bann and drowned in the water below. Joseph stood helplessly watching from the other side. To overcome his sorrow, he began to wander. By age 25, his travels had taken him to an area near Port Hope, Canada. There, he tutored some of the local children in their schoolwork. He often served for no wages and even shared his clothes with those less fortunate than himself. Ten years later, he received word that his mother, still in Ireland, was facing a crisis. Joseph drafted a poem and sent it to her. He met a wonderful young lady, Elisa Roche, and again fell in love. They had exciting plans to be married. However, tragedy reared its ugly head again, and she died of pneumonia before the wedding. On October 10, 1896, Joseph became critically ill. In his delirium, he rose from his bed and staggered outdoors, where he fell into a small creek and drowned at age sixty-six. His poem for his mother has become the famous hymn, 'What a Friend We Have in Jesus.'

On March 5, 1858, Fanny Crosby, the blind hymnist and America's "Queen of Gospel Songs," quietly married Alexander Van Alsteine. A year later, the couple suffered a tragedy that shook the deepest regions of Fanny's heart. She gave birth to a child, but no one knew if it was a boy or a girl. In later years, she never spoke about it except to say in her oral biography, "God gave us a tender babe, and soon the angels came down and took our infant up to God and His throne." Years later, musician Howard Doane knocked on the door of Fanny's apartment in Manhattan. "I have exactly forty minutes," he said, "before I must meet a train for Cincinnati. I have a tune for you. See if it says anything to you. Perhaps you can commit it to memory and compose a poem to match it." He then hummed the tune. Fanny clapped her hands and said, "Why, that says, 'Safe in the arms of Jesus!'" She retreated to the other room of her tiny apartment, knelt on the floor, and asked God to give her the words quickly. She had composed the poem within half an hour and dictated it to Doane, who dashed off to catch his train. During her lifetime, Fanny claimed the hymn was written for the bereaved, especially for mothers who had lost children – 'Safe in the Arms of Jesus.'

Carl Boberg had recently quit his work as a sailor and started working as a lay minister in his native Sweden. He would later go on to be a newspaper editor and a member of the Swedish Parliament. In 1885, he was inspired by the sound of church bells ringing during a wild thunderstorm and penned the poem "O Great God." Boberg's nine-verse poetry didn't catch on and seemed destined to be forgotten. However, three years later, someone out there liked it enough to match the words with a traditional Swedish melody. When Boberg found out about it, he quickly published the poem again in his newspaper in 1891, with the musical notation added. Fast forward a few decades to the 1930s. Somehow, this poem put to music had traveled across borders, and English missionary Stuart Hine heard the song (in Russian) while in Poland. Deeply moved by the song, he translated it into English, tweaked the musical arrangement and some of the wording, and took it home with him to England. In English, the song was now called 'How Great Thou Art.' How astonishing that this song, recorded over 1,800 times in the last 50 years, had its origins as a poem in a small town in Sweden, written by a sailor turned lay minister, and somehow wound its way around the globe. Such are the stories of hymns.

A pharmacist named Sanford Bennett filled prescriptions in Elkhorn, Wisconsin, when his friend Joseph Webster entered the store. Joseph was a local musician who suffered from periods of depression. Joseph was unusually blue on this particular day, and his face was long. Looking up, Sanford asked, "What's the matter now?" "It's no matter," Joseph replied, "it will be all right by and by." An idea for a hymn hit Sanford like a flash of sunlight. Sitting at his desk, he began writing as fast as he could. The words came almost instantly. Two customers entered the drugstore, but no attempt was made to assist them. Sanford was too absorbed in his poem, so they walked over to the stove and visited with Joseph. Finally, Sanford rose and joined them, handing a sheet of paper to his friend. "Here is your prescription, Joe," he said. "I hope it works." Picking up his fiddle, Joseph played a melody over a time or two, then spoke to the others, "We four make a good male quartet. Let us try the new song and see how it sounds." And, for the first time, 'Sweet By and By' was being sung.

The best way to tell how "I Need Thee Every Hour" came to be is through Annie Hawk's own words. "I remember well the circumstances under which I wrote the hymn. It was a bright June day, and I became so filled with the sense of the nearness of my Master that I began to wonder how anyone could live without Him, in either joy or pain. Suddenly, the words I need thee every hour flashed into my mind, and very quickly, the thought had full possession of me. Seating myself by the open windows, I caught up my pencil and committed the words to paper - almost as they are today. For myself, the hymn at its writing was prophetic rather than expressive of my own experiences. It wafted out to the world on the wings of love and joy instead of under the stress of great personal sorrow, with which it has often been associated. At first, I did not understand why the hymn so greatly touched the throbbing heart of humanity. Years later, however, under the shadow of a great loss, I understood something of the comforting power of the words I had been permitted to give out to others in my hours of sweet serenity and peace." When Annie's husband died sixteen years later, she found her hymn – 'I Need Thee Every Hour' - among her most incredible comforts.

When Dr. P. W. Philpot was pastor of Moody Church in Chicago, he received a frantic phone call from the Stephens Hotel at about two o'clock in the morning. The voice on the line pleaded with him to come, for a young lady was extremely ill and disturbed. He spent some time with her and eventually led her to the Lord in salvation. For the remaining years of his stay in Chicago, he heard nothing of this woman or her family. In time he moved to California, where he became pastor of the Open Door in Los Angeles. One Sunday afternoon after the service, the three people he had met in Chicago came to see him. The lady who had come to salvation years before thanked him for leading her to Christ. She told him she used a God-given talent to write gospel songs. With that, she handed the pastor a manuscript of a new song, saying, "I have written this, especially for you for introducing me to the most wonderful person I have ever known." As the pastor opened the manuscript, he saw the beautifully written song she had identified as 'Jesus Is the Sweetest Name I Know.'

These are beautiful stories of how God uses His people to heal broken hearts and cause faith to soar. It is lovely to hear music that has come from the heart of God. It is even more wonderful to send it back to Him! As I read these narratives and others like them, I think, "What impact am I making on the kingdom of God? Whose life is influenced by the Holy Spirit's work in me?" Stories like these are regulated more than just yesteryear. Our Lord continues to work in those willing to spend a lifetime for something greater than life itself. God specializes in using surrendered hearts, not for man's sake, but for His glory. Today, my prayer is simple: "Dear Lord, by your grace, I want to be a blessing to those around me. So, use me for your will and purpose, whether in joy or pain. In Jesus' name, I pray. Amen."

Live Well and Finish Strong

To illustrate what it means to seize the day: A young soldier and his commanding officer got on a train together. The only available seats were across from an attractive young woman traveling with her grandmother. As they engaged in pleasant conversation, the soldier and the young woman kept eyeing one another; the attraction was mutual. Suddenly the train went into a tunnel, and the car became pitch black. Immediately two sounds were heard: the "smack" of a kiss and the "whack" of a slap across the face. The grandmother thought, "I can't believe he kissed my granddaughter, but I'm glad she gave him the slap he deserved." The commanding officer thought, "I don't blame the boy for kissing the girl, but it's a shame that she missed his face and hit me instead." The young girl thought, "I'm glad he kissed me, but I wish my grandmother hadn't slapped him for doing it." And as the train broke into the sunlight, the soldier could not wipe the smile off his face. He had just seized the opportunity to kiss a pretty girl and slap his commanding officer - and had gotten away with both! That young man knew how to seize the day.

Time is like a river. We cannot touch the same water twice, for the flow that has passed will never pass again. Life is short at best, and we cannot boast of tomorrow (Prov. 27:1). In what is believed to be the oldest psalm in the Bible, Moses wants us to recognize the brevity of life (Ps. 90:12). He tells us to make wise choices. He says to live each day for God's glory - not ours. And to perfectly manage the time allotted, we must develop a godly point of view. Without an eternal perspective, we misinterpret life. We see things that would hinder our comfort and convenience as a nuisance, even an enemy. We reject hardship because we do not want to accept that we are only a tiny part of a universal plan established by a sovereign God.

Now our brother Paul had a way of interpreting his circumstances with a wide-angle lens (2 Cor. 4:16-17). He saw his afflictions as a momentary assignment for a more glorious future. In times of testing, he could say with the ancient prophet Job, "I cannot see him: but he knoweth the way that I take; and when he hath tried me, I shall come forth as gold. My foot hath held his steps, his way have I kept, and not declined. Neither have I gone back from the commandment of his lips; I have esteemed the words of his mouth more than my necessary food" (Job 23:9-12). By faith, these men could see as God sees, to value as God values. This kind of faith comes only by surrendering to the Word of God (Rom. 10:17). Paul's desire to be with the Lord changed his view of difficult circumstances, and he rejoiced in all things (Phil. 4:1-7).

A well-known Christian author puts it this way: "Present sufferings must be seen in the light of the promise of eternal happiness in God. The scales cannot be balanced in this life alone. We do not pass our peaks in this life. The best is yet to come. New and better opportunities will replace missed opportunities. Do not wait until you are near death to believe that. Believing it now will change how you think, how you view the people around you, and what you do with your time and money, which are God's." With heaven in view, we are more likely to live each moment for God's purposes. Time is limited. Every life is a storyline of choices. The Psalmist says, "we spend our years as a tale that is told" (Ps. 90:9). In the parable of the talents, we learn about using God's wonderful gifts most effectually (Matt. 25:14-30). Through the study of the Word, we understand what God values most. And once we know, we can fix our priorities based on a Bible that must always have the last word on any subject. A well-lived life is the discipline of Scriptural doctrines, and I pray we will allow the Holy Spirit to help us live each day in the light of God's grace!

Some opportunities will present themselves only once. The apostle Paul spoke of a "great door" for practical work that was open to him, only for a while (1 Cor. 16:9). Evangelist Billy Graham was at a hotel in Seattle, fast asleep, when he suddenly woke with a mighty burden to pray for Marilyn Monroe, the American actress, and sex symbol. Graham understood something of the urgency of the Spirit's prompting. He began to pray, and the burden was just as substantial the next day. He had his assistants try to contact Monroe over the phone, but her agent made it difficult. She was too busy, the man said, but she would meet with the evangelist – sometime. "Not now," said the agent. "Maybe two weeks from now." Two weeks later, the headlines of America shouted out the news that Marilyn Monroe had committed suicide. She would never have that opportunity to find peace in her soul.

D. L. Moody, the famous evangelist, was preaching in Chicago on October 8, 1871. It was one of the largest crowds he had ever addressed, and his topic was "What will you do with Jesus?" He focused on the decision that faced Pilate, and Moody concluded by saying, "I wish you would seriously consider this subject, for next Sunday we will speak about the cross. Then I will ask you, 'What will you do with Jesus?'" The service closed with a hymn, but the melody was never completed. The unpleasant sounds of fire-fighting equipment filled the auditorium. The streets erupted in panic. The famous Chicago fire of 1871 broke out that night and almost burned Chicago off the map. The sermon on the cross never came. Moody often said afterward, "I have never since dared to give an audience a week to think about their salvation." The questions haunted him: "How many were ready? How many windows of opportunity closed on that fateful night?"

Jonathon Edwards led a remarkable life. His preaching launched the first two revivals ever to sweep America. Edwards had made the following covenant with himself: "I resolve to live with all my might while I do live. I resolve never to lose one moment and to improve my use of time in the most profitable way possible. I resolve never to do anything I wouldn't do if it were the last hour of my life." This man's legacy lives on because he honored God with the precious moments given to him. Dr. F. B. Meyer (1847-1929) was a Baptist pastor who touched the world through his pulpit and print ministry. His biographer explains how he would redeem the time, "If he had a long railway journey before him, he would settle himself in his corner of the railway carriage, open his dispatch case which was fitted as a sort of stationery cabinet, and set to work on some article, quite oblivious of his surroundings. Often at lengthy conventions, and even in committee meetings, when the proceeding did not demand his undivided attention, he would discreetly open his case and proceed to answer letters." Dr. Meyer explains Psalm 90 this way, "Moses' complaint about the shortness of life indicates that he was no idler. The days were not long enough for all he had to do; therefore, life seemed to pass so quickly through his hands. But amidst all that made him sad, he found solace in the thought that what he did would last."

Most of us desire to rise above the ordinary to distinguish ourselves. No one wants life to be mediocre. By nature, we want our lives to be whole. We want our lives to count for something yet greater. This is a worthy goal, but only if we live in the light of eternity. This is what makes life valuable. God created us for His glory (Isa. 43:7) and worked all things after the counsel of his own will (Eph. 1:3-14). We should be motivated to bring glory to God in everything (1 Cor. 10:31), for this is the chief purpose of our existence (Rev. 4:11). Glorifying God involves our worship (Ps. 100:2-3). It is praising Him as our Creator and Savior. It is living in a relationship and faithful service. It is pointing souls to the cross of Calvary. We are created for His pleasure, and the only worthwhile life is one of surrender and obedience to our Lord (Eccl. 12:13-14).

Today I ask God to keep me focused on His purposes. I want to screen out all distractions of life that do not bring Him honor. Only two things are eternal: people and God's Word. And it is time I invest heavily in both. When the Psalmist tells us to "number our days" he is not speaking of a mathematical calculation but a call to wide-awake living. Regardless of age, we never know how close we are to the finish line. Our purpose is not to count our days but to make our days count. Ask yourself these questions, "What do I want to see happen in my life? What small step can I take today toward that purpose?" With the Holy Spirit's help, I pray we live well and finish strong!

A PERFECT HEART AND
A WILLING MIND

According to the Bible, the Psalmist David had a perfect heart, not because he never sinned or failed God, but because he never turned away from the Lord. He quickly confessed and repented when he was made aware of his sin. David was not perfect in heart because of his performance, but because he had an abiding love for God. He said, "I will delight myself in thy commandments, which I have loved… and I will meditate in thy statutes." When we read Psalm 119:47-48, it's easy to see David's adoration for God and His Word. In 1 Chronicles 28:9, King David instructed his son Solomon to serve God with "a perfect heart and a willing mind." He prayed that Solomon would also keep the commandments, testimonies, and statutes of God (1 Chron. 29:19). This was his earnest desire. But then, in 2 Chronicles 25:2, we read of another king who "did that which was right in the sight of the Lord, but not with a perfect heart." How can this be? Simply put, there are times when we do the right things for the wrong reasons.

Perfection toward God is unconditional devotion offered by those whose motives are pure. Our priority is not in the doing - but in our relationship with God. Even as the Son of man came not to be ministered unto, but to minister… (Matt. 20:28), every follower of Christ is called to a life of service. Jesus did not seize on the privileges that were rightfully His, but He came to this earth in great humility to serve. We are called to do the same, and He is the One who examines our motivation for serving (Prov. 16:2).

What does it mean to have a perfect heart? First, it does not imply a sinless, flawless existence. Our nature is to judge perfection by outward performance. Still, God judges the heart (1 Sam. 16:7). He is interested in what we do – but equally important to Him is why we do it (Prov. 21:27, 1 Cor. 4:5). God calls us to position our hearts toward Him, for He sees the unseen motives. In Scripture, perfection is completeness, uprightness, and obedience. By the strength of the Holy Spirit, we can walk blameless in the beauty of what Jesus has done through His death, burial, and resurrection. A perfect heart and a willing mind cry out with David, "Search me, O God, and know my heart: try me, and know my thoughts: and see if there be any wicked way in me and lead me in the way everlasting" (Ps. 139:23-24). The Lord searches our hearts, and He understands all the imaginations of our thoughts (1 Chron. 28:9). Yet the Spirit's searching is not vindictive but redemptive. His purpose isn't to condemn us by resurrecting some old transgression. It prepares us to come into His holy presence to enjoy the sweet fellowship! In Psalm 24, the question is asked, "Who shall ascend into the hill of the Lord? And who shall stand in his holy place?" Then the answer, "He that hath clean hands and a pure heart."

Throughout the ages, people of God have emphasized the need to love and serve the Lord with heart, soul, mind, and strength (Mark 12:30). Some have failed in this quest because they have turned from God and accepted the philosophy of the world. But righteous men and women have consistently applied their hearts and minds to understanding and obeying Biblical principles. How does this understanding come? Through the study of the Word, faith, and earnest prayer. David said, "I will behave myself wisely in a perfect way... I will walk within my house with a perfect heart" (Ps. 101:2). God prescribes a perfect way of life through Scripture. David expressed a desire to act wisely and a purpose to do it. Our fellowship with God affects our perception of what happens in and around us. As we seek the Holy Spirit's leading, we view our time on earth and eternity as God does. Godliness is living our faith with an eternal perspective, which becomes apparent through our obedience to the Bible. A perfect heart is a receptive heart, responding to the Word of God without hesitation or compromise. A willing mind is a meek and teachable spirit fully tuned to the voice of God through Scripture. The Lord said to Abram, "walk before me and be thou perfect" (Gen. 17:1). God said to Israel, "Thou shalt be perfect with the Lord thy God" (Deut. 18:13). Jesus said, "Be ye therefore perfect, even as your Father which is in heaven is perfect" (Matt. 5:48). The apostle Paul adds, "…that ye may stand perfect and complete in all the will of God" (Col. 4:12). The Bible says that although King Amaziah did what was right in the sight of God, his heart was not perfect. Too often, we define Christianity based on good deeds. Amaziah knew the law well, and he followed the law. This king had every opportunity to serve God fully and encourage his people to serve God faithfully. Yet, he did not seek the perfect will of God. Instead, he acted on self-made plans. God sent a prophet to warn him to repent, but he would not listen. Amaziah, the king of Judah, whose name means "strengthened by God," could have had a long, successful reign had he continued following the Lord. But his story became another narrative of the fate of those who turn from God.

A perfect heart is filled with the love of God - and love for God. The apostle Paul said he could not claim that he was perfect but was pursuing perfection (Phil. 3:12). By what means? He had an open heart, transparent and honest before God and others. He was willing to receive correction because he wanted to do things for the right reasons. He was associated with God's truth and sensitive to His authority (Ps. 34:18). Whatever we do for the Lord, the heart from where it comes and the attitude with which we carry it out matters. A perfect heart is yielded, and we can know the mind of God only through the study of Scripture. A perfect heart rejoices in the opportunities for forgiveness and mercy (James 4:8), developing a purity of spirit and revulsion to sin. Righteous living flows from a divine relationship where we no longer measure behavior against outward rules. A person whom Jesus Christ has redeemed will not live a life characterized by continuous, willful sin. Their discomfort with sin is evidence of their new nature because they want to please the Lord. Good deeds are not a precondition of faith. They are a consequence. And the work of the cross should compel us to serve a good God who wants the best for us.

Perfect: complete and not defective. Willing: determined and desiring. A perfect heart longs for the Holy Spirit to expose everything that is not like Christ. A willing mind has the desire to be pure before the Lord. These are marks of the Spirit dwelling within. I ask myself, "Are my motives pure? Whose praise do I desire?" Jesus knows the temptation we face, and He speaks to this natural impulse in Matthew 5:16, where He said, "Let your light so shine before men, that they may see your good works, and glorify your Father which is in heaven." Our lives should be such that when the world looks on, they will know God is being glorified. This is a choice, and it all depends on the intent of our hearts. If we act to please others, we will never bring glory to God. But if we seek opportunities to honor Him, sinners will experience God's saving grace. The key to having a perfect heart is Jesus Christ, for He alone can cleanse and forgive sin!

God is looking for a perfect heart, not a perfect performance. The Pharisees prided themselves in following all of the laws and performing brilliantly, but their hearts were far from truthful. Without love for God and others, the external observance of the commandments becomes empty. Speaking to religious leaders of His day, Jesus specifically warned of this danger: "Woe unto you, scribes and Pharisees, hypocrites! For ye make clean the outside of the cup and of the platter, but within they are full of extortion and excess... for ye are like unto whited sepulchers, which indeed appear beautiful outward, but are within full of dead men's bones, and of all uncleanness" (Matt. 23). May we keep our hearts pure (Matt. 5:8). May we not allow offense, pride, or bitterness to disturb our relationship with God, nor let ourselves fall under condemnation (Rom. 8:1). Honor God. He will show Himself strong on your behalf. It is possible to minister from impure motives (Phil. 1:17). But God is not impressed (Matt. 6:1). Selfish intentions can hinder our prayers (James 4:3). Here are some questions to help us evaluate our motives: If other people never know of my giving and serving, would I still do it? Would I joyfully serve in a lesser position in the local church? If others misunderstand my heart, will I stop serving? If those to whom I minister never show gratitude, will I continue? Do I determine success based on a comparison to others? God looks at our motivation for evidence of righteousness in our hearts (Heb. 4:14), and the greatest freedom we will ever know is the blessing that comes from our love and commitment to God.

LET YOUR LIGHT SHINE

As a child, I remember singing in Sunday School, "This little light of mine, I'm gonna let it shine… let it shine, let it shine, let it shine." It was a simple song then, with an even greater message for me today. The song's origin is unknown, but its theme is taken from remarks Jesus made to His followers in Matthew 5:14-16, "Ye are the light of the world. Let your light so shine before men, that they may see your good works, and glorify your Father which is in heaven." What does it mean to let our light shine in the world? The light speaks of a surrendered disciple of Christ, revealing a gospel message dispelling sin's darkness. The central truth of the gospel is that God provided a way of salvation for all who believe in the death, burial, and resurrection of Jesus Christ (Rom. 5:8-11, 1 Cor. 15:1-8). The brightness of God in us is expressed through a manner of living made possible by the Holy Spirit's power. In 1 Peter 4:10-11, we read, "As every man hath received the gift, even so, minister the same one to another… that God in all things may be glorified through Jesus Christ." Never doubt that people are watching us. They are watching - and they are evaluating. Someone has said, "Preach the gospel at all times and use words if necessary." This is not to imply a more excellent spiritual value assigned to good deeds over preaching (1 Cor. 1:21). But good works should complement our preaching to the extent that people are convinced of the truth and excellency of the Bible. What a great responsibility we bear when we say we are followers of Christ. What a privilege. The Holy Spirit is the treasure of God dwelling in earthen vessels (2 Cor. 4:7). The apostle Paul said, "How beautiful are the feet of them that preach the gospel of peace and bring glad tidings of good things!" (Rom. 10:14).

Marilyn, a former atheist, writes about her conversion: "For years, I held the belief that there was no God, not expecting it ever to change.

But then I met someone who caused me to become interested in the possibility of God. She was caring, kind, and brilliant. It bothered me that someone so intelligent could believe in God. She talked about God like he was her closest friend. She was convinced he deeply loved her. I knew her life well. Any concern she would take to God, trusting him to work it out or care for her in some way. She would tell me, quite candidly, that she was merely praying that God would act upon her concerns. For over a year, I regularly saw answers to her prayers. I watched her life through a myriad of circumstances, and her faith in God was unwavering. I wanted to believe in God because I admired her life and love for others." Marilyn continues, "When I think of the value of knowing God, it is this: that we can understand life, we can proceed with clarity. We can avoid pitfalls, we can be led by God, we can know truth, we can be given strength, hope, peace, and enjoy the most important relationship with One who will be faithful to us in love. Until we come to know Him, we will always be searching, always testing other possibilities and find them lacking. But when we respond to God's offer to be in relationship with Him, we are satisfied and complete. We now are equipped to live this life with a plan and with Someone who can lead us in it."

A young man writes, "By the time I turned fifteen, I was neck-deep in the mire of my teenage rebellion, hanging out with a bad group of friends. One day at school, we saw two classmates coming toward us, each with a Bible. I tried to move out of their way, but for some crazy reason, my feet would not budge. How strange. I can still picture the nervous tension etched on their faces as they walked toward us. Despite their fears, they began sharing things like sin, hell, heaven, and faith in Jesus Christ. My friends and I blasphemed, joked, poked fun at, and challenged those two Christians with questions like, "Oh yeah….so who made God then?" I don't remember much else from that ten-minute, divinely orchestrated conversation; only the thoughts raced through my mind as they walked away. I remember being jealous and thinking, "I wish I had what they had." My buddies and I began discussing the conversation a few minutes later. We agreed that it took guts to go around and talk to people like that. Although we were thoroughly unrepentant, we couldn't help but be impressed. That first gospel seed was planted in the soil of my teenage heart, and seven years later, while a senior in college, the Lord decided it should bear fruit. I remain convinced that if God's children were obedient to the great commission (Matt. 28:19), the Lord would do His work!" Christian friend, we cannot accomplish anything of eternal value unless the Holy Spirit works within us. And just because someone isn't interested in a spiritual discussion today doesn't mean that the Spirit cannot soften the most complex heart over time. Our job is to help people take one step closer to Christ, leaving the results and timing to God (John 6:44).

When did you first experience Jesus? How did you come to know Him? For me, the light of an earthen vessel was reflected by my parents. Their faithfulness to the Lord - and His to them - persuaded me to want a relationship with God. In the book of Acts, everyone was not always in agreement, but enduring love and respect was the source of unification for members in this local church. All labored for the cause of Christ. They threw their houses open to hospitality and united worship. They stood ready to help a foreign brother or sister. The poor, the sick, and the friendless were the cause of their care. God often uses the witness, the strength, and the encouragement of people to accomplish His will. Sometimes we need to take a step back and look at the big picture of our lives to see His hand in it. Share it with others if you have known God's love and guidance. Be the source of hope and love they so desperately need. Pray and ask the Lord to open doors for you to take His love to others. Share your salvation story by asking, "Can I tell you about the greatest thing that ever happened to me?" Your spoken testimony - and the way you live it - is powerful. God manifests in the world through our prayers, hospitality, service acts, love, and compassion for people (Matt. 25:31-46).

We cannot convince people to receive Christ. We are called to introduce them to the Lord through intelligent conversation and let God do the convincing (2 Cor. 7:10). Now, it is our duty to witness to everyone we meet with sound judgment. The story is told of an old eccentric member of a particular church, a barber, who quickly told others of the emotional fire burning within him. But very often, he needed to be more careful in his approach. After lathering a man for a shave, the concerned barber picked up his razor and said, "Sir, are you prepared to meet your God?" The customer was last seen running down Main Street with a lather on his face! But honestly, we are to make the most of the opportunities that come our way and trust that God will use us to lead people to Calvary. Remember again what Jesus said: "Let your light so shine…" (Matt. 5:16). Behavior that reflects Christ will be our witness (1 Pet. 3:15-16). This is the treasure of the earthen vessel. Sometimes we declare the truth of who Jesus is, and those who hear will immediately become His disciples (John 1:35-50). There is no argument. No long discussion. No back and forth. God has already been at work, and the response is, "Yes, I want that for my life!" Others will not immediately follow the Lord. They, like Nathanael, are cynical at first. The call of Philip and Nathanael to discipleship is recorded in the first chapter of John, beginning in verse forty-three. Jesus went to Galilee and found Philip, who then went to Nathanael, his friend. Philip told Nathanael that he had found the One Moses wrote about in the Law and about whom the prophets also wrote - Jesus of Nazareth, the son of Joseph. Nathanael was skeptical. His mocking question was, "Can there any good thing come out of Nazareth?" Notice that Philip does not engage in Nathanael's cynicism. He only responds with three words, "Come and see."

"Come and see" is an invitation and a promise to people everywhere. Come and see Jesus for yourself. Come seeking to know Him, and through Scripture, I promise you will find Him as the risen, redeeming Savior of the world (Eph. 1:7). Come and see, and you will recognize Him as the conqueror of sin and death at Calvary; the Christ of the empty tomb (2 Tim. 1:10). Come and see Him as the Holy God of heaven (John 17:11), the One who takes away the sins of the world (John 1:29). Come and see, and in your coming lay your burdens at His feet (1 Pet. 5:7). See Him as King of kings and Lord of lords (Rev. 19:16). Recognize the Sun of righteousness who will come again with healing in His wings to set His people free (Mal. 4:2). Let Him wrap you in His redeeming love. Your life will never be the same!

A college student writes, "I was born and raised in the church. I saw religion as something I had to do, like going to school. I didn't have any relationship with God. I barely knew Him. They say your view of God determines everything else in your life. This was true for me. I believed God was a mighty being whose sole job was to punish me for wrongdoing. This fear also led me to believe God didn't love me or care for me. He wasn't with me, and I was on my own. Therefore, I was always afraid and worried, and I had no reasonable expectations or hope for the future. But glory to God, I am not that person anymore! I want to share with you how

Jesus changed me. During my first semester in graduate school, a friend invited me to an on-campus Bible study. But I had all kinds of excuses for not going. I was tired and had a headache, and Bible study was not my thing. It happened that the guy I had a crush on was going, so I sought an opportunity to spend time with him. I went to that Bible study expecting to learn more about my crush than God. However, the teaching was so exciting and captivating that I quickly forgot about the boy next to me and paid full attention to what was being said. It was the first time in my life that I enjoyed a sermon. From the way the director spoke, I could tell he loved God. For the first time, I heard God's message of love. I learned of God loving me and saw someone express their love for Him. During that study, I learned three truths that changed my view of God. I learned that I am a depraved sinner in need of God's grace (Rom. 5:8). I learned that He gives His grace freely and that I can never earn it (Eph. 2:8-9). And I learned that Jesus loved me enough to die for me (John 3:16). I never knew of this loving God. I wanted to know Him and come to love Him. That is why on January 1st, 2016, I gave my life to Jesus."

A Christian inmate tells his story, "My new cellmate said to me, 'So, not only do you work on radios, but I see you counsel people, too.' He had overheard me talking to an upset man outside our cell. His comment gave me pause because I hadn't even realized I was counseling the man. In my eyes, I had just let him vent about his problem and then offered insight on how to look at his situation. I had been getting tired of his complaining and was wishing he would go away and leave me in peace. But God gave me the patience and love to care enough to listen. Most of the time, listening is what people need the most. Laying an open ear can alleviate another person's burden when something is weighing heavily on their mind. Listening is a straightforward way to fulfill Galatians 6:2, which instructs us to 'bear ye one another's burdens, and so fulfill the law of Christ.' Amazingly, God cares for my needs when I compassionately tend to the needs of others. Here's why: when I focus on other people rather than myself, I become God's workman, a vessel through which His love can flow. The same is true for you."

As we tell of God's grace, we need to observe the interests of others. Before the plane took off, Scott engaged in polite conversation with a woman sitting in the window seat and discovered she was an artist. But she grew quiet and returned to her book when she learned Scott was a Christian. He closed his eyes and tried to rest. When the plane reached cruising altitude, the prompting of the Holy Spirit interrupted his nap. Scott opened his eyes and noticed that his seatmate was staring at the breathtaking sunset. "Beautiful, isn't it?" he commented casually. "It's amazing how God paints us a new work of art every evening, and no two are alike." Her response surprised Scott. For the next hour, she told him more about her life. They talked about what the Bible says about God's ability to meet her needs in the difficult circumstances she was facing. People need to trust the messenger before they will trust the message.

At just 12 years old, Bill Wilson was abandoned by his mother on a street corner in Pinellas Park, Florida. He sat and waited for her in that same spot for three full days, but she never came back for him. Countless people walked by this young boy sitting out on the street corner. Finally, a man on his way to see his son in the hospital stopped and asked him if he was okay. After learning of his situation, the man got him some food, made some calls, and was on a bus headed to a Christian summer camp within five hours. Bill's family hadn't been religious, so that camp was the first time he had heard about God or Jesus. Much to his dismay, Bill discovered that at that "Christian" summer camp, nobody would pray for him at the altar because of how badly he looked and smelled. Instead, all alone, he went to the altar and attempted his prayer: "My mother doesn't want me," he told God. "The Christians do not want me. But if you want me, here I am." God's response to Bill instantly resounded: "YES, I want you!" That moment forever changed him. Thousands of people had walked by a 12-year-old orphan. It took just one person stopping to ask if he was okay to change the course of his life forever.

There is a lesson here: God wants unwanted people! The days of religious rhetoric are over. People have to see the reality of the gospel. They must know the integrity and compassion of Christianity. Every believer has a testimony that stands without question. It is a personal experience that will not suffer debate. And it is ours to share. You and I are the only Scripture some are reading, the only sermon they hear. God has a unique plan for every life. Love people however you can. Tell them the most beautiful words, "I love you, and Jesus loves you." This is what it means to let our light shine for the glory of God and His gospel!

The Cornerstone of Life

Ephesians 2:19-22 speaks of individuals who are "made nigh by the blood of Christ" as the household of God, built upon the foundation of the apostles and prophets, and Jesus Christ himself being the chief cornerstone. Concerning architecture, a cornerstone is traditionally the first stone laid for a structure, with all other stones laid in reference. The total weight of an edifice rested on this particular stone, which, if removed, would collapse the whole structure. A cornerstone marks the geographical location by orienting a building in a specific direction. Cornerstones have been around in some form for ages. Speaking prophetically of the coming of Jesus, the Old Testament patriarch Isaiah said, "Thus saith the Lord God, Behold, I lay in Zion for a foundation a stone, a tried stone, a precious corner stone, a sure foundation" (Isa. 28:16). The New Testament writers recognized this stone as Jesus Christ (Matt. 21:42, 1 Pet. 2:6), the foundational Rock of God's church.

One way we can understand the importance of a biblical worldview is to think in terms of a foundation, specifically the foundation's cornerstone. We begin with the foundational truths of God's Word. In these turbulent days, as our world turns its back on Christianity, it is more important than ever that we understand Jesus as our cornerstone; everything must rest against His character. There are Biblical requirements for accurate measurement, and all are based on the attributes of God made manifest in the life of Jesus. If a cornerstone isn't located properly, if Christ does not occupy His rightful place in our hearts, then everything measured from that location will also be in the wrong place. The cornerstone of the Christian faith is Jesus Christ, God incarnate who died, was buried, and rose again. He is the only atonement for sin! We find our identity in Him, for we are the other stones that build the spiritual household of faith (Eph. 2:21).

The Bible tells us that we are "fitly framed together." This speaks of the unity of purpose that we are to have in Christ. Pisa is a small town in Italy with about 91,000 residents. There, on a grassy field known as the "Square of Miracles," the tower of Pisa, constructed of white marble with a foundation only ten feet deep, was built in 1173. It was intended to stand 185 feet vertically. But due to poor foundations, the tower began to lean shortly after construction began. For this reason, construction was halted in 1178, resumed in 1272, and halted in 1284. In 1319 the seventh floor was completed. When construction continued, the engineer in charge sought to compensate for the lean by making the new stories slightly taller on the short side, but the extra masonry caused the structure to sink further. Increasingly, people are sacrificing enduring truth for quick fixes. We can learn from those building eight hundred years ago that you will have settlement issues if you have a poor foundation on deficient soils. Anything you attempt without the Holy Spirit's power will fail. Or finances, our friendships, our relationships, and all other things about life must be established and maintained according to the precepts of the Bible. In 1990 the tower was closed as engineers undertook a major straightening project. The work was completed in May 2001, and the structure was reopened to visitors. Experts will say the tower should remain stable for many years. But they also say that one day it will have leaned too far and will collapse onto a nearby restaurant where scientists now gather to discuss their findings. So, it becomes clear that, without a proper foundation, the building will always be compromised.

David and Holley Snow decided to build their new Chick-fil-A franchise location in Marshall, Texas, on the Bible — literally. The foundation of their building was poured over a Bible opened to Joshua 1:9: "Have not I commanded thee? Be strong and of a good courage; be not afraid, neither be thou dismayed; for the Lord thy God is with thee whithersoever thou goest." At the time of construction, the Snows said, "When the first concrete was poured on the restaurant site, it was important to us that a Bible be laid into the foundation of Chick-fil-A Marshall. We opened the Bible to Joshua 1:9 - a verse that has stuck with our operator and his family through all their endeavors." The Snows carry the faith-filled legacy of Chick-fil-A founder Truett Cathy, who started the restaurant franchise. "While we serve delicious food, people are most important to us. Our purpose here is simple — to glorify God by being a faithful steward of all entrusted to us and to positively influence all who come in contact with Chick-fil-A," the Snows said. In a previous interview with Pure Flix, Truett Cathy's daughter, Trudy K. White, said that her parents always instilled in their family the values of being a blessing and serving others, something that the Snows share. "We feel blessed so that we can be a blessing to others. And so, we are merely a channel of God's love to other people, a demonstration of His faithfulness and blessing," she said. "So, we just want to be an extension of His love to others. And that's really the way we manage the things that God has given us."

Jesus Christ is the foundation of true Christianity. He is the chief cornerstone of the church, and the gates of hell will not prevail against it. Just like bricks and mortar are placed around a cornerstone of a building, so must we be permanently bonded to Christ. And when we are rightly connected to Him, we will also be rightly related to other people. The world hates Christianity. Why? Because the gospel allows for no other way to God apart from Jesus alone. Speaking of Christ, Peter tells those gathered, "This is the stone which was set at naught of you builders, which is become the head of the corner. Neither is there salvation in any other; for there is none other name under heaven given among men, whereby we must be saved" (Acts 4:10-12). Although the world despises the Lord, He is precious to those who know Him!

Storms are an inevitable part of life. And if we want to ensure that we can weather life's most tremendous storms no matter how strong the winds or how torrential the rains are, we need to step out of convenience and onto the bedrock of lasting truth. Jesus, a carpenter and the builder of humanity, provides explicit instruction on building a rock-solid foundation for our lives. Jesus focused on the fundamentals of the faith. Forget the theological complexities that many of today's teachers focus on. The belief that Jesus taught was profound enough to set the religious establishment of His day on edge yet so simple that a child could understand it. Being deeply rooted is having a genuine desire to know and love Christ, submitting to His lead, and trusting His power. Jesus preaches a personal relationship far more profound than the rhetoric often heard in some Christian circles today. He speaks of a relationship and a fellowship with God that is life changing. Foolish people of our day build their lives on the sands of relativism, humanism, and liberalism. They put their trust in the monetary system, the political system, and society in general. But all of these will disintegrate in the storm. Blindly accepting the world's philosophies will lead to confusion and drifting further from the revealed truth of God's Word. There will always be many areas of potential confusion. But as Pastor Rick Warren said, "Much confusion in the Christian life comes from ignoring the simple truth that God is far more interested in building our character than he is anything else." Satan will try to confuse us when we are down. He will try to make us think that God is incapable of making a difference in a particular situation; it has been so since the beginning. But we can rest entirely on Jesus and the truths He has revealed to us. Don't turn from the Lord because of the pressures of society to conform to their way of thinking. Do not fall to their belief systems. If there is one thing I want my life to be identified by, it is my relationship with Jesus. He is my cornerstone, and I have chosen to build my life on Him; for He is truth. As the prophet Isaiah said, He is a tried stone, a precious stone, a sure foundation. When life demands bear down on you, there is only one cornerstone capable of handling the weight. That cornerstone is Jesus Christ. Trust Him with every aspect of your life, and you will find that He never fails!

THE ESSENTIAL NATURE OF THE LOCAL CHURCH

To some Christians, going to church is something to do when there's nothing else competing for their time. But meeting regularly with fellow believers would be high on that list if you were to make a list of the essential elements of the first-century church. They understood the importance of the church because they understood the ownership of the church. The church belongs to Jesus Christ, for He purchased it with His precious blood (Acts 20:28). Our English word 'church' originated from a Greek word that means "belonging to the Lord." The local church is central and essential to the effectiveness of Christianity.

Of the 117 times the word church is mentioned in the New Testament, 113 instances refer to the local church as a visible body of believers. When Paul told Timothy that the church is the "pillar and ground of the truth (1 Tim. 3:15)," he said it is a place of truth that provides biblical exhortation and ministry for those attending. The church is meant to elevate and display God's truth to the world (Phil. 2:15-16). The church's message is Jesus, His deity, and our redemption at Calvary. Churches in the New Testament met together. The writer of Hebrews tells us to use our time together to give encouragement and receive admonition (Heb. 10:24-25). The command of Jesus Christ is "Go ye into all the world" with the gospel, and nowhere else is the grand vision of God displayed than in those who labor in His church. We know that to love God, we must love people. He is the One who will bring actual change to their lives, and our responsibility is to minister in the best way possible. Our care for others is our grateful response to the love Jesus Christ proved to us at Calvary. There can be no other response. I am so thankful we can be a part of God's work in the world. Let us show our love for Him by serving people.

I think about church pastors and their commitment to serving God's people. It is so important to be aware of what they are facing and try to encourage them. Following are a few words from a pastor that we all should consider. He said, "When we underdeliver and consistently give to the Lord that which is not our very best, we dishonor His name, and the kingdom of God suffers a great loss. But there is a level of commitment where we find reliable and trustworthy people. Having a strong sense of duty, they are always there on time to complete their responsibilities no matter what. Responsible members encourage faithfulness around the church. Yet another level of commitment is the generosity of those who go way beyond what is expected because they have a deep love for God and people. These are individuals who generate excellence in what they do." The pastor continues, "God has called us to something even greater than generosity and kindness. Here we find people who understand that they were saved to serve the body of believers (Matt. 20:26). They are filled with a deep sense of urgency for the gospel and want their churches to become useful for the Kingdom. And the best way they know how to make it happen is to become an example themselves. It is amazing to see accomplished professionals cleaning church bathrooms, picking up trash, and janitors delivering sermons that bring people to Christ. And they do it with joy, love, and excellence. Have you ever met someone kind and loving, always ready to serve with a big smile and without any hidden agenda? Please take the opportunity to tell them that they inspire you. Jesus committed Himself entirely to us—can we commit ourselves entirely to Him?"

I love the people of God. It is my joy to fellowship with those who have deliberately chosen to follow Jesus and serve others. I love my local church. I love the sights and sounds, the worship, the singing, the teaching, the preaching, and the friendships! When visitors walk into our church, it doesn't take long for them to see that we are ordinary folks who love people and worship God (1 Cor. 1:26–31). We sit together because of Him. We rejoice together because of His glory. We worship together because He is worthy (Ps. 95:1-3). We lift His Word and our hearts heavenward, praying in the name of Jesus. I associate with like-minded believers to help me avoid sin and a worldly lifestyle. The house of God is where I am spiritually fed by the teaching and preaching of the Word (Eph. 4). It is where I meet with others and share my life with them, and they, with me. It is a place where I grow in faith and accountability. I have attended church since birth. But I have not always valued the people of God as I should, nor have I understood what a privilege it is to be part of them. But this I know: Jesus loves His church, and the power of death and hell will never destroy it (Matt. 16:18). God's Church will last forever. The Psalmist David said, "I was glad when they said unto me, let us go into the house of the Lord" (Psalm 122). What a privilege it is to "enter into his gates with thanksgiving, and into his courts with praise" (Psalm 100:4). In the house of God, we learn how to offer grace — and to receive it. Indeed, God's church is my family.

Someone listed why they no longer attend sporting events: "Every time I went, they asked me for money. The people sitting in my row didn't seem very friendly. The coach never came to visit me. The referees made a decision I disagreed with. I was sitting with hypocrites who only came to see what I was wearing. Some games went into overtime, and I was late getting home. The band played songs I had never heard before. The games are scheduled on my only day to sleep in and run errands. My parents took me to too many games growing up." Do these reasons sound familiar? J. C. Penney said, "If a man's business requires so much of his time that he cannot attend the services of his church, then that man has more business than God intended him to have." A healthy local church is to a Christian what potting soil is to a plant. It provides an environment for more grace and spiritual growth. It is a place to learn, both from those in leadership roles (Eph. 4:11-12) and also among the membership. It is a place of help. God did not design life to be lived in isolation. Even the most mature and grounded Christians need the godly influence of their brothers and sisters. The church is meant to be where those who need help receive it and those who can give service provide it (Gal. 6:10). It is a highly relational gathering of people to serve as the Savior called them to do. The church needs you, and you need the church. Jesus called His disciples to walk with Him, eat with Him, to serve alongside Him. Throughout His ministry, Jesus affirmed that togetherness is essential to the Christian life. A vibrant, biblical church directly impacts the community in which it exists. Christians in any society are meant to be lights in the dark world, and local churches are essential for the future of this or any other nation (Matt. 5:13-14).

A grandmother told her granddaughter, "Tomorrow, we're going to Sunday school." "I don't like Sunday school," said the granddaughter. "We need to learn more about God," replied the grandmother. The girl said, "I learned about Him last week." "I've been going to church all my life, and I haven't learned enough," said the grandmother. The granddaughter replied, "Well, maybe you weren't paying attention!" I do not doubt that one day this sweet little girl will understand that churches are for mending lives. Does anybody know the name of the man who was president for a day? President James Polk spent his last day as president on March 3, 1849, and Polk was out of office at midnight. But his successor, Gen. Zachary Taylor, a staunch churchgoer, refused to be sworn in on March 4, 1849, because it was a Sunday. He said, "Going to church is a higher priority than becoming president of the United States." He postponed his inauguration until Monday, March 5. So, for one day, Senator David Atchison of Missouri was president pro-tem of the United States. Can you think of anything more critical than becoming president? Zachary Taylor could – it was going to church.

Our hope as Christians is Christ. But our hope for a spiritual awakening in our nation or any community is a faithful local church that stands for truth and reaches people with the gospel's message. Throughout history, the church has faced difficulties and hardship, yet it has continued in the face of all opposition. We have the promise of Jesus that the church will not be defeated, and history is filled with examples of its triumphs. Christianity was not legal in the Roman Empire for about 300 years, during which time there were periods of intense persecution. During the Dark Ages, Roman Catholics repressed God's Word; yet underground local churches continued. In the repression of early America, the preaching of men like Jonathan Edwards and George Whitfield brought about the First Great Awakening. In the 1960s, China's Mao Zedong forced thousands of missionaries to leave the country, and most church buildings were destroyed. But even in the face of continuing persecutions, threats, jail, torture, and even executions, the number of professing born-again believers in China today is around 200 million. Is the church essential? Jesus believed it was. He loved it and gave Himself for it! I pray that each of us will recognize the importance of our local church!

WALKING WITH GOD

The highest calling of life is to walk with God. After describing every conceivable pleasure of life, King Solomon concluded by saying the whole duty of man is to fear God and keep His commandments (Eccl. 12:13). Charles Spurgeon said, "We are never right unless God is the friend of our pilgrimage, the companion of our thoughts, the rest of our weariness, the home of our delight, the very element of our life." In Exodus 33:13, Moses prayed to the God he knew so well. He said, "If I have found grace in thy sight, shew me now thy way, that I may know thee, that I may find grace in thy sight." The Bible says God "made known his ways unto Moses, his acts unto the children of Israel." The Israelites saw the ten plagues in Egypt, the pillars of cloud and fire, the parting of the Red Sea, the manna in the wilderness, and many other miraculous deeds. They saw the things God did. But Moses discovered the ways of God through a greater understanding of His very nature. Moses desired to know God in a deeper relationship. He was unsatisfied with the conversations he and God had in the tent meetings. He wanted something more. God has not changed. He will be found of us when we seek Him with all our heart (Jer. 29:12-14).

In the Spirit-filled life, we learn to pray, trust, obey, and not look back. We look up. We look to a Savior to do what we cannot do for ourselves (2 Cor. 5:14-19). Enoch walked with God (Gen. 5:24). Abraham was a friend of God (James 2:23). David sought after God (Ps. 27:7-8). The apostle Paul wanted to know God (Phil. 3:7-8). These men walked in agreement with God. They lived according to the word of God. They gave the Lord permission to speak into their lives. They walked by faith, and God rewarded them all! God could have defined his relationship with us in any terms he desired, yet he chose to describe himself first and foremost as our Father. This reveals the kind of relationship he wants with you and me. Christian author Max Lucado says, "If God had a refrigerator, your picture would be on it. If He had a wallet, your photo would be in it. He sends you flowers every spring and a sunrise every morning. Whenever you want to talk, he will listen. He can live anywhere in the universe, and he chose your heart. Face it, friend. He is crazy about you." When the Bible speaks of "walking," it often refers to a lifestyle (Eph. 2:1-10, Col. 3:1-10). To walk with God is to eliminate everything that does not glorify Him from our lives. The apostle Paul said, "Whatever ye do, do all to the glory of God" (1 Cor. 10:31). It is not hard to identify people who walk with God. Their lives are a stark contrast to the world around them. Through the Holy Spirit's power, they manifest love, joy, peace, longsuffering, gentleness, goodness, faith, meekness, and self-control. These attributes of Christ are the evidence of salvation, described as the fruit of the Spirit (Gal. 5:22-23).

Have you ever walked with a person who was distracted by things going on around them? Compare that experience to when you enjoyed someone's company, walking side by side in the same place and sharing the joy of being together until you reached your destination. Which experience most resembles your relationship with God? It's an important question. God desires a journey with us where we consistently communicate through the joys and sorrows of life. Dallas Willard once said, "I want to live so close to God that when I die, I will barely notice." Close relationships do not just happen. There is a choice to be made, a deliberate choice. People will ask, "Why do you walk with God?" My answer is quite simple: "Because without the Light of the world, there is only darkness (John 8:12). Walking with Him makes things possible. Not necessarily easy, but possible. Walking without Him is an unnecessary struggle. Jesus Christ is my comfort. And because of His resurrection power in me, I can overcome" (Ps. 23, 1 Cor. 15:57). From the beginning of time, God wanted a walking partner. He walked with Adam and Eve in the cool of the day (Gen. 3), and He still longs for companionship, unbroken communication, intimacy, and mutual delight. Enoch was likely the first man to uncover the true joy of walking with God because he nurtured a friendship for a lifetime, one that Adam did not experience. Jesus went on walks with His disciples, which deepened their friendship. Today, Christians who enjoy a close relationship with God desire a God-ordered life. They recognize their human frailty and humbly call Him to order their steps (Ps. 119:133). And when the strength of God is expressed in their lives over and again, their faith increases. They have confidence that the Lord will again be with them the next time they face a trial.

Dr. J. Vernon McGee tells about a flight he took from Los Angeles to Phoenix years ago. He said, "The plane hit rough air and began to bounce around. The pilot tried to get us out of it by going higher, but it only got rougher up there, so he leveled off. At times, the plane would drop, and it seemed to me like it would never stop. I grabbed the seat in front of me and held on for dear life. Of course, the seat in front of me dropped just as fast as the one where I was sitting! A fellow traveler aboard, who had been around the world by air several times, stated that this was the roughest trip he had ever experienced. I concurred with him thoroughly, for it surely was my roughest trip - and, as I felt then, my last trip by air. But across the aisle from me sat a man who had fallen asleep before the plane took to the air. When we hit that turbulence, he was merely annoyed by all the disturbance and turned over and went back to sleep. After we landed, I had to ask the man what gave him such assurance. He said, 'You all haven't flown over Germany surrounded by enemy fire yet.' Now, whatever security that plane offered was mine as well as his. We both had faith enough to enter the plane, but he had assurance that I didn't have. Why? Because he had an understanding through life experience that I didn't have." The Bible speaks of a progressive, growing development of faith (Rom. 1:17, 2 Cor. 3:18).

Walking with God means moving through life with Him in unity and trust. To describe what it means to walk with God, think about being with a friend. What do you expect from that person? How do you speak and behave when you are together? When you take a walk, you are traveling in the same direction. Your steps move at a similar pace, so neither of you leaves the other behind. You speak directly to them in the kindest of terms, and your attention is not distracted. The Bible is the foundation for living a godly life. It is the voice of God. Scripture is the guide that keeps us from harmful missteps. Through prayer, we have a close, personal connection with God. Think again about how you behave when walking with a friend. You may walk in silence sometimes, but the conversation is the means of sharing what is in your heart. Prayer is the means of talking, laughing, and crying with God. Jesus said, "Lo, I am with you alway, even unto the end of the world" (Matt. 28:20). When we recognize that His presence is with us, to know He shares our joys and our sorrows, and to be confident that He will supply all we need, we have an incredible quietness and confidence of spirit. Sometimes, God may interrupt the usual flow of things in a significant enough way that it seems He is changing our path. It appears this way because we had predetermined the course. The signs of providence can be subtle sometimes, so keep your heart open to discern them. Consider the story of Isaac and Rebekah. Abraham's servant went to look for a bride among Abraham's relatives in his homeland. God brought Abraham's servant to a well, and while the servant was praying for the right girl to arrive, Rebekah offered him and his herds a drink of water - a chosen sign. The meeting was too important to be a coincidence merely. It was providence. God had brought Rebekah to the well at the right time and guided her to perform the right actions (Gen. 24:15-20).

In Psalm 25, David prays, "Shew me thy ways, O Lord; teach me thy paths. Lead me in thy truth and teach me." The Psalmist understands life as a difficult journey that can only be traveled successfully with the Lord's guidance. We need instruction that comes through the knowledge of Scripture. Instead of inventing a life (which is a typical response to the difficulty in a rudderless world), why not employ the words of God that teach us how to live? For David, Jehovah was not just an impersonal authority but his Savior, the One who had protected him and delivered him. Let's analyze our steps and consider the way we are living. Times will come when we realize we should have listened to the prompting of the Spirit instead of stubbornly walking ourselves to trouble and danger. Catch the vision of your Leader. Lay aside the distractions, the people, and the weight of things that create an enormous drag on your spiritual growth. I know of which I speak. The greatest joy is in finishing well. Remember, we are walking alongside a God whose path is much better than ours! People who walk similarly are a blessing from God, so fellowship with those who share your dedication to God.

Now there are times when God seems absent when we have no sense that our prayers are being heard. With no relief in sight, there seems to be no comfort in the theological knowledge that God is omnipresent. The Psalms often speak of these times. Read Psalm 6. The reality is that

God's most devoted followers go through dark times when things happen without warning or underlying reason. In these times, we can pray as David did, "Turn thee unto me and have mercy upon me; for I am desolate and afflicted. The troubles of my heart are enlarged: O bring thou me out of my distresses" (Ps. 25:16). Loneliness feeds depression. And to be both lonely and oppressed is the lowest state one can reach emotionally. But we cannot wallow in our despair.

Do not believe Satan's lie that you are alone or that God doesn't understand how you feel. There was a time when David and those with him raised their voices and wept until they had no more strength to weep (1 Sam. 30:4-6). Elijah asked the Lord that he might die (1 Kings 19:4-5). Hannah wept and would not eat. The Bible says she was deeply distressed and wept bitterly (1 Sam. 1:7-10). Paul was so utterly burdened that he despaired of life itself (2 Cor. 1:8-10). But in Psalm 121, David says the eyes of the Lord are upon us, and he hears our cry. He said the Lord is near those heartbroken, that He hears and delivers them out of all trouble. Looking unto the hills where he had known the presence of God, the Psalmist gives us this assurance, "The Lord shall preserve thy going out and thy coming in from this time forth, and even for evermore." Never doubt in the night what God revealed to you during the daylight hours. The Christian journey is a cleansed life. It is a yielded and holy life. It is a radiant and victorious life. It is a satisfying life. And it is a life that can be ours when we faithfully walk with God!

THY WILL BE DONE

When Jesus taught His disciples to pray, "Thy will be done in earth, as it is in heaven" (Matt. 6:10), and again, his prayer in Gethsemane, "Not as I will, but as thou wilt" (Matt. 26:39), He graciously provided insight into the way we should communicate with Him. When we pray, we should keep the high principle in mind: God is sovereign, and He is in charge. If we are followers of Christ, we are progressively formed into His image (Phil. 3:20-21). Our Lord does not want to merely be our helper. He wants to be our life. He doesn't just want our work. He wants to do His work in and through us. Corrie ten Boom said, "Follow the pathway of obedience, and you will be used by God far beyond your own powers." God can indeed arrange life so much better than we can!

"Thy will be done" should never be a sigh of resignation at the end of a thought or a prayer. It is not a catch-all phrase of futility (Eph. 3:20-21), nor does it render our faith or prayer useless. "Thy will be done" acknowledges God's right to rule. It is a recognition of the fact that He knows best. Praying for God's will to be done demonstrates our desire for Him to increase righteousness on the earth, draw more to repentance, and for His kingdom to come fully. The apostle James said God resists the proud but gives grace to the humble, so "Submit yourselves therefore to God" (James 4:6-7). A prayer of faith - yet humility - is what He wants to hear (Matt. 8:1-13). The disciples asked the Lord for a lesson on prayer because it did not come naturally to them. Likewise, for us. We depend on God and must learn to communicate with Him effectively. Jesus is the vine, and we are the branches. Without the Holy Spirit, we can do nothing. South African Pastor Andrew Murray said, "Let me say I am here by God's appointment, in His keeping, under His training, for His time."

At the age of fifteen, W. Ian Thomas felt convinced that he should devote all of his life to the service of the Lord Jesus. He told God he would become a missionary. He began preaching in the open air, even at that early age. He was also actively engaged in Sunday School work, and life began to be a round of ceaseless activity. Many years later, in 1956, Mr. Thomas shared with his students at Wheaton College the following account of those early years of fruitless pursuit. He said, "I was a windmill of activity. Every moment of my day was packed with doing things: preaching, talking, counseling. The only thing that alarmed me was that nobody was converted. That gets a little discouraging after a bit. The more I did, the less happened, and it was not a question of insincerity. The prospects and environments were good; there was plenty of ammunition and targets, but nothing happened! I became deeply depressed because I loved the Lord Jesus Christ with all my heart, and I wanted to be a blessing to others. But I discovered that forever doubling and redoubling my efforts to win souls, rushing here and dashing there, taking part in this campaign, taking part in that campaign, preaching in the morning, preaching in the evening, talking to the Bible class, witnessing to this one, counseling with another, did nothing, nothing to change the utter barrenness, the emptiness, the uselessness of my activity. I tried to make up with noise what I lacked in effectiveness and power. Then, one night just at midnight in my room at home, I got down on my knees before God and wept in sheer despair. I said, 'Oh, God, I know I am saved. I love Jesus Christ. I am perfectly convinced that I am converted. With all my heart, I have wanted to serve You. I have tried to my uttermost, and I am a hopeless failure. As far as doing anything more, I am finished. It is useless for me to continue like this. I hate this double life!' That night, things happened. This was the moment God had been waiting for. For many years He had watched me running around in the wilderness. I heard His voice: 'To me to live is Christ… I am the way, the truth, and the life.' To me, to live is Christ! I told God, 'I will thank You, for You are my life, my victory, my strength, my power, and my future.' Then I went to sleep. I got up the next morning to an entirely different Christian life. The Lord said, 'This is my life. It is not a new technique that you have learned. It is simply My life, being what I am, doing the inevitable. You cannot have My life for your program. You can only have My life for My program.'"

Thus, step by step, God led His trusting and obedient servant into paths he did not foresee nor choose but pathways of satisfying service. Major Thomas testifies: "It was just His victory. It was just what He was. I found that the simpler I could make it, the more blessing He gave; whenever I tried to be complicated or clever, He closed down. Only as I related situations to Him did I find that He undertook. As soon as I related a situation to myself, He retired into the background. So, I soon learned to count upon Him. That is the secret; it is so simple! To take everything to the Lord Jesus and take our hands off – to stand back and say, 'I thank you, Lord.'" To the young students at Wheaton, as well as to others, Major Thomas says, "It is all in Christ, and all of Christ is yours. Commit yourself totally to Him. Tell the Lord you want no other program than the life He is prepared to live through you."

Prayer is not about bending God's will to get what we want. Instead, to be thankful, seek God's will and then align our desires with His. And when we want something desperately, this is not an easy thing to do. But Jesus understands our human struggles. So, pray honestly, yet fully convinced that His way is perfect! Corrie ten Boom says, "Returning to Holland after my release from the German concentration camp at Ravensbruck; I said, 'One thing I hope is that I will never have to go to Germany again. I am willing to go wherever God may want me to go, but I hope He will never send me to Germany.'" But she continues, "If we want to experience the guidance of God in our lives, we must accept one condition: obedience to Him." Jeremiah 18:3-6 says, "Then I went down to the potter's house, and behold, he wrought a work on the wheels... behold, as the clay is in the potter's hand, so are ye in mine hand, O house of Israel." The song was inspired in 1902 by the simple prayer of an older woman overheard at a prayer meeting. This was her prayer: "It doesn't matter what you do with us, Lord," she said. "Just have your way with our lives." Can I stop here and speak mainly to the elderly folks reading this piece? Satan would have you believe your days of godly influence are over. They are not. Keep telling of the grace of God and how He has kept you these many years. The enemy is a liar! Keep singing. Keep praying. For you, life experience has proved the truths of the Bible. Keep encouraging your generation. Keep telling the younger generation about the faithfulness of God! Little did the woman know how her prayer would come to bless tens of thousands of people for many years. She was pouring out her heart to God, and He did the rest!

How can we know the will of God? First, we must commit any decision to Him (Phil. 4:6-7). We look to the Bible to understand God's heart and His nature (Jer. 9:23-24). God's Word never promises to answer every human question. Still, it offers a principle that will apply to every situation of life (2 Tim. 3:16). Scripture is the basis of truth for understanding all things (Ps. 19:7-14). The Bible is all we need to equip us for a life of faith and service. Understand your circumstances as best you can and seek godly counsel (Prov. 15:22). Lean on the peaceful control of the Holy Spirit (Isa. 30:21). Acknowledge God in all your ways, and He will make the path straight (Prov. 3:5-6). Prayer is for the glory of God, so our motivation to pray should be God-centered (1 John 5:14-15). When we follow the Lord's way, He will do amazing things in and through us. Moses is a fitting example. After unsuccessfully trying to rescue the Israelites with his strength, he fled and spent forty years in the wilderness. At that time, his pride, self-reliance, and self-will were broken. Sound familiar? I can certainly identify with this. Humbled, Moses was now someone God could use to accomplish the great deliverance of God's people from Egypt. Through this man, the Lord demonstrated what remarkable things He can do through one yielded person (Ex. 3:21-22).

When you pray, try not to see everything only in your past experiences. The Israelites could not see God's vision for their lives in the wilderness. But God had promised them a land flowing with milk and honey, and He wanted them to catch the new vision. God's words through the prophet Isaiah are these, "Remember ye not the former things, neither consider the things of old. Behold, I will do a new thing; now it shall spring forth; shall ye not know it? I will even make a way in the wilderness, and rivers in the desert" (Isa. 43:18-19). If you want to see change happen, get a vision beyond what you have already seen and experienced. An excellent place to look for that vision is in the hundreds of promises contained in God's Word. You can claim each of them through obedience to His Word for yourself. Surrendered people obey God even when it does not seem to make sense. Abraham followed God without knowing where it would take him. Hannah waited on God's timing without knowing when she would have a child. Mary expected a miracle without understanding the mystery that was taking place inside her. Joseph trusted God's plan without knowing the reason for complex circumstances. Each of these people we read about in the Bible surrendered to God. And the result of their surrender was a victorious fulfillment of God's promises. How did this happen to them? They lived in the spirit of "Thy will be done."

With My Whole Heart

Our love for God begins with God Himself. We love Him because He first loved us (1 John 4:19). Salvation from the penalty of sin is only available through faith in Jesus Christ. And it begins with a surrendered heart (Acts 4:12, Rom. 10:9-13). Jesus said the greatest of all commandments is to love God with our whole heart, mind, body, and soul (Mark 12:30). How is it that this needs to be a commandment? Because the Lord knows we are not capable of such love without the Holy Spirit's power. We tend to be forgetful and distracted away from the things that matter. We need constant reminders, guidance, and correction of Scripture to live a godly life. Certainly, living according to Biblical precepts is the will of God, and a righteous lifestyle will give us a wonderful sense of fulfillment. But as we endeavor to honor God through words and deeds, sometimes we hold back the most important thing: our heart. A dear lady writes, "As I sat quietly, I saw that picture of Jesus knocking on that big wooden door before me. Indeed, I had opened the door, for I was saved by grace. But I had replaced the door with a glass door that I repeatedly washed with window cleaner. The Lord showed me that I was always so busy letting Him see into my heart that I didn't allow Him full access. The missing element was that I was trying to bring about His presence in my life by keeping the glass door clean. But dying to self is breaking down that door, risking everything to allow the Lord continual access and residence into the depths of my being." She said, "It isn't about continually trying to clean the door. It's about breaking down all the barriers that I have erected."

The heart is our innermost part. It is the control center of our personality, will, and emotions. It is the place of decision, the core of who we are. It is where we choose life or death (Prov. 18:21). God wants our hearts. Anything less is not enough (Luke 10:27, Deut. 6:5). Repeatedly, the Bible instructs us to surrender fully to the will of God. Samuel tells us to serve the Lord with all our heart (1 Sam. 12:20). Joshua says to walk in all His ways and keep His commandments (Josh. 22:5). Ezra instructs us to serve Him with a whole heart and a willing mind (1 Chron. 28:9). Moses says we will find Him if we search for Him with all our heart and soul (Deut. 4:29). David said he would praise God and keep His precepts. How? With his whole heart (Ps. 119:69, 138:1). As servants of God, we surrender complete rule over our every word, action, thought, and dream. It's easy to talk about this matter theoretically; however, it can be challenging to live a surrendered existence. I must embrace the reality that my family and home are not mine. My finances are not mine. My health is not mine. My abilities are not my own. Everything the Master has given to me is on loan. It all belongs to Him. I have been bought with a price (1 Cor. 6:20), which ultimate price for my redemption was paid at Calvary. My past, my present, and my future - all belong to Him. I must surrender to the Lord everything and anything that keeps me up at night. I will trust the God of the Bible, for He honors such faith.

We all want to control our lives. We want stability and security. This is human nature. But God's design is that we depend on Him. The Psalmist said, "He only is my rock and my salvation: he is my defense; I shall not be moved" (Ps. 62:6). And, although He gives us the freedom to choose, without Christ, we deceive ourselves into thinking our way is best. The Christian journey of spiritual growth involves becoming more like Jesus (1 John 2:6). The apostle John said, "He must increase, but I must decrease" (John 3:30). The Bible says the profit of living for the things of this world will be nothing compared with an eternal loss of one's soul (Luke 9:24). It has been said that the primary mark of a Christian mind is that it cultivates the eternal perspective. That is to say, a yielded heart looks beyond this life to a much better one. Yes, we plan; we organize and build. We pursue goals and dreams. But we do so in light of eternity to the glory of God (Luke 12:16-21).

Loving God means serving Him with our life; a joyous, faith-filled, and purpose-driven life. If we live daily in a relationship through prayer and Scripture study, we are compelled to take the gospel message to a frantic world desperate for love and redemption. I ask myself: How diligently do I seek God and read His Word? Do I walk with Him and share the experience of my salvation? Am I proving the perfect will of God (Rom. 12:2) by renewing my mind? The heart, that spiritual part of us where our emotions and desires dwell, is mentioned 826 times in the Bible. And by the grace of God, a new heart is created within us (Rom. 10:10). Love is active. Love is more than emotion or words to repeat. Apostle Paul said He who is rich in mercy loved us when we were yet dead in our sins (Eph. 2:4-8). Are you enthusiastic about seeing lost souls saved? Is your earnest desire to glorify God? Sometimes I have sought the rituals of religion rather than God Himself. It is easy to focus on the things created instead of the Creator, to seek the gift, not the Giver. Surrender is the act of giving back to God the life He has given to us. It is relinquishing control, rights, power, direction, and everything we do and say, resigning ourselves to Him to do with us as He pleases. Jesus said, "If any man will come after me, let him deny himself, and take up his cross daily, and follow me" (Luke 9:23). This is where we relinquish personal control and give Him full attention. Instead of finding solace in earthly things, we go to God for every provision. David said, "My soul, wait thou only upon God; for my expectation is from him" (Ps. 62:5).

The spirit of obedience is this: yielding to the sovereign claim of a righteous God. The all-powerful, all-knowing, all-sufficient Creator of the universe is worthy of all praise and devotion. We are prone to surrender only when a crisis forces us to. But living daily in His presence, we will ask, "What now, Lord? What would You have me do? I surrender my agenda, goals, and expectations to You." This is a manner of living where Kingdom work is our priority. And as we relinquish our circumstances to God, He becomes our delight (Ps. 37:4). Peter Forsythe was right when he said, "The first duty of every soul is to find not its freedom but its Master." And if He is our Master, obedience will follow. 'Where our Captain bids us go, 'tis not ours to murmur 'no;' He that gives the sword and shield chooses too, the battlefield.' Roger Staubach, who led the Dallas Cowboys to the World Championship in 1971, admitted that his position as a quarterback who didn't call his signals was a source of trial for him. Coach Landry sent in every play. He told Roger when to pass and when to run. Even though Roger considered coach Landry to have a "genius mind" regarding football strategy, pride said he should be able to run his own team. Roger later said,

"Once I learned to obey, there was harmony, fulfillment, and victory." We are delighted with what God does when we lean on extraordinary grace. When we love, serve and worship with our hearts, He will show Himself faithful, never forsaking us!

Jesus said, "Whosoever he be of you that forsaketh not all that he hath, he cannot be my disciple" (Luke 14:33). People, priorities, and possessions can consume our minds and keep us from being utterly devoted to Him. We must die to ourselves and crown Jesus King, for He uses only surrendered vessels to accomplish His work. I enjoy reading about people of faith who have done remarkable things for God, and I think, "Why did God use them so abundantly? How was it that the power of the Spirit was so wonderfully manifested in their lives?" It seems the first thing that accounts for God using them so mightily is that they were fully surrendered to His will (Ps. 62:11). They chose to be available to anything God wanted to do in and through them. They were not perfect. No one is. They made mistakes. Everyone does. They just lived, knowing that all power and glory belong to Him. Many Christians are brilliant and wonderfully gifted but have stopped short of absolute surrender.

Our God desires availability over ability. And if you and I are to be effective in growing the Kingdom, we must put all that we have - and all we are - into His hands. Dr. B. J. Miller once said, "It is a great deal easier to do that which God gives us to do than to face the consequence of not doing it." When God is our priority, we will faithfully do everything He bids us to do. And in so doing, we will discover the faithfulness of God and the joy of serving Him with our whole hearts!

A LIVING HOPE

Hope is a word that represents the possibility of a positive outcome. These days, hope expects something to happen, while not entirely sure it will. It is more like a wish or a desire. For example, we might hear someone say, "Oh, you know, hope springs eternal" when they buy a lottery ticket or want their favorite team to win the championship. The Merriam-Webster Dictionary defines hope as "to cherish a desire with anticipation; to want something to happen or to be true." In this sense, the definition rests in doubt and uncertainty. But the hope of the Bible is vastly different. Biblical hope is knowing for sure that the desired outcome will happen. It is not wishful thinking but a confident expectation. The Greek word translated hope first appears in the New Testament in Matthew 12:21, meaning to anticipate with pleasure; to welcome. It is trust. It is an expectation of what is guaranteed. We look to the future with joy and peace despite our circumstances because we know we have a God that works all things for our good (Rom. 8:28).

The resurrection of Christ is the cornerstone of the Christian faith. Apostle Paul said in 1 Corinthians 15:14 that if Jesus has not risen, then our faith is empty. But Christ is risen, and in Him, we can confidently expect to rise on the last day. In 1 Thessalonians 4:16-18, we read, "For if we believe that Jesus died and rose again, even so them also which sleep in Jesus will God bring with him. For the Lord himself shall descend from heaven with a shout, with the voice of the archangel, and with the trump of God: and the dead in Christ shall rise first: then we which are alive and remain shall be caught up together with them in the clouds, to meet the Lord in the air: and so shall be ever be with the Lord. Wherefore comfort one another with these words." Christ is our living hope, the fulfillment of everything we wait for in this life. He is coming to make all things new, and we who are saved expect His return with joy. We have the promise of a resurrection! We are "looking for that blessed hope, and the glorious appearing of the great God and our Savior Jesus Christ" (Titus 2:13).

The apostle Peter said, "Blessed be the God and Father of our Lord Jesus Christ, which according to his abundant mercy hath begotten us again unto a lively hope by the resurrection of Jesus Christ from the dead" (1 Pet. 1:3). For the redeemed, this passage of Scripture speaks of a living hope; the confidence of a guaranteed resurrection. It is a sure hope (v3), an eternal hope (v4), and an enduring hope (v5). Nothing can disappoint us in this life when the confidence of being with Jesus burns brightly in our hearts. This lively hope is great and glorious. It is an optimistic hope – a hope anchored in the unchangeable promises of God. The writer of Hebrews speaks of this hope as an "anchor of the soul, both sure and steadfast" (6:19). It does not rest upon the fleeting philosophies of men. It is embedded in the solid rock of Jesus Christ. It is a hope that becomes our strength to endure and enjoy life (Matt. 24:13, Phil. 1:6). It is a taste of God's tomorrow instilled in our hearts.

Because we have experienced sunrises and sunsets, we have confidence that they will occur repeatedly. Based on our experience with gravity, we know that if we drop something, it will fall to the ground. Such is our absolute confidence in God's promises for our future, shown to us through past experiences. God has blessed us with a hope that produces joy in challenging times. It creates more extraordinary perseverance, faith, love, and stability. Hope is never subjective or conditioned upon circumstances. This living hope is not established on positive thinking or wishful dreams. This hope of which Peter speaks is the outcome of being born again through the resurrection of Jesus from the dead (1 Cor. 15:19-22). Living hope is locked up with our Savior, who lives forevermore, and death cannot diminish it. Jesus said He is the resurrection and life and that we who believe in Him shall also live (John 11:25). This is the assurance of eternity in heaven made possible by the finished work of Christ at Calvary. It is an inheritance imperishable and undefiled that will not fade away, reserved in heaven for one who is born again (1 Pet. 1:4). Hope is alive through Jesus Christ our Savior. Hope is secure and everlasting through Jesus Christ our Savior!

For the Soviet leader Leonid Brezhnev and his wife Victoria, the Church did not exist. From 1964 to 1982, he used the KGB to quell any opposition to his repressive regime. They never spoke of religion and certainly never practiced it. Brezhnev imprisoned priests and Bible believers, closing seminaries and churches whenever they got in his way. Both in public life and at home, he and his wife were communist atheists. Faith was nowhere to be found. When Mr. Brezhnev died in 1982, United States Vice President George H.W. Bush attended the funeral. He remembers being moved by Victoria's actions that day, which was to be her last public appearance. She stood without moving by her husband's coffin until seconds before it was closed. Then, just as the soldiers touched the lid, Victoria leaned over her husband's body and made the sign of the Cross on his chest. At the center of an atheist empire, she traced the image of our hope and salvation on the body of the man she had loved for 54 years. Perhaps she hoped that her husband was wrong, that there was another life, and that God might yet have mercy on him. God reaches out to us with unrelenting love. Through years of life in a godless regime, our Lord reached out to Victoria through her love for her husband. We can never know the workings of God in someone else's heart, but maybe He kindled the light of hope for her that day.

The Book of Psalms is replete with hope (Ps. 31:24, 39:7, 62:5, 71:14) that is not mixed with speculation but a joyous anticipation for what God will do. Even Job, in his unthinkable circumstance, declares his confidence in God (Job 13:15). His life was an expectant demonstration of trusting the Lord forever. The writer of the Book of Hebrews tells us that hope is not a momentary emotion - nor a gamble (10:23). But it is foundational to faith (11:1). Hope is a gift from God deposited into us by the Holy Spirit (Rom. 5:1-5). In the Old Testament, God is the basis of hope because of His known character, His past deeds of salvation, and His covenant with His people. The New Testament repeats this truth, fulfilled in the ministry of Christ. What assurance is there of this hope? God promised it from all eternity, and He cannot lie (Titus 1:2). Christ is the ground of hope. Just as His second coming is the central object of hope, His first coming is the motive of Christian hope. He is its author, its foundation, and its guarantee. The hope of the Bible does not spring from our minds. Christian hope is securely founded in the atoning death and resurrection of Jesus Christ! When Sir Michael Faraday, an English scientist of the 1800s, was dying, some journalists questioned his speculations about life after death. "Speculations!" he said, "I know nothing about speculations.

I'm resting on certainties. I know that my Redeemer liveth, and because He lives, I shall live also" (Job 19:25). Richard Sibbs authored a book based on Psalm 42:5 where the psalmist is preaching to himself: "Why art thou cast down, O my soul? And why art thou disquieted in me? Hope thou in God." What was the reason for this dialog the psalmist had with himself? It is because trusting in God does not come naturally to us, and we must speak forcefully to ourselves. Fear corrodes our confidence in God's goodness. Panic fills our world, but it does not have to fill our hearts. Mark 4:35-41: "… and there arose a great storm of wind… and he (Jesus) arose, rebuked the wind, and said unto the sea, 'Peace, be still'. And the wind ceased, and there was a great calm." God always manages a great quaking with a great calming! Take him at His word when He says 'fear not' 365 times in the Bible. William Carey said, "Expect great things from God." These are a few of my favorite Scripture verses about hope: Romans 15:13 – "Now the God of hope fill you with all joy and peace in believing, that ye may abound in hope, through the power of the Holy Ghost." Titus 3:7 – "That being justified by his grace, we should be made heirs according to the hope of eternal life." Isaiah 12:2 – "Behold, God is my salvation; I will trust, and not be afraid: for the Lord Jehovah is my strength and my song; he also is become my salvation." Psalm 31:24 – "Be of good courage, and he shall strengthen your heart, all ye that hope in the Lord."

The ministry of Jesus was one of hope. He welcomed the outcasts, healed the sick, restored the afflicted, and forgave sinners. Wherever Jesus went, people felt the spirit of a new day. American theologian Ted Jennings (1942-2020) says of Jesus, "He comes to liberate. He liberates the blind from darkness, the lame from immobility, the sick from disease, and the possessed from madness. He shatters the bonds of custom and class and breaks open legalism's iron constraints. He summons the dead to life. He transforms water into wine and death into life. He announces deliverance to the captives and sets at liberty those who are oppressed." Hope means that our past need not limit our future. Hope means that God's love has sufficient power to unleash our deepest potentials. Hope is captured in the biblical word "salvation;" salvation that is ours through faith in that moment of transparent honesty as we admit our brokenness, our sin, and our pain to Jesus (Rom. 10:13). May we open ourselves to the healing and redemption that comes only from God. For indeed, He is our living hope!

Finding God Instead of Learning Why

As all parents know, every child's favorite question is, "Why?" The truth is, our "why" questions, though now of a more severe kind, continue into adulthood. When a relative dies in a tragic accident, a parent is afflicted with a disease, or our children are plagued with problems, we will ask the same question. Our favorite question at the beginning of great trouble is, "Why?" But in all forty-two chapters of the Book of Job, God never answers the question. Instead, He shows us that if we get to know *Him* in times of difficulty, any 'why' will be okay (42:1-6). Like a parent who has come to the end of a child's string of questions with, "Because I said so," God says to us, "I am your heavenly Father. Trust me; not only when you do not understand, but *because* you do not understand. Live by faith; not just with the first step of your Christian journey, but with every step" (Ps. 46:10). In time, Job said of God, "Though he slay me, yet will I trust in him… He also shall become my salvation…" (13:15-16). Job questioned God's actions, but he never stopped trusting.

When a struggle comes our way, it is our nature to ask God why it happened. Moses asked, "Lord, wherefore have I not found favor in thy sight?" (Num. 11:11). David asked, "O Lord, why hidest thou thyself in times of trouble?" (Ps. 10:1). Habbakuk asked, "Why dost thou shew me iniquity?" (Hab. 1:3). Job asked, "Why has thou set me as a mark against thee?" (Job 7:20). The disciples asked, "Master, who did sin, this man, or his parents, that he was born blind?" (John 9:2). We tell God how we feel, for He wants to bear our burdens. Jesus said, "Come unto me, all ye that labor and are heavy laden, and I will give you rest" (Matt. 11:28). We know that God welcomes a sincere question from a sincere heart. The Psalmist said, "The eyes of the Lord are upon the righteous, and his ears are open to their cry" (Ps. 34:15). When in distress, David cried, "Hear my prayer, O Lord, give ear to my supplications: in thy faithfulness answer me" (Ps. 143:1). The apostle Paul says, "Be careful for nothing, but in everything by prayer and supplication with thankfulness let your requests be made known unto God" (Phil. 4:6). In Matthew 7:7 Jesus tells us to ask, seek and knock. And I am so thankful for the privilege of coming before the throne of God to "obtain mercy and find grace to help in time of need" (Heb. 4:16)! At issue is not whether we should ask God why, but in what manner and for what reason. Some have a relentless need for answers, even to the point of demanding explanations. They want to live the abundant life spoken in John 10:10, forgetting that Jesus also said we would face tribulation (John 16:33). In light of the Cross, anything we experience ceases to be a liability. Rather, it becomes an asset to be used for God's glory. What is your chief joy? Is it to be healthy, happy, and prosperous? Indeed, these are blessings from God. But our chief joy should be to do the will of God and to finish the work He has designed for us. This was the passion of our Lord (John 4:34), for Jesus said, "As my Father hath sent me, even so send I you" (John 20:21). No matter the circumstance, we are to glorify God.

The Christian experience is a journey of faith. What is this way of faith? It is that we find the world of the unseen more convincing than this one. In the uncertainties of life, there is certainty in what God has promised: "Which hope we have as an anchor of the soul, both sure and steadfast… even Jesus" (Heb. 6:13–20). Let us hold fast the profession of our hope without wavering, for He is faithful that promised (Heb. 10:23). He is with me to accomplish His perfect will in my imperfect life. Truly, I have found a faithful friend and Savior! When trouble comes, our faith changes. It either diminishes or deepens because it has been challenged. We want to figure things out and understand the reasoning behind everything that is happening. But there are so many things we cannot understand. And for those who are suffering, any intellectual response seems inadequate. Yes, we experience pain and confusion. But in times of trouble, we need more than logic. We need hope. Jesus Christ is that hope! Do not stumble at the mysteries of life where there is no explanation. Rather, find comfort in the knowledge that you are a child of God, living by faith with heaven in view (Rom. 1:17). Jesus taught us to live one day at a time (Matt. 6:11). I

Remember the man with an infirmity lying beside the pool called Bethesda for thirty-eight years? He was waiting to be healed. And when Jesus saw him there, He had compassion (John 5:1-15). But notice the Lord did not ask the man, "Do you need to get well?" The need was evident, and the situation seemed hopeless. The question was, "Do you want to get well?" God knows our hearts, and He understands that deep sorrow can rob us of the willingness to do anything about it. He wants to see if we desire the healing strength to help us pick up and walk by faith. The question that was asked that day speaks volumes. I have met those whose continual questioning has become an excuse for not accepting the sovereignty of God. Why? Because it is easier than submitting to His authority and yielding to His lordship. The first thing Adam and Eve did after they sinned was to hide from God (Gen. 3:8). To be free from the God who calls sinners into accountability has been a constant goal of humanity throughout history. A life spent requiring answers will not bring glory to God. He is glorified through our obedience and praise (John 15:14, Ps. 150:6). We read in Psalm 100:3: "Know ye that the Lord he is God; it is he that hath made us, and not we ourselves… be thankful unto him, and bless his name." Sometimes asking "Why?" suggests a hostility toward God's character or that He cannot be trusted. Truthfully, He is God, and we are not (Ps. 100:3). There is a difference between questioning God and asking Him a question. And the difference is found as we humbly acknowledge that His thoughts are not our thoughts; neither are His ways our ways (Isa. 55:8).

The human mind will never fully understand the grandeur and authority of God. But enough is written in Scripture that we do well to know all we can about His nature, His power, and His majesty, for we gain both the strength and the freedom to trust. God has no rival. He is subject to no other power, and He reigns supreme. Heaven is His throne, and the earth is His footstool (Acts 7:49). The vast universe is evidence of the glory of God. He is clothed with majesty, and His throne is established forever (Psalm 92:8). He is Almighty on the throne. All will bow before Him whose grandeur no one can surpass. His majesty is displayed with lightning and thunderous voices going out from the throne proclaiming His holiness (Rev. 4:5). He is God

Almighty. He always has been, is now, and forever will be (Psalm 90:1–2). Power and glory are His. His dominion is everlasting, a kingdom that will never pass away nor be destroyed (Dan. 7:14). All authority in heaven and earth belongs to Him (Rev. 4). None can fully describe the attributes of God, the manner of His existence or manifestation. His power to create, to produce something out of nothing, is beyond human understanding. The foundation of the earth and the heavens are the works of His hands (Heb. 1:10). He is the Creator and sustainer of the universe (Gen. 1). He owes His existence to no one. God is not subject to, altered, or aged by time. He is eternal in nature (Psalm 90:2). In Him, there is height and depth that human intellect cannot measure. God is infinite. There is no limit to His being; therefore, He cannot be compressed into any particular definition. In His hand is the soul of every living thing and the breath of all humankind (Job 12:10). God's work is majestic in creation. He has all authority to free people from the curse of sin. God's power will affect how we live and save us for eternity. He is love. He is truth. He is life. His transforming Spirit is released into our lives, and the power of the gospel is regeneration. His grace changes how we live here and gives us the assurance of eternal salvation in heaven (Acts 11:16–18). God is not subject to human limitations. The angels of heaven cry, "Holy, holy, holy, is the Lord of hosts: the whole earth is full of his glory."

The Old Testament patriarch Job understood that he could not demand anything from the Lord (Job 23:13). Many heroes of the Bible experienced trouble for decades before they saw God's plan. And for some, the reasons were never made known. Do not continue with a lifetime of questions where there is no spiritual growth. Somewhere deep inside, the repeated questioning and lack of answers feed a sense of entitlement. And when that sense of entitlement grows, it usually leads to bitterness. I have seen the effects of anger in the hearts of good people, and so have you. Do not live with an angry, quarrelsome attitude (Eph. 4:31). There is a better way to live. Focus on the goodness and majesty of God! Make an intentional decision to believe that He is teaching you something for your ultimate good (Phil. 3:8). Knowing there is something to learn in a trial makes it easier to bear (James 1:2-12). The answers we think we must have may never be known in this lifetime. The Bible does not promise it, and we are not entitled. We read in Romans 9:20, "Shall the thing formed say to him that formed it, Why hast thou made me thus?" He is the potter; we are the clay. We are "the work of His hand" (Isa. 64:8). Jehovah says, "I am God, and there is none else... my counsel shall stand, and I will do all my pleasure" (Isa. 46:9-10). God does not suggest that our stories will make sense in and of themselves. But He does promise we will one day find our greater purpose in light of His eternal plan of redemption (Eph. 3:9-13, 2 Cor. 1:3-6). Oh, friend, our faith in God must be stronger than our need to know. If we want peace, we must give up the need to understand. Knowing that God's glory can be displayed even in the brokenness of our lives will bring hope, and those around us will be encouraged. We will find more purpose and joy if we set aside the question "Why?" and begin to worship Him with our lives.

How might God use your circumstance to display His glory? Can He use your heartache to show His power? What can He reveal about Himself in your trial? Will you allow Him to turn your mess into a message and make you a person who walks by faith and not by sight (2 Cor. 5:7)? For every child of God, there has been – or there will be – an experience that will change Romans 8:28 from a memorization quote to a belief system. Will you allow your prayer to move from "God heal me" to "God, use me for your glory and help me cope?" Only then will you find that joy can indeed co-exist with uncertainty, pain, and confusion. Thank God because He is worthy of praise (Ps. 18:3). Glorifying God is expressed by a lifestyle. He is perfect in truth, holiness, love, power, and wisdom. Praise Him for what He has done. Worship Him for who He is!

Truly, God can use your situation to show you the peace that is found only in Jesus Christ (John 14:27). He can use the death of your loved one to stir the hearts of others and show them the importance of surrendering their lives to Him (John 11:45). We cannot see the big picture. We cannot see around the corners. But we know that God will never leave or forsake us (Deut. 31:6). We also know He loves us. He hears our cries, and He cares (1 John 5:14-15). So, take a moment and ask for divine wisdom in moving forward with your life (Prov. 4:7). Trust God. Commit your cause to Him, and He will work things out according to His plan. We must trade understanding for peace. When we visualize Him in majesty and power, we will find that God is in complete control without needing to understand why things happen. He is with you!

A RENEWED MIND

It is said that where our minds go, our behavior will follow. Today, I realize more than ever that my mind is a battlefield. I have a choice to make. I can allow my thoughts to go with the flow of life, or I can think about the things of God. And what I feed my mind becomes a mindset that will control me. In Romans 12:2, the apostle Paul tells us not to be conformed to the world but to be transformed by renewing our minds. In Philippians 4, we learn that we must always rejoice in the Lord to have God's peace. Sitting in a prison cell, Paul tells us to think about things that are true, honest, just, pure, lovely, anything that is virtuous and of a good report. The apostle was in pain, and the cell doors were locked, but he set his mind on his Lord. Isaiah 26:3 tells us, "Thou wilt keep him in perfect peace, whose mind is stayed on thee." The circumstance may not go away, but in Christ, we can rest when we trust in His provision, sovereignty, guidance, and protection. God truly has all things under His control. The prophet Isaiah said, "For the Lord of hosts hath purposed it, and who shall disannul it?" (Isa. 14:27). In the Old Testament, Joshua tells God's people to be strong and of good courage (Josh. 1:9). The Psalmist David speaks of the blessing of God on those who will continually meditate on what God has to say in His Word (Ps. 1:1-3).

Renewing the mind means interpreting life through the truth of God's Word rather than through the lens of experiences, preferences, or feelings. It is viewing life each day from an eternal, Kingdom perspective. Unless we learn the value of "bringing into captivity every thought to the obedience of Christ" (2 Cor. 10:5), we will continue to live in confusion and defeat. Proverbs 23:7 says, "…cease from thine own wisdom… for as (a man) thinketh in his heart, so is he." Our thoughts fuel our beliefs. So, if we want to live differently, we must think differently. When I open my Bible, I ask the Holy Spirit to help me capture each troublesome thought or a personal opinion and replace it with a Scripture verse. It has taken me some years, but I am learning to let God design His will for my life instead of trying to do it alone. Through many failures, I have found that God's way is the best way to live!

Roy Rogers (1911-1998), affectionately known as the "King of the Cowboys," and his wife, Dale Evans, were two of the earliest TV stars in Hollywood. They had a large family. But the only child Dale gave birth to during her marriage to Roy was baby Robin. Robin was born with down syndrome and passed away from complications with the mumps before her second birthday. Roy and Dale adopted Deborah Lee Rogers after becoming an orphan during the Korean War. Sadly, she passed away when she was 12 years old in a bus accident with other children from her church. John David "Sandy" Rogers was adopted shortly after the loss of Robin when Roy and Dale were visiting an orphanage. He entered the U.S. Army, but sadly he choked to death when he was just 18 years old. And yet, "Happy Trails" is their signature theme song. Dale wanted a song that said a cowboy had to ride the trails no matter the weather, especially if the trails were not sunny. This famous couple showed us that faith could overpower pain. Roy and Dale chose how they wanted to live. They were not ashamed to boldly witness for the Lord! And in doing so, with renewed minds, they inspired tens of thousands!

Some will say that the path to God is through mind manipulation. This is not true. Nowhere in the Bible will you find this nonsense. The Word of God clearly states that our forgiveness from sin is made complete by the atoning blood of Jesus Christ (Eph. 1:7). The apostle Peter boldly declares, "Neither is there salvation in any other; for there is none other name under heaven given among men, whereby we must be saved" (Acts. 4:12). Salvation can only be received by faith in the grace of God that was revealed on the cross of Calvary (Eph. 2:8). Even so, our mindset will influence how we will feel, speak and act. For example, you may live for money or human approval because of what you believe money or people's praise will bring you. The things we expose ourselves to and the people we associate with will begin to shape us. Have you been so consumed by the day's culture that you start to believe the lies? The Bible tells us how to guard our thoughts. Ephesians 6:10-20 speaks of the armor of God. We must let the word of Christ dwell in us richly, setting our minds on things that are above and not on things of earth (Col. 3:2,16). This does not happen by accident but by resolution. The words we say and the thoughts we hold have incredible power. Therefore, it will take God's Word and the Holy Spirit working in us to make us more like Christ. We hear things daily that attempt to influence how we see ourselves and life. But if I open my heart to early-morning prayer and Scripture reading, I can lay the foundation for what I will believe and think for that day.

Change comes in many forms. For example, Randy was unsure about his choice of clothes for church, so he sought some advice from his wife. He asked, "Do you think I should change?" She immediately took advantage of the opportunity and replied, "It depends. Are you talking about changing your shirt or making a sweeping change as a human?" Then there's the story of someone who dialed the wrong number and got the following recording: "I am not available right now, but I thank you for caring enough to call. I am making some changes in my life. Please leave a message after the tone. If I do not return your call, you are one of the changes." But in all seriousness, the Bible will come alive, and we will experience extraordinary transformation through the leading of the Spirit within us. Choose to have faith in God's promises.

Early in life, John D. Rockefeller, Sr. (1839-1937) determined to earn money. At age 53, he was the wealthiest man, but he could only digest milk and crackers. He could not sleep, and he enjoyed nothing in life. The doctors predicted he would not live past another year. Those sleepless nights set him thinking. He realized with a new light that he "could not take one dime into the next world." Without delay, he surrendered His life to Christ. The following day, he awoke a new man. He began to help churches, the poor, and the needy. John began to sleep well, eat and enjoy life. The doctors had predicted he would not live over age 54. He lived to be 98 years old. As he neared the end of his life, he learned how to tango, hired a caddy to help with his golf swing, and passed out dimes to children who passed his house. Understand divine intervention is deep within the soul, but it begins with a thought. Former heavyweight boxing champion George Foreman said, "The truth is, my relationship with God is the reason I have such a positive outlook on life. Before I found Christ, I was blind...but when Jesus came into my life, He opened my eyes and started showing me all the good things I couldn't see before. God changed my heart and altered the way I view everything." Foreman said, "Granted, it is possible to think positively without having Jesus in your heart. But without Him, you'll never have His eternal perspective on the issues you're dealing with."

Meditate on the words of Scripture that stand out to you. Allow them to change the way you think, feel, and act. Reflect on a passage of the Bible that seems relevant to what you need, for you will never have a better day than when your mind is renewed by what God is saying to you! The context of Romans 12 is about resisting conformity to the world and living a life pleasing to God. As believers, we are no longer part of the world order (1 John 2:15-17, Col. 1:13). The world is an ungodly atmosphere that will lead to a broken life full of disappointment. But we who are in Christ can be taught by the Holy Spirit. That is, we allow the Word of God to dominate our thoughts and minds, after which we conduct ourselves accordingly. Transformation happens when the Bible becomes our guide for living. Why do we need a renewed mind? We "may prove what is that good, and acceptable, and perfect, will of God" (Rom. 12:2b). There is a way that we all live by default. The renewing of our mind is a process. Paul writes that we must change how we think if we want to understand the will of God for our lives. He encourages us to look at life with new questions: What does God want for me? What does He want from me? How can I use my life for His purpose and glory? God has a "good, acceptable, and perfect will" for each of us that should be proven by how we live.

Sir John Templeton encouraged people to think of the mind as a garden and themselves as responsible for tending it. He said if we exercise no control, something that should be a place of beauty will become a weed patch and a source of shame and misery. Gardens are not made in a day. God gave us one lifetime for the job, and He promised to help us get it right (Matt. 21:22). The Bible will help us recognize our thoughts for what they are. God presents a stark contrast between two options, and then He urges us to make a choice (Deut. 30:19, Matt. 7:13-14). This is a function of the brain. We cannot spiritualize everything. Some things require intentional determination. As believers, we are called to live on this earth surrounded by human society yet to display a very different system of values and a way of life.

Nearly all his life, former heavyweight boxing champion George Foreman had been an angry, hateful man. His mind was continually steeped in bitterness and rage. George was not ignorant of Christianity. Although he had never embraced Jesus as his Savior, he had been slowly evolving in his view of God. Thus began a renewing of his mind. And the change was seen in George's sudden desire to patch up relations with people he had hurt or who had hurt him. In the following months, he looked up old enemies and people he had mistreated to apologize. He went to his old neighborhood to ask forgiveness from old friends he felt he had ignored once he became wealthy and famous. And from his lips, both to family, friends, and people he once hated, now came the words, "I love you." Few could understand the new George. Many thought this was some con game he was playing. Some asked him, "Why are you doing this?" Others made it plain that they wanted nothing to do with him. But getting right with people was only part of the equation. George Foreman was transformed from one who scorned Christianity to one obsessed with all things Christian. He began going to church regularly. Here we see how anything we say or do starts with a thought. From there, salvation is a divine intervention, sealed by the power of the Holy Spirit (Eph. 1:13). Soon, George was sharing his conversion experience. He and a friend began preaching Christ on the streets. He just wanted to help people. Foreman is a happy man. He has been incredibly blessed by the influence for which he has become. The transformation of life by Christ is a beautiful thing. George Foreman is one more testimony to the reality that "If any man is in Christ, he is a new creation" (2 Cor. 5:17). Indeed, we have a choice. And our selection begins first in our minds and then in our hearts. I want God to be the central focus of my life. For by grace, we are saved through faith; and that not of ourselves. Jesus Christ becomes the Master of a renewed mind and a surrendered heart!

FOR THIS, WE NEED JESUS

Cuts and scrapes happen all the time. From a backyard mishap to a fall on the playground, we have bandages on hand to treat minor wounds. Then there are more extensive injuries that require pain medication. And if the drugs are not adequate, someone will say, "Oh, we need a stronger prescription for that." There are even more severe injuries where we say, "For this, we need professional help." Perhaps a few sutures to close the wound – maybe even surgery. Finally, we all recognize the most severe conditions that can only be treated successfully when a medical team says, "For this, we need a complex and long-term care plan." I use this opening to illustrate the varying hardships we face and how we can use our knowledge and ability to bring relief. But there are times when we are brought to circumstances so desperate that our talents and skills fail. These are the times when we have to say, "For this, I need Jesus!"

In Matthew chapter eight, we read about seasoned sailors, disciples of Christ who had faced storms that were common occurrences in the region. So, when Jesus got into the boat, they followed Him. These men thought nothing of it. They had done this many times in their fishing days, and they knew what they were doing. They drew from years of experience being on the water in stormy weather. They had bandages for that kind of trouble. But this time, "there arose a great tempest in the sea, insomuch that the ship was covered with the waves" (v24). This storm was different. This time their knowledge and strength were not getting the job done. They needed the One who healed blindness, unstopped deaf ears, and brought the dead back to life (Matt. 11:5). Yes, they were followers of Christ, serving Him with the mind, soul, and spirit. But now, the strongest of winds swept across the water. The sea, which a few minutes before was smooth as glass, was now boisterous with the white crests of the foaming waves. The ship was filling with water, and they were surely sinking. Have you experienced a time of smooth sailing that was interrupted when a fierce storm descended upon you without notice? Such was the case for these men. This tempest rocked their world, and the fierceness of this particular storm caused them to cry out, "For this, we need Jesus!"

Those who travel with Jesus will face storms. Those who travel without Jesus will face storms. No one escapes the trials of life. Sometimes we become so fearful that only our Lord can help us endure. And when He speaks peace to our troubled hearts, we become aware that we are in the presence of Almighty God! When the multitudes were hungry, and only a small sack lunch was found (John 6:1-14), someone might have said, "Oh, for this, we need Jesus." When Lazarus lay in a tomb (John 11:38-44), his sisters Mary and Martha said, "Our hearts are broken… for this we need Jesus!" When there was not another drop of wine at the marriage celebration (John 2:1-11), Mary said, "Okay, gentlemen, for this, we need Jesus." Do His miracles matter to you? Can you see Him working in your life? When Peter's mother-in-law was near death (Luke 4:38-40) when a man was possessed by demons (Mark 5:1-20), when two blind men sat on a sidewalk begging (Matt. 20:29-34) when an ear was severed from a soldier's head (Luke 22:50-51), what would you have done? What could you have done?

When you face a dire situation, and you feel as if you are suffocating, what then? What do you do when you cannot catch your breath in the middle of the night? When isolation causes you to feel like you are treading water alone in a vast ocean, what then? I know of which I speak and many of you do as well. Even though the memories of a loved one become wonderful treasures, our world still closes in with shades of darkness. Each day we wake up thinking, "Not even one of those days will ever happen for me again." Maybe your loss is different, but your midnight is just as black. We cannot prevent certain things, nor can they be fixed. These are the times of emotional pain when many of us cry, "For this, I need Jesus!" And when we do, He will especially attend to our needs (Ps. 23). Oh, how I thank God for His lovingkindness!

The occasions when we are most like our Lord tend to be in times of difficulty. We are more sensitive to the needs of those around us. We see brighter rays of sunshine in the smaller things – like a baby's laughter. We face each day with a softer heart. We are moved to create opportunities to show someone we care. It seems we have cause to make our way closer to God. This was the ministry of Jesus. The woman with the issue of blood suffered for twelve years, and this terrible illness caused her to put her faith in God (Luke 8:43-48). Many people have confessed their salvation in Christ, having gone through terrible hardship, overwhelming difficulty, the death of a loved one, or a life-threatening disease. Often, when we find ourselves in painful situations, we seek Him. And knowing He is near, we gain strength (Ps. 73:26). The stories of so many in the Bible remind us that in the most unpleasant conditions, the more we need to go to our Lord in prayer. There is contentment in the knowledge that our sovereign God controls all things. Maybe you feel overwhelmed and exhausted. After all the fear the disciples suffered, we see how these men exemplify the definition of courage in their preaching (Book of Acts). Those who were mere sailors and tax collectors are now courageous and bold for the cause of Christ. What caused this drastic change? It is the hope of the gospel of Jesus, the powerful means of victory for us all! But remember, before the disciples were sent out to share this good news, they spent a fair amount of time on a boat with Jesus. Who is in your boat? Have you had a time of nearly capsizing and being exposed to the elements? During those times, the disciples learned to keep their eyes fixed on the One who said they would have tribulations (John 16:33).

Where is your faith? We can read all the books that are available relative to coping with loss. And some are very helpful. We can check off all the lists of things to do to help brighten our days from a phycological point of view. We can read in-depth articles on 'What To Do When Trouble Comes' or memorize dozens of inspirational quotes about overcoming life's struggles, all written by those who understand deep grief. But in the end, only Jesus can satisfy our souls and bring peace to our minds. How does this happen? By humbly surrendering to God's terms whether or not we understand. And when we do (Prov. 22:4), His pleasure will not be because He won an argument but because we have won a victory!

Some time ago, a friend told me that, shortly after the birth of their son, any attempt to feed him was unsuccessful. He and his wife were aware that their infant was malnourished and that something must be done soon. He recalled the look of helplessness in his wife's eyes as she handed her son to him after several attempts at getting the baby to eat. He said it was one of the darkest days of their lives. Thankfully, their prayers were answered, and their son began to eat. Today he is a strong and happy boy. But I can only imagine what those days were like for young parents. Indeed, their hearts were broken. But, trusting in One who said He came to heal the brokenhearted (Luke 4:18), they witnessed the lovingkindness of God as they prayed those unforgettable words, "For this we need Jesus!"

In Psalm 139, David prayed the prayer of a believing heart. Our Lord is often closest to us when we feel the most alone. He is watching, He is concerned, and He cares (Ps. 121:4). The resurrection of Christ is that morning of history that gives us the courage to endure the hours of darkness, even the night of death. I do not pretend that faith is easy, but it is always worth the effort (2 Cor. 12:9). What is the way of faith? It is that we find the world of the unseen more convincing than this one. Difficult circumstances make us question the strength of our confidence and the certainty of God's faithfulness. But when we "call upon the name of the Lord" at an altar of worship as Abraham did in Genesis 26:25, we will – as he did – learn that God is trustworthy! Jesus loves and cares for us in our moments of distress. When you cry out, "God, it's not right. It is just not right!" will you still trust Him? Indeed, there was a day when everything went terribly wrong. God's creation would still be a perfect and sinless design if not for the willful fall of man from his first estate (Gen. 3:1-7, Rom. 5:12). Nevertheless, put your trust in Christ alone for He is making all things new (Rev. 21:5). Do you know that Jesus weeps with you (Luke 11:33-36)? The Bible says God puts your tears in a bottle because they are precious to Him (Ps. 56:8). The wonder of God lies in His power to create and in His willingness to heal broken hearts and revive wounded spirits!

Will you, like those who mourned Lazarus's death, though they cringed at opening an occupied grave, roll away the barrier to your miracle? Will you allow God's glory to manifest in you so that others may know Him? Who better to trust than an all-sufficient Savior who suffered a horrible death and rose again (Luke 24:46-47) to reveal His love for us? Is there anything more He could have done? He gave His all. Indeed, our Lord is the hope of all who seek Him, and He is not far from any of us (Acts 17:27). Therefore, as disciples in a storm-tossed boat, peace beyond human understanding (Phil. 4:4-7) will be ours when we humbly lay our burden at the Cross and say, "For this, I need Jesus!"

Jesus Makes Heaven Accessible

Geoffrey was a young homeless boy in the slums of London. He heard that an American evangelist named D. L. Moody was coming to the evening service of a church on the other side of town, and he wanted to listen to him preach. Geoffrey set out to find the church on the day of the meeting. He dodged rumbling carriage wheels, slipped through crowded streets, and wove his way through the hordes of hurrying pedestrians. He helped himself to an apple from a grocer's cart along the way, narrowly escaping the irate shopkeeper's angry grasp. Finally, just as the sun began to set, he looked up and saw his destination. He stopped in his tracks to stare in awe. The church was majestically situated on a hill, its stained-glass windows reflecting the setting sun with a glow that looked like the very glory of heaven.

In the stillness of the early evening air, he could hear hundreds of voices rising and falling with the thunderous swell of organ pipes in a stirring song of praise. The sight and sound seemed to reach out to him. Geoffrey did not hesitate. He bounded up the long, sweeping staircase that led to the massive wooden front door. Just as he was about to enter, a big hand descended out of nowhere, grabbed him by the shoulder, and asked sharply, "Just where do you think you're going, son?" Geoffrey responded stiffly but truthfully. "I heard Dr. Moody was going to preach here tonight, and I've walked across town to hear him." The big doorman looked down at the little boy with uncombed hair, unwashed face, dirty clothes, and bare feet, then declared emphatically, "Not you! You are too dirty to go inside!" The doorman then stood squarely in front of the door. Geoffrey squared his little shoulders, glared back at the doorkeeper, then stalked off the front steps. He was confident he would find another way into the church. But as little Geoffrey walked around the building, he found all the other doors solidly locked, and the windows were too high for him even to attempt an entry. He ended up back on the front steps, plopping down, weary and discouraged. Despite his street-cultivated toughness, tears began to run down his dirty cheeks. Suddenly his attention was caught by a black carriage that pulled up to the foot of the steps. A very distinguished-looking gentleman climbed out and began to climb the stairs quickly.

When he reached Geoffrey's step, he glanced over and noticed the curious interest in the young boy's eyes and the tear stains on his cheeks. He stopped abruptly and asked, "What's wrong?" For a moment, Geoffrey started to shrug and say, "Nothin'." But something in the man's demeanor caused Geoffrey to blurt out, "I came to hear Dr. Moody preach, but he says I'm too dirty to go inside," and he pointed toward the doorman. The gentleman looked down at the little boy, then extended his hand. "Here, take my hand," the man offered. Geoffrey took a long, hard look at the man, then let his eyes focus on his extended hand. Slowly, he lifted his grimy little hand and placed it in that of a stranger, who clasped it tightly and invited Geoffrey to "come with me." And Geoffrey did. Hand in hand, they walked up the long, sweeping staircase. When they came to the massive door, the very same doorkeeper who had formerly forbidden the boy to enter now hastily opened the door wide. With the man still gripping his hand, Geoffrey walked through the open door and down the center aisle of the church, already filled with worshipers, until they came to the front row. The big man walked up the steps to the platform, stood behind the pulpit, and began to preach. The man who made God's house accessible for this little boy was D. L. Moody!

Likewise, Jesus makes heaven accessible to us! Have you ever thought there is another way to heaven than through the Door (John 10:9)? Jesus is the only way. He alone has the power to forgive sin (Matt. 9:1-8). In Acts 4:12, we read, "Neither is there salvation in any other: for there is none other name under heaven given among men, whereby we must be saved." Or, like so many others, maybe you have questioned whether the Door is sufficient - because, like the doorman told Geoffrey, "Not you! You are too dirty to go inside!" Ephesians 2:8-9 answers it all. The apostle Paul says, "For by grace are ye saved through faith; and that not of yourselves; it is the gift of God; not of works [emphasis added], lest any man should boast." We contribute nothing to God's plan of salvation, not even our points of view (Rom. 3:10, 2 Tim. 1:9). Just as Geoffrey wove his way through the multitudes of noisy pedestrians searching for his destination, the varied opinions of men will make you weary and discouraged (2 John 1:9). They will keep you unsettled and guessing (Eph. 4:14, 2 Tim. 4:1-4). Jesus rebuked the religious elders of His day (Luke 11:37-52) insofar as their teaching was not established in biblical truth. When Satan tempted him in the wilderness, Jesus responded three times with "It is written" (Matt. 4:1-11). He did not respond with "Well, the church leaders have said" or "According to our handbook" (Matt. 23). Consequently, when Jesus came and extended His hand of grace to me (Matt. 14:31), I remember studying His hand before I stretched mine to His. But when I did (Ps. 50:15), I felt the firm grasp of His love and heard His kind words, "Come with me." And because I accepted His offer (John 1:12), He will walk with me hand in hand, not only through my journey down here but through heaven's gates that will open wide for me (2 Pet. 1:10-11). By faith in the death, burial, and resurrection of Jesus (Acts 2:23-36), heaven is made accessible. There is hope for everyone who calls on His name (Rom. 10:8-13). How wonderful the grace of God!

Anne Graham Lotz tells this story, "A few years ago, I found myself groping for a way to explain that the blood of Jesus is sufficient to a woman who had been on death row for multiple murders. She would be executed within ten hours of my visit. Tears glistened in her eyes as she looked at me beseechingly, needing assurance of the salvation she had claimed by faith six years earlier. That very night she would be stepping into eternity, she was desperate for reassurance of her forgiveness from God. I asked her if she had ever been to the ocean, and she nodded. As she walked along the shore, I asked her if she had seen small holes in the sand where ghost crabs had darted in and out. Again, she nodded yes. I then asked if she had seen any larger holes, like those made by children digging a deep moat around a sandcastle. She looked somewhat puzzled and said she had seen holes like that. I persisted as I probed gently to see if she had ever seen huge holes created by machines dredging a channel or burying pipelines on the beach. Her brow began to furrow as she again acknowledged a quiet yes. I then leaned toward her and pressed my point, 'Velma, when the tide comes in, what happens to all those holes? The little ones made by the crabs, the medium-size ones made by children, and the great big ones made by machines?' A soft light began to gleam in her eyes, and a smile played at the corner of her lips as I answered my own question: 'All the holes are covered equally by the water, aren't they? The blood of Jesus is like the tide that washes over the holes of your sins and covers all of them equally (Rom. 5:6-11).' Velma stepped into eternity that night, reassured of her forgiveness by God and with a welcome into her heavenly home based on nothing but the blood of Jesus!" Ms. Graham Lotz continues, "Praise God for the blood of Jesus to cover all of our sins! All of them! Little sins like losing your temper. Medium-size sins like gossip. Big sins like murdering your mother. They are all under the blood of Jesus, and we are free to enjoy complete forgiveness!"

At one point in Jesus' ministry, many of His followers, having heard a sermon difficult to accept, turned their backs on Him. Jesus turned to the Twelve and asked, "Will ye also go away?" Peter's reply is exactly right: "Lord, to whom shall we go? Thou hast the words of eternal life. And we believe and are sure that thou art that Christ, the Son of the living God" (John 6:67-69). There is a widespread belief that one will get into heaven as long as one leads a good life. This viewpoint contradicts the truth of the Bible. The prophet Jeremiah says, "The heart is deceitful above all things, and desperately wicked; who can know it?" (Jer. 17:9). In Psalm 51:5, David makes the point even stronger: "Behold, I was shapen in iniquity; and in sin did my mother conceive me." According to Romans 3:23, we all have fallen short of the glory of God. In Acts chapter 2, the apostle Peter speaks of the indwelling of the Holy Spirit as the only way to have everlasting life in the presence of God. We must humbly submit to God, turn from our transgression, and accept Christ as both Savior and Lord (John 3:1-21). 1 John 5:20 tells us, "And we know that the Son of God is come... this is the true God, and eternal life."

After a busy day at a camp meeting in western New York, Fanny Crosby, the blind author of so many wonderful hymns, sat with John Sweney resting on the porch of a hotel. After a bit, John asked, "Fanny, do you think we'll recognize our friends in heaven?" She responded, "John, that's not what you really want to know. You wonder how an old lady who has been blind all her life could even recognize one person, let alone her Lord and Savior. Well, I've given it a lot of thought, and I don't think I'll have a problem. But if I do, when I get to heaven, I'm going to look around, and when I see the one whom I think is my Savior, I'm going to walk up to Him and say, 'May I see your hands?' When I see the nail prints in the hands of my Savior, then I'll know I've found my Jesus." "Oh, Fanny," John said, "that would make a great song." "No, thank you," she replied. "I'm tired; I'm going to bed." Well, the following day, bright and early, Fanny met John for breakfast, and before they went their separate ways, she dictated the words of this great hymn: "I shall know Him, I shall know Him; and redeemed by His side, I shall stand. I shall know Him, I shall know Him, by the prints of the nails in His hands." Do you know Him? Have you been redeemed? Crosby also wrote this wonderful verse: Someday the silver cord will break, and I no more as now shall sing. But, O, the joy when I shall wake within the palace of the King! And I shall see Him face to face and tell the story, saved by grace. Oh, friend, Jesus has made heaven accessible to me (Eph. 4:30), and how I look forward to the day when I will be with Him there!

LOVING OTHERS

In the days of Jesus' earthly ministry, a road connected Jerusalem and Jericho, the oldest continually inhabited city in the world. This path descends more than 3,300 feet in elevation in just seventeen miles. Given the isolated terrain, people on this road were easy targets for bandits who would have found ample hiding places and escape routes into the desert where no one would pursue them. When Jesus said, "A certain man went down from Jerusalem to Jericho," his listeners surely would have recognized the dangers of the journey. In desert-like conditions and without shelter from the elements, the familiar road was steep and rugged, with rocky valleys and passes. Until the fifth century, it was called the Way of Blood, and in the 19th century, people still paid safety money to local sheiks before they traveled on it. Undoubtedly, this was the road on which Jesus said a man was robbed, beaten, and left for dead. Two men traveling separately, with a mindset of superiority over those not part of their social and religious circles, walked by the dying man and did nothing. At points, the road was so narrow that a passerby would have had to step over a victim's body. Then a third man came along, a Samaritan who had sympathy for the man lying there. Racial tensions and religious differences gave way to heartfelt compassion. He stopped to help the best way he could (Luke 10:25-37).

It is no coincidence that Jesus chose this problematic road to illustrate the journey of life where compassion involves more than sympathy. What's the difference, you ask? Sympathy says, "I am sorry." Compassion says, "I am sorry and will help you." And on that day, a fallen man's wounds began to heal when he received mercy from an unexpected source. Does this sound familiar to you? It is the story of every believer! "For God so loved the world, that he gave his only begotten Son, that whosoever believeth in him should not perish, but have everlasting life" (John 3:16). We also have received mercy from One who loved us as we lay wounded at the hand of the enemy; and there, left to die in our sin! Oh, I thank God for His lovingkindness! The story of the good Samaritan begins with our Lord's response to a man who tried to tempt Him - and then justify himself. We're good at making excuses to ease our guilt, aren't we? But you see, Jesus knew the motivation behind the man's question, "Who is my neighbor?" God is always interested in our questions. But He is also concerned with the reason for our asking (Matt. 6:1-8).

Is it possible to pray with wrong motives? The apostle James says it is (James 4:3). Wise King Solomon says it like this, "All the ways of a man are clean in his own eyes, but the Lord weigheth the spirits" (Prov. 16:2). The key is for us to pray that God's will be done (1 John 5:14-15). I ask myself, where do I place myself in this story? Do I make excuses? Or do I accept the lesson of how I should involve myself in the needs of others? We live in a culture that could use a lot more friendliness. One night, a mother overheard her little girl praying, "Dear Jesus, please make all the bad people good and all the good people nice." Now more than ever, Christians should be kind to people regardless of their political views, social position, or religious beliefs. The second of the two greatest commandments in the Bible is to love our neighbors as ourselves. I believe God places this as the second and not the first for this reason: To be a good neighbor, we must first love the Lord with all our heart, soul, and mind (Matt. 22:34-40).

Every day is a test of whether we love God. And only when we love Him more than temporal blessings will we be able to communicate His heart to others. Christ's death on the cross demonstrates the love of God like no other event in history! And the apostle John says our love for each other is the overflow of God's love for us (1 John 4:7-12). In Matthew 14:14, Jesus was moved with compassion, and He healed those who were sick. In Matthew 20:24, He had compassion, healing folks who were blind. In chapter eight of Mark's gospel, our Lord compassionately fed thousands who were hungry. We know we have loved our neighbor well when we are moved to compassion, even when it's costly or inconvenient. What did Jesus mean when He used the word "neighbor?" Who is our neighbor? Based on the meaning of "neighbor" in the Old Testament book of Leviticus (chapter 19), Jesus' audience would have defined "neighbor" as any fellow Israelite or a resident alien that had been welcomed into the community. However, through the good Samaritan story, Jesus expands that definition to anyone who needs our help. The Lord illustrates a more exaggerated love than was required in the Old Testament - and then He commands us to show it. The literal meaning of the New Testament Greek word neighbor is "the one near." When we consider God's unconditional love for all people (John 3:16) and that He shows no partiality (Rom. 2:11), we understand that Jesus intends us to interpret "neighbor" as everyone we meet. The demonstration of love spoken of in John 13:35 is to show the world that we are disciples of Christ.

And if we believe there are no coincidences or chance happenings given God's sovereignty, then our neighbors are not limited to only those with whom we have something in common. Now that we know who our neighbors are, let's consider this question, "How do we love them?" Jesus leaves us no 'wiggle room' for how we are to love others. In John 13:34, He said, "A new commandment I give unto you, That ye love one another; as I have loved you, that ye also love one another." This is a straightforward command. In Mark 12:31, Jesus said to love them just as we love ourselves. That is, we look out for our welfare each day, ensuring our basic needs are met through food, clothes, and a comfy place to sleep. We take time to go for a walk or do something fun. We treat ourselves to special little things on occasion. We get to know ourselves by discovering what our values are and what we believe. We accept ourselves without the need for comparison. We focus on our strengths and not our weaknesses. We take responsibility for our behavior. We understand that we make mistakes, and then we forgive ourselves. We do not judge ourselves too harshly. Sometimes, we make fun a priority. We demonstrate gratitude for God's goodness to us. We want our opinions to matter. We surround ourselves with people who treat us with kindness and respect. And we associate with those who are concerned for our spiritual welfare. These are some of the ways we love ourselves. So, how to love others? In just the same way! I am familiar with volunteers who feed, clothe and minister to a large homeless population. They will tell you this: "If we wouldn't eat it, then we don't feed it. If we wouldn't wear it, we don't give it." And I will add another for myself, "If I don't live according to God's Word, then I won't teach it."

In R. B. Mitchell's story, The Castaway Kid, he writes, "It was February 1962. I was seven years old. I struggled to keep hope alive, but I lost that battle in the winter of second grade. Living in (an orphanage) with other abandoned kids, I cried until no tears were left. 'No one's going to rescue me. I'm alone, and I don't know why. What did I do wrong? I was only three when they left me here. What could I possibly have done to deserve this?' On that cold winter night, I hardened my heart. 'Nothing and nobody will hurt me this badly again. The big boys can beat me until I cry with pain, but no one is ever going to make me cry from my heart like this again.' It was only a little boy's vow. But it was all I had to protect me from the living nightmare that lurked around the corner. As I lay in bed that night, my stomach was full. But I felt as empty as ever." A few years later, I banged my fist on the desk of my new counselor, 'Who's doing this to me? Huh? Tell me! Who am I supposed to be mad at? I'm not that terrible a kid! I didn't ask to be born. I sure didn't ask for my psychotic mother! Why won't anybody take me? Why can't I belong to someone and have my own home?' He continues, "Like many kids at the Home, I tried to control situations by throwing authority figures off balance. Some did it with bad behavior or explosive anger. I preferred twisting the grown-up's words and getting a reaction I liked."

Sometimes we cross paths with people whose behavior is harsh and difficult to love. And so often, it is because they are hiding a heavy heart. But if we take the time to understand, we may find that inwardly they desperately want someone to care about them. How can we love people? First, don't offer a lecture to a person who needs a hug. Consider more fully the damage that is done when people suffer. Give not only resources but also your time (Gal. 6:2). A creative teenager tired of reading bedtime stories to his little sister decided to record several of her favorite stories on tape. He told her, "Now you can hear your stories anytime you want. Isn't that great?" She looked at the machine for a minute and replied, "Nope." "Why not?" "Cuz it don't have a lap." Practice hospitality and be friendly (Rom. 12:13). Share your wisdom (Luke 3:10-11). Nothing else offers the same protection, benefits, and blessings that wisdom does. Be ready to act on short notice (Prov. 3:27). Open your heart and hand wide (Deut. 15:11). Refresh the spirit of others (Prov. 11:25). Speak well of people (Isa.

58:10). Be an encourager (1Thess. 5:11). Be a good friend; establish a bond of trust (Prov. 17:17).

A British publication once offered a prize for the best definition of a friend. This was the winning definition among the thousands of answers received: 'A friend is the one who comes in when the whole world has gone out.' Defend the oppressed, take up the cause of the fatherless and plead the case of the widow (Isa. 1:17). Honor others above yourself (Rom. 12:10). Lead people to Jesus (Eph. 2:10). The Bible is saturated with God's instruction that we help others, care for the poor, and live an attitude of self-sacrifice. Someone wrote, If I had known what trouble you were bearing, what griefs were in the silence of your face; I would have been more gentle and more caring, I would have brought more warmth into the place. Yes, we must love people (Mark 12:30-31). But, even more, the pouring of ourselves into someone's life is an incredible testimony of what God has done for us and what He will do for them! Dear Lord, help us to love others, wherever they are - whoever they are - and however we can.

THE RELIABILITY OF THE BIBLE

We read in Paul's second letter to Timothy (3:16-17), "All Scripture is given by inspiration of God, and is profitable for doctrine, for reproof, for correction, for instruction in righteousness: that the man of God may be perfect (mature and complete), throughly furnished (sincerely and without reserve) unto all good works." The Bible is the revealed Word of God. It is God's letter to humanity, a collection of sixty-six holy books written by forty divinely inspired men with a wide range of backgrounds and occupations. Unlike other religious writings, the Bible is a factual news account of events, places, people, and conversations. God shows us who He is and how to know Him. The Holy Scripture contains hundreds of subjects penned in three languages on three continents over fifteen hundred years. Yet, the entire Bible has one single theme and purpose. This could only be achieved if a sole author inspired the Bible. Indeed, only one Author spans every age, language, location, and subject – God Himself. The Bible is divinely inspired by God, authoritative for all of life, and without error (Ps. 19:7-8, 119:160). 2 Timothy 3:16 speaks to the product. 2 Peter 1:21 speaks to the process. From beginning to end, the theme of the Bible is Jesus Christ!

Satan has waged war on the voice of God since the beginning of creation (Gen. 3) with this simple phrase "Hath God said?" The enemy of our soul is skilled at causing us to doubt, and the questioning of Scripture continues today. But the Bible is the Word of life (Phil. 2:16) that produces heart-penetrating conviction (Heb. 4:12) and offers messages of hope (Rom. 15:4). The writers themselves acknowledged that Scripture is God's words and not their own. David said, "The Spirit of the Lord spake by me, and his word was in my tongue" (2 Sam. 23:2). In the opening verse of the

Book of Revelation, John makes it clear that all revelation was given to him by God. New Testament writers quoted verses from the Old Testament, revealing their confidence that all passages are indeed the voice of God to humankind. The infallibility of Scripture is made evident primarily through its prophecy and fulfillment. Read the promise of the coming Messiah in Isaiah chapter 9; a glorious event prophesied about 700 years before it occurred. And there are many others. And, although the purpose of the Bible was not to record all of history or teach science, where it does give us facts regarding these things, it is without error. It's incredible to see how Scripture describes past events that modern-day historians are only now discovering and reporting. The Bible also recorded accurate scientific facts before they were revealed to man.

At her coronation on June 2, 1953, Her Majesty Queen Elizabeth II (1926-2022) was presented with an Authorized (King James) Version Bible with these accompanying words: "Our gracious Queen: to keep your Majesty ever mindful of the law and the Gospel of God as the Rule for the whole life and government of Christian Princes, we present you with this Book, the most valuable thing that this world affords. Here is Wisdom; This is the royal Law; These are the lively Oracles of God." And, with those words, she ascended the throne. Some two thousand years before that day, on a mountainside, the King of all kings declared, "For verily I say unto you, till heaven and earth pass, one jot or one tittle shall in no wise pass from the law, till all be fulfilled" (Matt. 5:18).

When Jesus resisted the temptation of Satan by relying on the powerful weapon of Scripture (Matt. 4:1-11), He let us know that the Word of God is the only answer to spiritual warfare. When Jesus read from the scroll in the synagogue (Luke 4:21), He said that the Old Testament promises of what God would do are now fulfilled in Him. Friend, the confidence of Heaven resides in the holy Scriptures. The sufficiency of all things is in God alone, meaning that the Bible is all we need to equip us for a life of faith and service. It demonstrates God's intention to restore the broken relationship between Himself and humanity through His Son, Jesus Christ, through the gift of faith. No other writings are necessary for this good news to be understood. No other words can give us abundant life here and everlasting joy in Heaven! Holy men of God spake as they were moved by the Holy Ghost (2 Pet. 1:21). The Bible is not an object into which God breathed something. It is that which God Himself breathed out. How are we to understand the expression "breathed out?" It means that the Holy Spirit entirely guided the writers of Scripture with perfect revelation. The Greek words theo (God) and pneustos (breath) are supernatural extensions of God Himself. Therefore, we can confidently say that what Scripture says, God says. Someone has said, "The words of God contain full authority only as we regard them as having sprung from heaven where they are spoken." Our words to God are essential for Christian living. But they pale in comparison to the importance of His words to us. Apostle Paul loved the Thessalonians because they received the Scriptures, not as the words of men, but of God (1 Thess. 2:13). A person yet unredeemed and without the indwelling of the Holy Spirit cannot understand the righteous precepts of the Bible (1 Cor. 2:14). Only through the Spirit's power can we know and employ for ourselves the character and righteousness of God (John 14:26). The Word of God does the work of God – in our hearts - by the Spirit of God.

In George Foreman's book, God in My Corner, the former heavyweight boxing champion writes: "In 1974, before I went to Africa to fight Muhammad Ali, a friend gave me a Bible to take along on my trip. He said, 'George, keep this with you for good luck.' I believed the Bible was just a shepherd's handbook, probably because the only verse I knew was 'the Lord is my shepherd.' But I was always looking for luck, so I carried that Bible with me. I had lucky pennies and good luck charms, so I added the 'lucky' Bible to my collection of superstitious items. After I lost the fight, I threw the Bible away. I never even opened it. The Bible didn't help me win, so why do I need it? I thought I'd get power simply from owning it; I didn't realize that I needed to read it and believe what it says. Since then, I've come to understand that the Bible is my road map, not my good luck charm."

When God gave His words to humanity, He preserved them so we would have God's truth forever. Josh McDowell said, "The Bible has withstood vicious attacks of its enemies as no other book. Many have tried to burn it, ban it, and outlaw it, from the days of Roman emperors to the present-day communist-dominated countries." Even as evil forces attempted to destroy Scripture forever, God not only foiled their efforts but Also used them to spread the Gospel further. And as we immerse ourselves in the Bible, we will grow in our relationship with God and become ready to do the work He has called us to. President Ronald Reagan said, "Within the covers of one single book, the Bible, are all the answers to all the problems that face us today – if only we would read and believe."

In 1908, a small group established Gideon's International – an organization to make a difference for the Lord disproportional to their size. A few years later, the group began distributing free copies of the Bible. They have distributed more than two billion copies of New Testaments and Bibles worldwide. Every copy of Gideon's New Testament contains the following statement: "The Bible contains the mind of God, the state of man, the way of salvation, the doom of sinners, and the happiness of believers. Its doctrines are holy, its precepts are binding, its histories are true, and its decisions are immutable. Read it to be wise, believe it to be safe, and practice it to be holy. It contains light to direct you, food to support you, and comfort to cheer you. It is the traveler's map, the pilgrim's staff, the pilot's compass, the soldier's sword, and the Christian's charter. Here too, Heaven is opened, and the gates of hell are disclosed. Christ is its grand subject, our good its design, and the glory of God its end. It should fill the memory, rule the heart and guide the feet. Read it slowly, frequently, and prayerfully. It is a mine of wealth, a paradise of glory, and a river of pleasure."

The Psalmist said the law of the Lord is perfect and more to be desired than fine gold; trustworthy, enlightening, and altogether righteous (Ps. 19:7-14). When you need answers, go to the Word (2 Pet. 1:3). When you see chaos in the news, focus your heart on God's truth (John 17:17). When you have a heavy heart, allow the words of Jesus to comfort you (Matt. 6:25-34). When you struggle with decisions, seek the wise counsel of the Bible (James 1:5, 3:17). The Bible is a living Book. The wisdom of the Bible is timeless. The message of the Bible is clear. God's words will endure forever; through them, in obedience (Luke 11:28), we are brought to new life in Jesus Christ!

REFLECTING GOD'S GLORY

"In the name of Jesus Christ of Nazareth, rise up and walk" were life-changing words to a lame man familiar to those who entered the temple gates daily. In a moment, God healed him through the ministry of Apostles Peter and John. All who witnessed the miracle were filled with wonder and amazement, looking to God's men as if, by their power or holiness, they caused the man to walk (Acts 3). What happened next? This was Peter's grand occasion to glorify God, and my, did he ever take advantage of the opportunity. The apostle preached one of the most God-honoring and convicting sermons in all Scripture! But while Peter and John were still speaking, they were arrested and set amid governmental and religious leaders who demanded to know, "By what power, or by what name, have ye done this?" (Acts 4:1-22). What did Peter do then? Well, he didn't stop preaching. The Bible says that he, "being filled with the Holy Ghost," boldly preached another sermon, one so convicting that many came to faith in Christ! Here is the message in this writing: People found salvation in none other than the name of Jesus Christ because someone glorified God for His mighty acts (Acts 4:12). Let us be that someone! When God uses us in any way, the best we can do is point people to the One who did the job.

God sits high upon the throne of heaven. He has no rival. He is subject to no other power, and He reigns supreme. Dominion and glory are His. The sights and sounds of heaven are more glorious than we can imagine. Yet the angels do not worship these things. They worship God. Streets of gold and gates of pearl are beyond human comprehension. But this does not inspire heaven's singers to sing. God alone is the inspiration for their music! The prophet Isaiah was overwhelmed by a visual revelation of God's divine glory (Isa. 6). He saw heavenly beings crying one to another, "Holy,

holy, holy, is the Lord of hosts; the whole earth is full of his glory" (Isa. 6:2-3). In the Hebrew language, a repetition of words is a literary practice used for emphasis. The threefold repetition of the defining characteristic of God's nature is holiness (Isa. 6:3, Rev. 4:8). He is holy! The supreme purpose of our living is to glorify God (Micah 6:8). And if we want God's will to be done in earth as it is in heaven (Matt. 6:10), we will join the heavenly hosts in giving Him our highest praise!

I remember my childhood Sunday School teacher telling us that God has all power and glory. Then, in the "big church," as we called it, the preacher would say, "People of God, we need to give Him glory." Now one might think, "How can we give God any more glory than He already has?" Well, the meaning of the word glory is to "give weight or tribute to" or " honor." To add to God's glory is not possible (Isa. 48:11, Acts 17:24-25), for He upholds all things by the word of His power (Heb. 1:3). But we acknowledge His glory, and in His presence, we reverently bow our hearts (Ps. 95:6). How do we glorify God? The most honorable praise will be our obedience to His Word, surrendering our will to what He desires. Then we celebrate Him audibly. The Psalmist David said, "Because thy lovingkindness is better than life, my lips shall praise thee" (Ps. 63:3). Johann Sebastian Bach said, "All music should have no other end and aim than the glory of God." So, when you come up with words or a song that expresses your heart's gratitude, give them to the only One deserving! Apostle Paul tells us to glorify God in everything we do (Col. 3:17). Jesus said, "Herein is my Father glorified, that ye bear much fruit; so shall ye be my disciples" (John 15:8). We honor God by sharing the gospel of Jesus Christ (Luke 19:10) in obedience to Matthew 28:18-20.

The Duke of Wellington, the British military leader who defeated Napoleon at Waterloo, was not an easy man under which to serve. He was brilliant, demanding, and not one to compliment his subordinates. Yet even Wellington realized that his methods left something to be desired. In his old age, a young lady asked him what, if anything, he would do differently if he had his life to live over again. Wellington thought for a moment, then replied. "I'd give more praise." One day R.C. Chapman, a devout Christian, was asked how he was feeling. "I'm burdened this morning!" was his reply. But because his happy countenance contradicted his words, the person asking was surprised, "Are you really burdened,

Mr. Chapman?" "Yes, but it's a wonderful burden; it's an overabundance of blessings for which I cannot find enough time or words to express my gratitude!" In Psalm 68:19, David blessed the Lord from whom he received daily benefits, even the God of his salvation!

In times of blessing, we praise Him. When trouble comes, we depend on Him. When we fail, He is our righteousness. In weakness, He is our strength. And as we worship Him, our fear is put into perspective. What a privilege it is to give our highest praise to Almighty God!

The Psalmist said, "When I consider thy heavens, the work of thy fingers, the moon, and the stars, which thou hast ordained; what is man, that thou art mindful of him?" (Ps. 8:3-4). Many astronauts have experienced profound spiritual transformations when viewing the Earth from space, a phenomenon that has come to be called the "overview effect." Apollo 14 astronaut Alan Shepard recalled, "When I first looked back at the Earth, standing on the Moon, I cried." Looking out the window of his Apollo spacecraft, astronaut Edgar Mitchell described it as "a glimpse of divinity." He said he felt as if he momentarily became one with the universe. Another astronaut, Nicole Stott, told of her voyage into space, "I don't know how you can come back and not, in some way, be changed." In the awesome presence of God, we feel smaller. Not insignificant, but smaller. We sense that we are a piece of a greater whole; we have a place and purpose in the world. Consider the One who spoke all things into existence, the Creator who "divided the light from the darkness" (Gen. 1:4), and the God with authority to create something by simply saying He would. As the heavens declare the glory of God (Psalm 19:1), we also declare His glory through righteous living made possible by the power of the Holy Spirit (1 Peter 1:13–25). Our God cannot be a means to an end, but the end Himself; not merely useful, but worthy.

The wise King Solomon said the whole duty of man is to fear God and keep his commandments" (Eccl. 12:13). Whether we are aware or not, people around us are influenced by how we live. Therefore, it will be known when we are enthusiastic about our God. In his book Hope That Goes The Distance, Jud Wilhite tells this story, "I'll never forget being in a doctoral program and rooming with a sixty-year-old African American. He lived in the Northwest and worked as a school principal. I was a young pastor in my late twenties, serving a church in Texas. We couldn't have been farther apart in geography, background, race, or religion." He said, "Over the course of the week, I asked God to open a door for me to share with him the hope I have. I longed for an opportunity to present why I am a God-follower. At the end of our seminar, he invited me to have lunch with him. As we sat there, he placed his fork on the table, leaned forward, and, with the most concerned, serious look you can imagine, said, "Jud, tell me how to live my life." I had prayed for an open door; God kicked the wall down. As I shared my hope with him, he began nodding." Pastor Wilhite says, "What an adventure God calls us to! What a privilege to share our hope with the hopeless, the hurting, the broken, and the confused!"

The men who play baseball for the New York Yankees wear uniforms without a name, only a number. From the start, club organizers believed that putting players' names on the jerseys would call unnecessary attention to individuals rather than the team as a whole. What an excellent way to illustrate "Team Jesus," the collective body of believers worldwide. Paul said, "God forbid that I should glory, save in the cross of our Lord Jesus Christ" (Gal. 6:14).

A song written by Margaret J. Harris (1865-1919) goes like this:

I will praise Him! I will praise Him!
Praise the Lamb for sinners slain;
Give Him glory all ye people,
For His blood can wash away each stain.

While writing this devotional, I was impressed to write something to a friend who has also endured tremendous loss. I said, "For every child of God, there has been – or there will be – an experience that will change Romans 8:28 from a memorization quote to a belief system. Your prayer will move from "God heal me" to "God use me for your glory and help me cope." And then you will discover that joy can coexist with uncertainty, pain, and confusion." A few days later, I asked God to give me a song for those who would hear this message the following Sunday. After napping one evening, I awoke with a simple chorus in my heart,

I will glorify the Lord; I will glorify the Lord;
My song I'll bring, I will praise the King; I will glorify the Lord!"

We praise God because He alone is worthy to be praised (Ps. 18:3). He is perfect in truth, holiness, love, power, and wisdom. We praise Him for the beauty of His creation, grace, mercy, and forgiveness. We reflect the radiance of God's character (Luke 2:9) by yielding to the Holy Spirit through the written Word of God. Whether child or adult, the most powerful witness of God's grace is for someone to see the outpouring of a grateful heart. Thankfulness is contagious! The Psalmist said, "O magnify the Lord with me, and let us exalt his name together" (Ps. 34:3). Praising God is an expression, an outward manifestation of thanks, happiness, and awe. Glorifying God is expressed by a lifestyle. We praise God for what He has done and worship Him for who He is!

A Heart For God

The heart is mentioned over eight hundred times in the Bible. It is often characterized as the spiritual expression of our existence, the place where emotions and desires dwell. It is the center of understanding (Prov. 4:23), created for fellowship with God (1 Sam. 16:7). The heart is a spiritual place. We are in spiritual warfare (Eph. 6:12). The heart bends toward what the eye sees (Matt. 6:22-23). The enemy will surely make it his business that we see - and desire - the things of his choosing (1 Pet. 5:8). Our heart is the source of everything we do (Prov. 21:2). The Bible tells us to "be strong in the Lord, and in the power of his might"… putting on "the whole armour of God" that we "may be able to stand against the wiles of the devil" (Eph. 6:10-11). Following the leading of the Holy Spirit is a matter of the heart (2 Chron. 16:9), and it begins with a heart exam. Scripture tells us our hearts are "deceitful above all things and desperately wicked" (Jer. 17:9, Rom. 3:23). Therefore, to have a heart for God, we must first believe in Jesus, who alone can forgive and cleanse us from all sin (Acts 4:12, Rom. 10:9); and then understand that we cannot live a godly and righteous life without the indwelling of the Holy Ghost (Acts 2:37-40).

How can we live a life that is pleasing to God? Consider David, the second king of Israel, the man after God's own heart (1 Sam. 13:14). When we study David's life, we discover that a heart for God is not a mystical gift; nor is it merely an emotional one. It is a surrendered lifestyle made up of God-honoring choices. A person with a heart for God will hold Him in the highest esteem (Ps. 42:1, 145:3), made possible only through prayer and the study of Scripture. Someone asked their pastor, "Which is more important… praying or reading the Bible?" The pastor replied with a question of his own, "Which is more important… breathing in or breathing out?" Both are essential.

So, what does it mean that David was a man after God's heart? Certainly, it doesn't mean he was blameless. In 2 Samuel 11, we are told of the terrible sins he committed for which he suffered great sorrow. But the Bible also says, "David did that which was right in the eyes of the Lord and turned not aside from anything that he commanded him all the days of his life, save only in the matter of Urijah the Hittite" (1 Kings 15:5). I believe the reason God spoke so highly of this man is found in Acts 13:22. There we read, "I have found David, the son of Jesse, a man after mine own heart, which shall fulfill all my will." David devoted his life to fulfilling God's purposes. He loved what God loved. In Psalm 119:47, he said, "I will delight myself in thy commandments, which I have loved." He was compelled to act upon whatever God desired. Yes, he was flawed. Who among us is perfect? Not one! We are all sinners needing a Savior (Rom. 3:10-23). But in humble submission, David asked God to bend his heart toward righteousness (Ps. 119:33-40). And with a continuing spirit of repentance, he received new mercies and forgiveness (Ps. 51). He loved the ways of God (Deut. 5:33). He loved the law of God (Ps. 119:97). When God spoke, he paid close attention. He wanted to live according to all that God intended for him. Psalm 119:2 says, "Blessed are they that keep his testimonies, and that seek him with the whole heart." David wanted to follow the Lord with a clean heart and a right spirit (Ps. 32:5). This is a great testimony of what God desires in us!

Does God love everybody? Oh, yes! John 3:16 settles that question. If you know nothing of the Bible, start with this verse. If you know everything about the Bible, return to this verse: He loves. He gave. We believe. We live. The Bible is clear that God does not demonstrate favoritism (Rom. 2:6-11). But He does grant special favor to certain people for specific callings. For example, who would argue that God didn't establish a special covenant with Noah (Gen. 6), or that He didn't have a special friendship with Abraham (James 2:23); or that He didn't favor Mary over all the young Jewish girls in Judea (Luke 1:25-28); or that He did not place a special blessing on an obscure shepherd boy named David (1 Sam. 15)? In at least two verses of Scripture, we recognize men who enjoyed a special companionship with God. In Jeremiah 15:1, God tells the prophet that even if Moses and Samuel were to stand before Him, His heart would not be with these people, so great was their sin. The implication is that these two men usually had exceptional influence, although in this case, even they would not prevail. Look at Ezekiel 14:14, where God tells Ezekiel that even if Noah, Daniel, and Job were to pray for these people, He would not grant deliverance except to these men alone. Clearly, Noah, Daniel, and Job had connections with God. Firm in their faith, these men stood apart from the world and alone with God. The first step of discipleship is to place God's plan ahead of our own. Faithful, surrendered people have always moved the heart of God.

Among the many virtues in the life of David, there is humility. It is easy to see how God loves this character trait: Psalm 138:6 says, "Though the Lord be high, yet hath he respect unto the lowly: but the proud he knoweth afar off." Psalm 147:6 says the Lord will lift the meek and cast the wicked down to the ground. James tells us that God resists the proud. Still, He gives grace to the humble (James 4:6). The apostle Peter says, "Humble yourselves therefore under the mighty hand of God, that he may exalt you in due time" (1 Pet. 5:6). Humble people who are willing to work toward God-honoring goals stand the best chance of reaching them. We see courage. Courage was the difference between Caleb and the others who were also chosen for the work of the Lord. Read Numbers 14:24, "But my servant Caleb, because he had another spirit with him, and hath followed me fully, him will I bring into the land…" And just like Caleb, David was different. He was courageous. We see a heart of obedience. This was David's prayer, "Teach me. O Lord, the way of thy statutes; and I shall keep it unto the end. Give me understanding, and I shall keep thy law; yea, I shall observe it with my whole heart" (Ps. 119:33-34). Another wonderful attribute is loyalty. Satan's attacks will come. And when they do, our loyalty is put to the test. David remained committed to the Lord, and he won God's favor in the process.

Samuel Truett Cathy passed away on September 8, 2014, at ninety-three, having lived a remarkable life. He started his professional life at a small café near Atlanta called Dwarf Grill. There he developed a chicken sandwich that became the foundation of his successful restaurant chain, Chick-fil-A. Mr. Cathy wrote five books. He won numerous awards and honors. But more importantly, he was committed to humble service. He helped young people in many ways. He sponsored summer camps and supported foster homes for children and scholarships for their education. Perhaps the most remarkable of all is that for more than 50 years, Mr. Cathy taught a Sunday School class of teenage boys. This successful businessman and financial investor knew the excellent value of investing in people and God's Word. He had developed a heart for God.

One of David's most outstanding qualities is revealed in Samuel's statement, "David inquired of the Lord" (2 Sam. 5:19). The shepherd, psalmist, warrior, and king repeatedly sought God's counsel and direction. For example, nine times in the Books of Samuel, we read where David asked for divine wisdom. And each time he inquired, the Lord graciously gave him a clear and definite answer. Our Lord is honored, and we are blessed when we seek His counsel (Prov. 3:6). David communicated with God! The apostle Paul said, "Be careful for nothing, but in everything by prayer and supplication with thanksgiving let your requests be made known unto God" (Phil. 4:6). In humility, David saw himself as a sinful man, helpless without God. He acknowledged the sovereignty of God. He accepted everything God ordained or allowed. To David, meekness was essential to life because it opened the door to more of God's grace (Prov. 3:34, Matt. 5:5). A teachable spirit is essential to spiritual growth. The importance of humility is that it denies a prideful mindset that will undoubtedly separate us from God (James 4:6). For me, the theme of the Book of Psalms is this: God is good and what He does is good. Therefore, like David, I will "give thanks unto the Lord; for he is good: for his mercy endures forever" (Ps. 107:1). I will rejoice in the works of the Creator and Sustainer of the universe (Ps. 92:4). I will give thanks to the God who does great wonders; He who rules by day and night and remembers me in my low estate. I will praise the One who has redeemed me (Ps. 136). I will look up through the skies to the Almighty, enthroned above all!

The Psalmist David continues to be a blessing in today's world, for, in his Spirit-led writings, we find comfort in verses like these: "Yea, though I walk through the valley of the shadow of death, I will fear no evil: for thou art with me" (Ps. 23); and "The Lord is nigh unto all them that call upon him" (Ps. 145:18); and "God is our refuge and strength, a very present help in trouble" (Ps. 46:1). In the revelation of that day, David saw what God was like, and he molded his heart into the likeness of what he saw. He looked through the window God had given him and beheld His beauty. Today, Calvary stands as the supreme event of all time and eternity. Through the life of Jesus, God proved his desire to be known. Through the death and resurrection of Jesus, He demonstrated his passion to be received (John 17:1-5). Jesus is the most significant expression of God's heart, for He is indeed the "good tidings of great joy, which shall be to all people" (Luke 2:10-11). Jesus Christ is the Savior of the world!

We who believe in God's love, wisdom, and sovereignty can see His hand in everything we experience. Therefore, with every celebration and struggle, every success and failure, every joy and sorrow, we can - as David did - put complete confidence in our father, protector, teacher, and Savior. And as we seek His presence (Ps. 34:4), as we learn His ways (Ps. 25:4-5), as we declare His praises (Ps. 139:14) and serve His purposes (1 Cor. 15:58), we will indeed be counted among those who have a heart for God.

A STRONG TOWER OF REFUGE

If we live the truth that Jesus is everything to us, we will treasure Him above anything the world offers. We will love God even more than we love His blessings – for He will be our reward. When Abram looked upon the spoiled wealth of this world with contempt, God said to him, "I am thy exceeding great reward" (Gen. 14:21-24, 15:1). Abram had determined all of the credit for his wealth, success, and witness would go to God alone. Such a great testimony! If God is everything to us, we will invest in people and Scripture, for these only are of eternal value. Sometimes we are so bent on holding tightly to our time, possessions, ideas, and comfort that we are no different from those who do not profess Christ to be Lord of their lives. But with a surrendered heart comes a sense of how to live as Jesus did. And yet, to live this way does not happen by accident, nor even by the design of salvation itself. Failure is the product of self-willed responses to 'Thus sayeth the Lord' (Isa. 48:17, James 1:13-16). It is always our choice to follow the leading of the Holy Spirit through obedience to the Word of God (Deut. 30:15-20). Remember, we walk by faith and not by sight (2 Cor. 5:7). Our Lord generally offers us more wisdom than answers (James 1:5). Why? Because the Christian life cannot be lived without trusting God in all things (John 15:5). In this game of living, keep your eyes on the Coach. And when it's your turn to bat against the devil, be strong in the Lord and in the power of his might (Eph. 6:10). Our Coach knows every pitch. He has seen it all before.

I think about Psalm 31:15, a song of surrender where David said, "My times are in thy hand." The Psalmist understood that everything in the hand of God is where it may be left without anxiety. Martin Luther once said to a friend filled with useless worry, "Philip, let the reign of Philip cease." In Psalm 73:24-25 we read more about the man whose heart God loved, "Thou shalt guide me with thy counsel, and afterward receive me to glory. Whom have I in heaven but thee? and there is none upon earth that I desire beside thee." Again, David expressed his confidence in the One who arranges and appoints all things according to His holy purpose (Acts 17:24-26). In his second letter to Timothy, Apostle Paul says, "For I know whom I have believed, and I am persuaded that he is able to keep that which I have committed unto him against that day." Let's consider what it means to say, "Jesus is my everything."

Before anything else, He must be our Savior (Ps. 18:2, 27:1). To understand Jesus Christ as Savior, we must recognize our desperate need to be saved. We will never come to the Cross of salvation without being persuaded that we cannot save ourselves. All have sinned against God (Rom. 3:23), and the inherent sinful nature has put us on a path to eternal separation from God in a terrible place called hell. Without Christ, we are hopelessly enslaved and rightly condemned for our sins (Eph. 2:1-3). But Jesus came to earth to die a gruesome death and shed His blood that we might have never-ending life with Him (Rom. 6:23, 1 Pet. 2:24). He raised himself to life, thereby establishing the victory over the power and penalty of sin, the sting of death and the torment of hell (1 Cor. 15:45-58). Jesus alone makes heaven accessible to us. And to all who will accept Him with a repentant heart of faith, He becomes Savior. For by His grace, not by our works, we are saved unto eternal life with God where we will worship Him forever (Eph. 2:5-10). Jesus Christ is our Savior!

God is loving; He is our Father (Ps. 89:26). Adoption into God's family is made perfect through Jesus Christ (Eph. 1:7, Gal. 4:4-7). Born again to a new life in Jesus (Rom. 6:4), we become the children of heaven. And we delight in the unique connection and love only a father and his children can enjoy (John 1:12). Never let the world or the enemy shake the foundational love of your heavenly Father. Your faith under pressure will give sinners reason to believe - and saints reason to rejoice. No failure, weakness, or sin could ever change the fact that you are loved, valued, and accepted (John 3:16). He is our Father. He gives us life (2 Tim. 1:9-10). He rewards our efforts (Luke 6:35) and corrects us lovingly (Heb. 12:3-11). He communicates with us through His Word (1 Thess. 2:13) and wants us to share with Him through prayer (Matt. 6:9). What joy!

When we are adopted into the family of God (Rom. 8:15), we are forever His children. To illustrate: we could stop talking to our biological father tomorrow, and it would not change the fact that he is our dad. I am most assuredly a child of God (Rom. 8:14-17). I am an heir to all the privileges of adoption, which include a provision (Luke 12:24), protection (Ps. 34:7), and position (Gal. 4:6-7). I am no more a servant but a son. And positionally, this can never change. When He is our Father, we live and die in the promise of everlasting life (1 John 5:11-13). This personal relationship with Jesus is spoken of in Scripture (Eph. 1:3-14). Fellowship with God is conditional, for our choices can damage it. But the relationship does not end, for we are His offspring (Acts 17:28-29).

God is our strength (Ps. 18:1-2). Sometimes our Lord will allow difficult situations. Why? To reveal our helplessness and prove His sufficiency (2 Cor. 3:5). He is looking for our willingness to surrender, by which we gain strength. When Jesus performed His first recorded miracle at the Cana wedding, he required that a few earthen pots be filled with water and made available. As we make ourselves available to the Master, He will, for His glory, do extraordinary things in our lives! In the book Surprise Endings, Pastor Ron Mehl writes about a woman in his church who was utterly overwhelmed by her limitations. Energy had used her up. She had hit the bottom of some black abyss and could not even move, let alone crawl out. She was trying to paint her picture without the Artist. Then something remarkable happened. She said, "When I turned the tools of creation over to my Creator, He began to put rich color back into my life." Let your Creator put rich color back into your life! Jesus loves digging us out when we are buried in failure and uncertainty. A marvelous restoration began just a few days after the apostle Peter tragically disowned Jesus (Luke 22:54-62). Our Lord did not say, "Simon, are you sure you are now failure-free? Are you sorry? Do you vow never to fail me again?" No. Jesus valued the relationship too much to ask those questions. Instead, He asked a simple yet profound question (John 21:15-17), "Peter, do you love me? Am I everything to you?" The reason life seems larger than we are is because it is. We are not meant to live without God's help, for only in Him can we live, move, and have our being (Acts 17:28). We are limited in power. God is not. We know many things. God knows everything. We can do many things. God can do anything!

The Lord is our hiding place, a strong tower of refuge in times of trouble (Ps. 32:7, 59:16, 61:3). We all have a favorite hiding place. Some create a false self they show to God and the world. It is their "happy mask." Others hide in their isolation. They put up a wall between themselves and others, even between themselves and God. The thinking is, "I'm tired of being hurt. Therefore, they can't make me feel bad if I don't let anyone get too close." Others use chemicals to numb themselves to the pain they feel inside. Do you associate with friends in high places, hoping others will also see you as a significant someone? Do you hide behind social media, making things seem better than they are? Do you buy friendships because you feel unloved or lonely? Pain is real. The delicate nerves of self-esteem are sensitive, and the hurt goes deep (Ps. 22:1). But things will not get better by hiding in the wrong places. It's not a question of the size of the load but of the best of our hearts. Ask yourself the question, "Is Jesus my Lord?" Indeed, He wants to be that "desired haven" spoken of in Psalm 107: 28-30.

Almighty God offers to be our rest, our protection, our refuge! David called on the Lord, "Deliver me in thy righteousness, and cause me to escape... be thou my strong habitation..." (Ps. 71:2-3). The Old Testament prophet Nahum said God is a refuge in times of trouble (Nahum 1:7). Jesus Christ is our hiding place. He said, "Come unto me, all ye that labor and are heavy laden, and I will give you rest." It is a privilege to communicate our most personal thoughts with our Creator. We are His workmanship (Ps. 139:1-16). Therefore, He understands our longings better than we do. He also knows that we need a safe place to feel protected. The amazing reality is that we can make God that safe place! God is our provision and comfort (Ps. 119:57, 119:76). Matthew 6:11, Jesus teaches us to pray that God would give us daily bread. We know that bread was a staple in the diet of the Jews. But greater still, the bread of the Bible was – and is - a powerful symbol of God's provision in every area of life. After the Korean War ended, orphanages were full of children who, even though they had three meals a day provided for them, were restless and had difficulty sleeping. To help resolve this problem, the relief workers in one particular orphanage decided that each night when the children were put to bed, the nurses would place a single piece of bread in each child's hand. The bread was not to be eaten. It was intended to be held by the children as they went to sleep, to remind them that there would be ample provision the following day. We also find comfort in knowing that the Bread of Life (John 6:35) will refresh our restless and weary hearts.

Our Lord will bring people into our lives by perfect design to help us bear a burden and give us new hope for the days ahead. And because of the friendship, the sufficient joy of what was taken from us by the curse of sin and death is restored beautifully. The compassion of God will never fail (Lam. 3:22-23). His mercies are new with every sunrise! And as we see His plan unfolding, we recognize the Holy Spirit saying to us, "This is one of those good and perfect gifts coming down from the Father of lights I told you about in James 1:17." Greater still, the special gift is often preceded by a time of loneliness and pain. Never doubt; when we wait on the Lord, He will lift us high on the winds of grace (Isa. 40:31). Friend, when you ask for a specific God-honoring desire, expect a particular God-honoring answer (Mark 10:46-52). Turn your thoughts into prayers, your fear into faith. Jesus Christ invites us to ask for bread in its many forms. I am so thankful that, according to His will and purpose, God is faithful to give us what we need when the time is right. Know this: great peace and contentment will come to us when Jesus is our everything!

GOD'S MEASURE OF SUCCESS

Some will say success is measured by acquired wealth, influence, or power. Others describe it as having a fulfilling career, a profitable business, close friends, or a good family. Still, others might say success is enjoying a long and healthy life. And for a child of God, any accomplishment or relationship will involve a Biblical perspective. When it comes to wealth, the Bible says, "The rich and poor meet together: the Lord is the Maker of them all" (Prov. 22:2). The declaration here is that God is the giver of all things to all people. Regarding the skills and abilities that lead to success in various fields, we see the same emphasis in the Bible: God is the giver (1 Cor. 4:7). Consider the issue of influence and power. In John 19:11, after Pilate tells Jesus he can set Him free or crucify Him, Jesus answers, "Thou couldest have no power at all against me, except it were given thee from above." So even earthly authority, by which some measure success, is a gift from God. John the Beloved summarizes this in 3:27 of his Gospel: "A man can receive nothing, except it be given him from heaven." In 1 John 2:15-17, things are put in perspective: "Love not the world, neither the things that are in the world." If we pursue worldly successes with the belief that they will bring joy and satisfaction, both will be lacking.

Gain of this world can be a blessing (Deut. 8:18) or a curse (Dan. 4:30-31, Luke 12:13-21), but it is never God's measure of success. The Psalmist David experienced wealth, influence, authority, family, and good health. Yet this is what he says in Psalm 16:11, "In thy presence is fulness of joy; at thy right hand there are pleasures for evermore." David achieved many things. But he found joy only in the presence of and through his obedience to the authority of God. Each day we live will only be successful to the extent we have walked with God. Why? Because traveling means we have chosen to follow the holy Road Map to a heavenly destination (John 14:6). We have decided to walk "worthy of the Lord unto all pleasing, being fruitful in every good work, and increasing in the knowledge of God" (Col. 1:10). Remember, our journey of loving the Lord and other people will be evaluated one day (2 Cor. 5:10, Rev. 16:5-7).

The word success appears only one time in the Bible, and here is the context in which it is mentioned, "This book of the law shall not depart out of thy mouth; but thou shall meditate therein day and night, that thou mayest observe to do according to all that is written there: for then thou shalt make thy way prosperous, and then thou shalt have good success" [emphasis added] (Joshua 1:8). Notice that success is the result of Bible study and obedience to the Word of God. In Matthew 16:26, Jesus said, "For what is a man profited, if he shall gain the whole world, and lose his own soul?" Worldly success focuses on that which is temporal - while ignoring the eternal (Ps. 102:3, James 4:14). Our nature is to emphasize our promotion. Still, Biblical success centers on the exaltation of God (Rom. 13:14, 1 Cor. 10:31). May we all seek a clearer understanding of what it means to be successful. It is a concept that will only become a reality for us through the revelation of the Bible. God delights to give good gifts to His children (Deut. 1:25, Matt. 7:11), but only against the backdrop of Matthew 6:19-20 where Jesus says, "Lay not up for yourselves treasures upon earth... but lay up for yourselves treasures in heaven..." then verse 33, "But seek ye first the kingdom of God, and his righteousness...."

Speaking of pride, envy, strife, and the love of money as a snare, our brother Timothy says, "But thou, O man of God, flee these things; and follow after righteousness, godliness, faith, love, patience, meekness" (1 Tim. 6:3-11). Any degree of victory or success we achieve comes by the grace of God working in us for His glory (Eph. 2:8, 1 Cor. 15:10). The great lie of our society is this: "If you work hard enough, you can be anything you want to be." To be the master of one's destiny has become the prize of our culture. But the Bible instructs such a misguided concept. Where? In the parable of the talents found in Matthew 25. Here, Jesus teaches us several things about His measure of success. First, we learn that God is the provider of everything, which is an important lesson! Then, we read where the Lord gave the same response to both the five-talent and the two-talent servants. So, we know that (1) we are not all created equal in success and (2) God measures success by the degree of effort over results. Indeed, God is the owner of all things. We are just stewards of the resources He allows into our lives. Next, this parable teaches that the excellence of stewardship measures godly success. That is, we use what we have to advance the kingdom of Christ. Finally, we understand that our one desire should be to hear our Lord say, "Well done, thou good and faithful servant… enter into the joy of thy Lord."

The dictionary defines success as "the accomplishment of an aim or purpose." So, the question becomes, "What are our aim and purpose?" I believe the greatest failure in life is being successful in the wrong assignment. Society says rich people are successful. God says obedient people are successful (1 Kings 2:3, Mark 10:17-31). Colossians 3:2 says, "Set your affection on things above, not on things on the earth." Worldly wealth and success are not signs of righteousness (Prov. 10:2, Luke 12:15, 21:1-4). The entire seventy-third Psalm deals with the suffering of the righteous and the prosperity of the wicked. David said, "It is good for me that I have been afflicted; that I might learn thy statutes" (Ps. 119:71). God graciously provides gifts, passions, resources, relationships, and circumstances to each of us so that we might use them to lead souls to salvation found only in Jesus Christ!

Christopher Parkening, one of the most gifted guitarists in the world, signed an international recording deal as a teenager. But by thirty, having achieved all the musical success he could imagine, Parkening felt empty. So, he moved to Montana and took up fly fishing as a hobby. Soon Parkening was not only one of the greatest guitarists in the world but also a world-class angler with all the money and time he could ever want. And yet, despite his success, his life was empty. He wrote: "If you arrive at a point in your life where you have the things you thought would make you happy, but you're not, you start questioning things." Then, visiting a friend, he attended a church meeting where 1 Corinthians 10:31 spoke to his heart, "Whatsoever ye do do all to the glory of God." Christopher explains, "I realized there were only two things I knew how to do: fly fish for trout and play the guitar. Well, today I am playing the guitar for the Lord, and my life has purpose." One day we will give an account of how we managed the things entrusted to us (Rom. 14:12), and God will judge success by our relationship, obedience, and faithfulness to do His will.

The apostle Paul gives excellent insight into the meaning of real success in the third chapter of Philippians. He says, "If any other man thinketh that he hath whereof he might trust in the flesh, I more: Circumcised the eighth day of the stock of Israel, of the tribe of Benjamin, a Hebrew of the Hebrews; as touching the law, a Pharisee: concerning zeal, persecuting the church, touching the righteousness which is in the law, blameless." In today's culture, Paul's version of accomplishment might sound like this: "A descendant of George Washington, I was born on the Upper East Side of Manhattan and baptized in the Episcopal Church. I attended Phillips Exeter Academy and then Harvard, where my IQ tested at 150, and I had a grade point average of 4.0. I was hired as a financial consultant at a major New York City bank and became a hedge fund manager on Wall Street. I had an apartment in Uptown and a summer home in the Hamptons. I was an elder at St. Luke's Cathedral and have been on the board of various charitable organizations." But listen to what Paul says, "I count all things but loss for the excellency of the knowledge of Christ Jesus my Lord... not having mine own righteousness... but the righteousness which is of God by faith" (Phil. 3:8-9). All that mattered to Paul was Jesus. Everything else was not merely less valuable—it was utter garbage (v8).

Even in the work of the Lord, it's easy to get sidetracked and measure success by large church attendance, notoriety, and attainment. Do not substitute another authority or standard for God's. Big is only sometimes better, and numbers alone do not equate to success. Refrain from buying into the mistaken philosophy of comparing your ministry with another. The devil's trick keeps us dissatisfied with our time and place. God calls people with different potentials to areas with various opportunities, and success is not always visible (Matt. 13:1-23). In the Gospel of Luke, the disciples argued over who would be the greatest in the Kingdom (Luke 9:46-48). Perceiving their thoughts, Jesus said, "He that is least among you all, the same shall be great." Live the Bible whether or not things turn out the convenient way; this is character. Enjoy God's blessings, and don't be discouraged; each step of service will be revealed to you by His design! Ministry involves God's timing, not ours. Success is doing His work His way - and - in His time.

Salvation Army founder General William Booth was asked about the secret of his success. After some hesitation, tears came to his eyes, and he said, "I will tell you the secret. God has had all there was of me." God uniquely creates us with unique gifts to use to grow His kingdom! So, how does God measure success? The answer is in the lives we touch and the people we influence for Jesus Christ.

GREAT AND PRECIOUS PROMISES

I love to read the Bible. It is the written expression of the mind and will of God. And with all my heart, I believe that "holy men of God spake as they were moved by the Holy Ghost" (2 Pet. 1:20-21). God's Word is the strength of my day, and nothing is more comforting than to know that the Creator of the universe is at work in my life! But admittedly, while I believe the entirety of Scripture, there have been times of circumstance when intellectually, I have struggled with God's promises. I have asked, "Is this promise of Scripture mine? Does it apply to my situation?" Therefore, this writing is for me, and you are invited to read along.

My journey is one of faith (2 Cor. 5:7), and there are occasions when I must ask the Lord to increase my capacity to trust what He says. The disciples did this in Luke 17:5, so I know I'm in good company. Joshua was a man of faith and obedience. Here's what he had to say about God: "There failed not ought of any good thing which the Lord had spoken unto the house of Israel; all came to pass (Josh. 21:45)." There it is! God was faithful to deliver on every promise He made to his people. In Romans 9:6-8, the apostle Paul tells us that what God has promised every believer, He will accomplish. In Christ, we are forgiven (Rom. 8:33-34). We are children of God, free from condemnation (Rom. 8:1-15), living in the promise of eternal life in heaven (Heb. 9:15). The future God has for us is infinitely greater than our imagination (1 Cor. 2:9). The promise of eternal life is so incredible that we cannot begin to understand it! And the promises of God - even those beyond our understanding - are to be believed. The writer of Hebrews says, "Let us hold fast the profession of our hope without wavering; for he is faithful that promised" (10:23). When nineteenth-century missionary Judson was imprisoned for his faith, a mocker asked him how his prospects were. He answered, "As bright as the promises of God." He lived by God's promises, not by His explanations. The missionary was living in the confidence that the promises of God would become a reality for him. He had learned how to live while waiting for the glorious return of Christ. Yes, we can live in the certainty of Scripture! The apostle Peter says we have exceeding great and precious promises. Why? That we might become partakers of the divine nature (2 Pet. 1:4).

There are victory days when believing comes easy. But why do we so often doubt the promises of God? It could be because we sometimes break our own promises. It could be because we have learned not to trust everyone who says, "Jump. I'll catch you!" Getting scammed in business and tricked in relationships are common occurrences. It could be that because God's promises are so far beyond our comprehension, we become skeptical. It's easy to have doubts when we do not see God working in our circumstances. We will say, "I asked for a solution, and nothing happened." But the Lord is not some celestial porter who jumps in response to our requests. He sees the past, present, and future. His invisible hand is already arranging the conditions to accomplish His will and purpose. In Isaiah 46:9-11 we read, "I am God, and there is none like me. My counsel shall stand, and I will do all my pleasure. I have spoken it; I will also bring it to pass; I have purposed it; I will also do it." Another cause for uncertainty is ignorance. If we are not familiar with God's nature, we will be disappointed with His response. Our prayers are often attended by expectations of how He will answer them. And when He fails to intervene according to our timetable or anticipated method, we begin to speculate. Questioning God can take us to the dark side of doubt, but it doesn't have to. Regardless of uncertainty, we can still live in the light of God's Word; this is the greatest joy of all!

We must move past the notion that when God says, "I promise," He doesn't mean, "I will try." The Bible shows that God's people were willing to ask for extraordinary things. At their requests, he stopped the sun, parted the sea, and raised the dead. He shook buildings, dropped walls, and destroyed armies when they prayed. Paul reminds us that God is "able to do exceedingly abundantly above all that we ask or think, according to the power that worketh in us" (Eph. 3:20). God's ways are not like ours (Isa. 55:8). Therefore, His promises are not like ours. We are known to break promises when we get a better offer. We want to change our minds when a person we promised to help hurts us. God doesn't work that way. His love is unconditional, and He has all authority to deliver. He is eternally unchanging and holy. Therefore, he cannot pledge something that will not be accomplished. From the beginning, God has proved himself faithful and trustworthy in the lives of millions. We, too, can live victoriously knowing that everything God says will be fulfilled according to his plan. Many of the promises of God have already become a reality. In some cases, the fulfillment of the promise was clear and undeniable, just as expected. On other occasions, God did the unexpected.

Sometimes we have a hard time recognizing how the Lord has fulfilled a promise, or we cannot imagine how he will do it. But God's sovereignty is not diminished by our difficulty to accept or understand it. He is God, calmly and powerfully working out his plan in ways and for reasons unknown to us (Isa. 55:8-9). Hebrews 11 lists several Old Testament saints who understood that God fulfills his promises according to his timetable. These people lived by faith. They believed that God would eventually do all he promised, even if they did not understand why the Lord delayed action for years or beyond their lifetime. When we look at life from a Biblical perspective, our faith will grow, and confidence in God's promises will be our reward!

The words, "Be still, and know that I am God" (Ps. 46:10), is an invitation to trust and not be afraid. God is working in the world. He keeps watching as much in darkness as in the light. It has been said that life can be compared to the mindset of a passenger on a voyage. Some travelers are good sailors; others are not. Some make their voyage easily, while others do not. But the ship's captain is equally concerned for the lives and safety of all. Do not blame the captain because the sea is rough. You do not see him on the bridge from your place below, but you are quite sure he is there. You saw him there during the fair weather when you were on the upper deck. You saw his vigilance when the sea was calm. You cannot imagine for a moment that his watchfulness is relaxed during the storm. As our relationship with Jesus becomes even more intimate through prayer and the study of Scripture, we will experience a love so deep that we could never imagine Him lying to us. God wants us to know we can trust Him in all things.

We read in Proverbs 3:5, "Trust in the Lord with all thine heart;

and lean not unto thine own understanding." Be encouraged by our Lord's message to His despairing apostles on that final night before His crucifixion. Their hearts were heavy, but Jesus made this promise, "I will see you again, and your heart shall rejoice" (John 16:22). We are prone to question God when our world is rocked by events that throw us off balance. To believe is to trust that a sovereign God still holds the answers to all of life's problems, regardless of chaos and disorientation.

Satan wants to destroy our confidence in God by making us fearful. Momentary fright is one thing, but to live every day with a troubled mind is to lose the battle of life. We dare not accept Satan's lie that our salvation is not secure, or our future is in question. In John 10:28-29 Jesus says we are safe in Him. He has promised a crown of life (James 1:12) and a home in heaven for all who will believe in His Name (John 1:12, 14:1-3). When God speaks, it's a waste of time to doubt what is being said. There is no mathematical probability or calculated likelihood involved in the promises of the Bible. The Psalmist said, "For ever, O Lord, thy word is settled in heaven. Thy faithfulness is unto all generations: thou hast established the earth, and it abideth" (Ps. 119:89-90). Therefore, to minimize or ignore the significance of God's promises is foolishness (Deut. 7:9). There is a verse of Scripture found in Numbers 23:19 that builds my faith: "God is not a man, that he should lie; neither the son of man, that he should repent: hath he said, and shall he not do it? or hath he spoken, and shall he not make it good?" I pray that nothing I face will overcome my confidence in what God says. He is mighty to save (Zeph. 3:17) and trustworthy!

An old gospel chorus comes to mind, "Every promise in the Book is mine; every chapter, every verse, every line. I am trusting in His love divine; every promise in the Book is mine." Among the promises are these: First, we are promised forgiveness of sin through the death, burial, and resurrection of Jesus, for it is "the power of God unto salvation to everyone that believes" (Rom. 1:16); and there is no greater blessing than a brand new existence in Christ (2 Cor. 5:17). God promises to protect His children (Ps. 121), and we have the assurance that His love will never fail (1 Chron. 16:34). He says we will be blessed if we delight in His Word (Ps. 1:1-3). He tells us all things work for our good (Rom. 8:28). We are promised comfort in times of hardship (2 Cor. 1:3-4). God says He will finish the work He started in us (Phil. 1:6). He promises peace, protection, and provision (Phil. 4:6-7). Jesus offers rest for weary hearts (Matt. 11:28-30), and He guarantees a never-ending life in heaven for those who trust Him (John 4:14). These are exceeding great and precious promises (2 Pet. 1:4) for us to claim!

The late Christian radio teacher Robert A. Cook tells about the day he told his two young daughters that he had budgeted enough money to buy a bicycle for them. The girls were so excited, and they ran outside to tell a friend they had a new bike! Mr. Cook said he overheard their skeptical little friend say, "You can't show it to me, so why did you say you have a new bicycle?" One of his daughters quickly answered, "Because Papa said!" I've never been to a place where sorrow and tears do not exist… but my Father said! I have never seen streets of gold and gates of pearl… but Father said! I've never looked into the eyes of my Savior… but Father said! All the promises of my Father find their ultimate fulfillment in Jesus, for he is "the express image of his person and upholding all things by the word of his power" (Heb. 1:3). God's power is beyond measure, His strength is without end, and His mercy never fails. I said I wrote this piece for myself… so now I am encouraged! And if you believe in Jesus Christ, you should be too! Why? Because the promises of God are great and precious; they are bright and true; they are "yes and amen" (2 Cor. 1:20). Oh, how amazing it is to know the Lord!

THE EXISTENCE OF GOD

Genesis 1:1 declares, "In the beginning God created the heaven and the earth." Nowadays, the word "God" itself suffers from vagueness. Since every culture has different gods and ideas about gods, the term is often too generic to have any real meaning. But in Romans 1:18-23, we see that the only God who exists has revealed Himself to humanity in specific ways. Some will outright deny God's existence, while others question and downplay His authority – especially His authority in their lives. If asked, many people will tell you they believe in the sovereignty and dominion of God in the universe. But few will say He is sovereign in the sense that He has absolute authority over their lives. According to Romans 1:19, the knowledge of the existence of God is something we inherently know. And for those who claim there is no God, the following is true: Because of their corrupt condition and hostility to the things of God, they, by sinful nature, do everything they can to suppress whatever revelation God gives of Himself to them (Rom. 1:20-24). God gave us a sense of morality, and to make value judgments is the imprint of God's image on our souls. Our moral understanding, values, and sense of right and wrong all point to the existence of God, as does our conscience (Eccl. 12:13-14), and He wants us to experience Him in a most personal way (Hosea 6:3, Heb. 11:6).

Some believe Christianity and science are at war. They are not. One way to erase the conflicts between science and Christianity is to view them as separate endeavors with different purposes, methods, and bodies of knowledge. Science only attempts to answer the question, "How?" Science will ask, "How can I know there is a God?" But Christianity never asks that question. Why? Because the Bible never tries to prove that God exists. It simply proclaims it from the very beginning. Indeed, the very first sentence of the Bible opens with the words, "In the beginning God…" (Gen. 1:1). Scripture declares the existence of God from the very outset. All knowledge (even the scientific kind) is the creation of God (Isa. 40:12-28). Therefore, science (a creation like any other) is not in a position to prove or invalidate the Creator's existence. Science involves observing things through the limitation of human understanding and conducting experiments. But faith involves the supernatural and its relationship to that which can be observed. Science and Christianity draw on different aspects of the human experience. For example, science is a powerful tool for understanding and explaining the dynamics of the physical universe. But science cannot explain the purpose of the universe. This is a question that falls under the theology of a faith that requires the supernatural influence of the Holy Spirit (Eph. 2:1). Dr. Francis Collins, a scientist who directed the National Institutes of Health from 2009 to 2021, wrote: "God's domain is in the spiritual world, a realm not possible to explore with the tools and language of science. It must be examined with the heart, the mind, and the soul."

If one does not believe in God, no explanation is sufficient enough. If one believes in God, no proof is required. Professor Edwin Conklin, a biologist at Princeton University, stated: "The probability of life originating from accident is comparable to the probability of an Unabridged Dictionary resulting from an explosion in a printing factory." The 17th-century physicist Isaac Newton constructed a solar system model, which he placed in his office. Sometime later, a friend and fellow scientist, who was an atheist, visited Newton, and he marveled at the model and asked who made it. "Nobody!" replied Newton. When his friend objected and charged him with being ridiculous, Newton asked, "If you accept that a model needs a maker, why do you have a problem when confronted with the actual universe?" The Old Testament prophet Isaiah wrote, "Who hath measured the waters in the hollow of his hand, and meted out heaven with the span? To whom then will ye liken God? or what likeness will ye compare unto him? To whom shall I be equal? saith the Holy One" (Isa. 40:12-26). The Bible says, "For the invisible things of him from the creation of the world are clearly seen… so that they are without excuse."

In light of what the Bible teaches in Romans 1:18-32, a person who claims to be an atheist knows there is a God. The problem is not that they don't know that God exists, but rather that they hate the God they know exists. Therefore, their issue is not an intellectual one but a moral one. They know God but refuse to honor Him as God (v21). A fallen man refuses to acknowledge what he knows is true. And unless the Holy Spirit accompanies the Christian argument and changes the heart of that person who hears the debate, they will never submit to the revelation and manifestation of God. All have seen sufficient evidence of God through creation, but many have suppressed the truth about God; "professing themselves to be wise, they became fools." They "changed the truth of God into a lie and worshipped and served the creature more than the Creator, who is blessed forever" (Rom. 1:18-25). On the other hand, for those who sincerely desire to know if God exists, this is what He says, "And ye shall seek me, and find me when ye shall search for me with all your heart" (Jer. 29:13).

God has revealed Himself to us in the person of Jesus Christ. Jesus, God manifest in the flesh, did what people cannot do. He performed miracles. He healed the blind, the disabled, and the deaf and even raised people from the dead. He had power over the natural world. God created food out of thin air to feed crowds of several thousand people. He performed miracles over His creation of nature! All of Jesus' teachings and miracles are evidence pointing to the existence of God. Unlike the leaders of world religions, Jesus did not say, "follow my words and you will find truth." He said, "I am the way, the truth, and the life; no man cometh unto the Father, but by me" (John 14:6). In Christ, there is freedom from the burden of guilt. A fabulous new life is a gift to all who will receive Christ, to all who repent in surrender to His lordship (Phil. 2:1-11). Friend, you can deny the facts and say God is just an illusion, that we are all an accident, a product of chance. You may believe He exists yet deny His deity. But seeing God in the world as Lord and Savior is a choice that we make, and everyone who has sought Him has caught a glimpse.

God reveals himself in and through creation. The Bible clearly portrays God as being involved on the stage of history - speaking, instructing, caring, and redeeming. God reveals himself because he wants to be known. We understand that knowing God entirely is impossible (Job 36:26-29). But even if we cannot know God completely, it doesn't mean we can't know him. The Psalmist said, "The heavens declare the glory of God" (Ps. 19:1). Just as a painting reveals something about the soul of the artist, so creation discloses something of the essential nature of God. Just as a great symphony testifies to the skill of the composer, the world and the universe testify to the wisdom and power of God. Wherever we see creativity, we know it started with God.

At the age of eleven, I reached out to God in prayer. And when He responded, I knew He existed. Even more, I knew He was the Savior of the world. God took me by the hand and said, "Come with me." After fifty-eight years, God continues to hold my hand and lead me on the path He has marked for me. You, too, can discover that God exists in a most personal way. How? By turning to Jesus Christ to receive forgiveness and eternal life (1 John 5:13-14). The apostle John said, "If we confess our sins, he is faithful and just to forgive our sins, and to cleanse us from all unrighteousness" (1 John 1:9). Someone may say that a poem is nothing but black marks on white paper. And such an argument might be convincing to an audience that could not read. But those who can read will understand that poems and the message they bring do exist. Russian cosmonaut Yuri Gagarin, the first man in space, orbited the earth in 1961 in the days when exiting the capsule would have meant sudden death. He reportedly said from orbit, "I don't see any God up here." Someone later pointed out that he would have had he opened the hatch. I am so thankful the Creator of the universe has chosen to make Himself known to me personally!

And now I want to speak especially to you who have followed Christ for some time, perhaps many years. Consider Thomas, one of the Twelve who walked and talked with God. He saw the healings, the miracles. He sat at the feet of Jesus and learned of Him. I have no doubt he and Jesus had an excellent relationship. But there came a time when, as never before recorded, Thomas proclaimed, "My Lord and my God." What happened that he would declare this confession in such a powerful way? It came by way of life experience (John 20:19-31). The situation was such that he was brought nearer to his Lord than ever before. And so, it is with us; we are free from the penalty of sin. Indeed, we have experienced the grace of God unto salvation. We know God through creation, even more through a personal relationship with Jesus Christ. We are recipients of His wonderful redemption.

So, my question to you who have been saved these many years is not "Does God exist?" nor "How does He exist?" It's not even, "How does God exist in Christianity?" Neither is it, "How did He exist in your life the moment you were saved?" My question is more pointed than that: "How does He exist in your life today?" Have the circumstances of life drawn you nearer to your Lord? Do His love and grace influence everything you say and do? If so, in what ways and to what extent? Do you still marvel at the grace of God? Are you still moved when you think of the Cross of Calvary? Dr. Bruce Shelley began a book with this statement, "Christianity is the only major religion to have - as its central event - the humiliation of its God." As we ponder the great and gracious Creator and Savior, may we do so with hearts of gratitude and faith. May we look forward to that day when a great multitude of all nations and languages will stand before the throne, clothed with white robes and palms in their hands. May we anticipate crying out with a loud voice, "Blessing, and glory, and wisdom, and thanksgiving, and honor, and power, and might, be unto our God for ever and ever" (Rev. 7:9-17). Truly, it will be a glorious day when we shall forever be in the presence of the God who exists for us in so many wonderful ways!

MUSIC LIFTS THE SOUL

People respond to music in a way that goes beyond culture, language, and geography. Henry Wadsworth Longfellow said music is "the universal language of mankind." Others have described it as a "sound that conveys emotion." Maybe you're listening to the radio in your car, and a song comes on that flips your happy switch. Immediately you are in a better mood and ready to face whatever the day brings. Music can bring individuals together who might otherwise have led a more solitary life. For the elderly, the emotional connection between memory and music is compelling because we are taken back in time. So, where do the rhythms, melodies, and harmonies come from? How can something so intangible have such an effect on us? Why does music exist, and why do we love it? Indeed, music is not a mere human invention. Music comes from God! Therefore, the Bible alone explains the origin of music and musical instruments. The apostle John was given a divine revelation of what is eternal in the heavens (Rev. 14:2-3). He said, "I heard the voice of harpers harping with their harps: and they sang as it were a new song before the throne." The Bible makes several references to music in connection with worshiping in the presence of God (Ps. 150:4, Rev. 5:8-9). John saw angelic hosts "having the harps of God" singing "the song of Moses the servant of God, and the song of the Lord, saying, Great and marvelous are thy works, Lord God Almighty" (Rev. 15:2-4). Then in Job 38:7, we read where music was given to us at the moment of creation "when the morning stars sang together, and all the sons of God shouted for joy."

God created us with the ability to sing and make music (Ps. 95:1, 98:1-6, Amos 6:5, Heb. 2:12). I was introduced to wonderful Christian music as a child. I continue to sing these days because there is something about sacred music that will reach places of the soul that cannot be achieved with conversation. Worship is possible without a song, but worshipful singing contributes to our receiving the Word of God. The Book of Revelation unveils a massive angelic choir of worshippers in heaven: "And the number of them was ten thousand times ten thousand and thousands of thousands" (Rev. 5:11). A song will make you feel a thought. Danish author Hans Christian Andersen said, "Where words fail, music speaks."

The Bible contains over four hundred references to singing, and at least fifty are direct commands to sing. In 2 Chronicles 5, we read how Shekinah's glory was a visible manifestation of God. Where? In the atmosphere of God-honoring, dedicated music, the priests could not stand to minister because of the cloud: the glory of the Lord had filled the house of God! When Johann Sebastian Bach read this verse in his Bible, he wrote in the margin, "At a reverent performance of music, God is always at hand with his gracious presence." Three-fourths of Bach's one thousand compositions were written for use in worship. He said, "All music should have no end and aim other than God's glory and the soul's refreshment." After being delivered from the enemy at the Red Sea, the people of Israel worshiped God in a song (Ex. 15). Why? Because singing was a part of their regular worship in both the tabernacle and the temple (1 Chron. 6:31-32, 16:42). The Book of Psalms contains a rich testimony of God's grace in the form of singing. Jesus and his disciples sang hymns (Matt. 26:30). The apostle Paul instructed the Colossians to sing psalms, hymns, and spiritual songs to God (Col. 3:16-17). For evangelist Billy Graham, it all came down to the invitation song "Just As I Am" at the conclusion of his crusades when he invited people to decide for Christ. This soul-moving hymn accompanied millions down the aisle to receive forgiveness from sin. These kinds of songs have been a blessing around the world for many years!

David said, "I will sing unto the Lord as long as I live" (Ps. 104:33). The singing of Paul and Silas in a dark prison was heard by many who were then saved that night (Acts. 16). The prophet Elisha called for music as a means of calming his troubled heart (2 Kings 3:15). King Saul called for music to give him relief from a tormenting spirit (1 Sam. 16:23). After Jesus and his disciples had sung a hymn, they went out to the Mount of Olives (Matt. 26:30). Singing continues to play a vital role in the life of God's people today. From its inception, when the morning stars sang together and all the heavenly beings shouted for joy (Job 38:7), to its culmination, when every creature in heaven and on earth will sing to the Lamb on the throne (Rev. 5:13), God's creation is musical. Music is an essential part of the body of Christ because it communicates a sense of worship in the presence of God. We tend to remember the theology that we sing more than preached theology. Apostle Paul said, "I will sing with the spirit, and I will sing with the understanding also" (1 Cor. 14:15). Songs consistent with Scripture will grow our faith, for they are an excellent source of spiritual renewal. A hymn correctly chosen can set the tone for a church service, and the closing hymn after a sermon can help us further reflect on what was preached.

A pastor writes, "In 1991, as the iron curtain was crumbling, I joined fellow Christians on a trip into the Soviet Union. Driving across a heavily armed border and passing under the shadow of heroic Soviet statues, it felt like I was crossing into a different world. For a child of the Cold War, stepping off the bus in Leningrad seemed like we were landing on the moon. A local contact led us to a Christian worship gathering the day after we arrived. I entered an unfamiliar place with unfamiliar faces speaking another language. But then the service began, and it began with a familiar hymn, "What a Friend We Have in Jesus." Instantly strangers became family, and our hearts united in our shared love for Christ." When Christians gather in separate congregations worldwide, singing the same hymns will bring a sense of connection beyond the local gathering. The Book of Psalms has the most profound history of any hymn collection, and the New Testament apostles praised the Christ who fulfills them (Luke 24:44-45). Music is a form of communication that touches the hearts of people everywhere. Singing is the light that illuminates the dark times. It is the tranquility that prolongs the good times. When words aren't enough, music will send the message directly to the heart.

When Karen found out that another baby was on the way, she prepared her three-year-old son for the arrival of his little sister. Day after day, Michael sang "You Are My Sunshine" to his sister in Mommy's tummy. But at birth, things didn't go well. The doctor told Karen and her husband to prepare for the worst. And though they had fixed up a room in their home for the new baby, they found themselves planning a funeral. For several days, little Michael begged to go into the hospital room and sing to his baby sister. But he wasn't allowed. Finally, Karen decided to take him whether it was allowed or not. "If he doesn't see his sister now," she said, "he may never see her alive." She dressed little Michael in an oversized scrub suit and took him into the ICU. A nurse bellowed, "Get that kid out of here now!" Karen, usually a mild-mannered lady, replied, "He is not leaving until he sings to his sister!" Michael began singing at his sister's bedside, "You are my sunshine, my only sunshine; you make me happy when skies are gray…." Almost at once, the baby girl responded. Her pulse rate became calm and steady. Karen said, "Keep on singing, Michael." Healing rest seemed to sweep over the little girl. The nurses began to cry, and Karen glowed as the ragged, strained breathing became smooth and steady. In a short time, everyone at St. Mary's Hospital in Knoxville, Tennessee, said it was a miracle that little sister was well enough to go home. Friend, there is healing in music and song!

The inspiration for music was not given just for us to have and to keep but to share with others. There may be a way to make music a significant part of your life, to share your piece before it is perfect. Please don't misunderstand. I am not promoting sloppy music, but I want us to accept our flaws and share what we have to offer to God and other people. Don't let the gift of music die with you because your expectation of perfection is too high. Singing is not so much a talent to develop as a gift to be shared! Pablo Casals was considered the most outstanding cellist ever to live. When he was 95 years old, he was asked why he continued practicing six hours daily. He answered, "Because I think I'm making progress." If singing affects you on a deep spiritual level, it will similarly affect someone else. My purpose for this writing is to encourage you to make music in your heart and return praise to the One from which it came! When we sing God's song, the story of our redemption will be obvious. It will magnify God's sovereignty, authority, and power.

Joseph Tson, a Baptist pastor and evangelical dissident, was expelled from Communist Romania for his Christian witness. He tells the story of Christian students at Romania's universities who, knowing it was illegal and dangerous to be a believer, wanted to locate and fellowship with each other. So, they learned to walk around the campus whistling tunes to hymns. The Communists, who didn't know the hymns, paid no attention. But Christians recognized the melodies so that they could meet their brothers and sisters in Christ. The Psalmist David said, "He hath put a new song in my mouth, even praise unto our God" (Ps. 40:3). Psalm 98:1, "Sing unto the Lord for He has done marvelous things." Music brings us together. In Colossians 3:16, Paul associates the wisdom of God with singing. Worshipful music reminds us of who we are and who He is! I encourage you today. Self-awareness will vanish when you sing as unto the Lord. If the melody in your heart speaks of God's love for the world, celebrate by lifting your heart and your voice in a measure of worship even beyond the song!

THE FREEDOM OF COMMITMENT

It is human nature to assume that commitments will somehow limit our freedom, but the Holy Spirit can help us with this. The hollow justification of people without resolve or purpose is usually, "I can't commit to that because I need to keep my options open. I don't want to miss the prospect of something better, should it come along." These folks seem unwilling to make the critical decisions necessary to do great things for God. They are unsettled and constantly searching, overwhelmed and paralyzed by many options. An undisciplined mind is easily swayed by worldly influence, but commitment leads to purposeful action. I recently spoke to a group of men, some of whom have a history of indecision in matters of lasting importance. But that evening, they were in a time and place where they could choose a better lifestyle through a closer walk with Jesus (Rev. 3:20). I told these men that establishing and achieving worthy goals is vital to successful living. I challenged them to strive for more essential things than anything they had ever experienced. Allow me to share a portion of what I discussed with these good men, all friends:

"Gentlemen let's read John 8:31-36. Jesus said, 'If ye continue in my word, then are ye my disciples… And ye shall know the truth, and the truth shall make you free… If the Son therefore shall make you free, ye shall be free indeed.' There are things Christ has freed you from. And there are things Christ has freed you to. First, He liberates us from the bondage, penalty, and guilt of sin (Rom. 8:1). You cannot have a vibrant, living, loving relationship with God or anyone else if you are holding on to the guilt and shame of your past. Jesus said in John 10:10, "I am come that they might have life and that they might have it more abundantly." The apostle James says, "Draw nigh to God, and he will draw nigh to you." But something needs to happen first. James continues, "Cleanse your hands, ye sinners; and purify your hearts, ye double minded" (4:8). He says a double-minded man is like a wave of the sea, blown and tossed by the wind... unstable in all he does (James 1:6-8).

A double-minded man tries to serve two masters (Matt. 6:24). As such, he is unbalanced, much like a drunken man trying to walk a straight line. He sways one way and then the other without any real direction. He lives by impulse, and as a result, he doesn't get anywhere in life. A double-minded person is restless and confused in his thoughts, actions, and behavior. Such a person can never lean into Christ confidently because he always looks elsewhere for solutions to his immediate dilemma. A double-minded person has one body and two heads. The world is ready to make a deal wherever you are, and you will always feel the tug! But maturity is the ability to make a decision and stand by it. Immature people spend their lives exploring endless possibilities; then, they do nothing. Live with a teachable spirit. You do not have as many answers to life as you might think, and neither do I. But this I know: There comes a time in everyone's life when they are presented with a choice to turn a corner... a choice between hope and fear (Ps. 27:1), an option to live or to die (Deut. 30:19). God is not interested in co-ruling with you. He wants His rightful place as Lord of your life. He is worthy of your faith and trust.

Secondly, what has Christ freed you to? God has a purpose for everything He does (Prov. 16:4). Ephesians 2:10 tells us we are God's handiwork, created in Christ Jesus to do good works, which God prepared in advance for us to do. We are saved by grace. Christ frees us, so our activity doesn't flow out of some sense of trying to win God's approval. Christ's approval doesn't come because of what you do but because of what He has already done at Calvary. He has freed you because He has a plan for your life. In Galatians 5:1-13 Paul tells us, "Stand fast therefore in the liberty wherewith Christ hath made us free and be not entangled again with the yoke of bondage... but by love serve one another." That God frees you from sin is not the end of the story. This freedom allows you to be the man God wants you to be. In Deuteronomy 30, the Lord speaks to his people about the rewards of repentance. Then, He gives this closing challenge in verse 15: "See, I have set before thee this day life and good, and death and evil: In that I command thee this day to love the

Lord thy God, to walk in his ways...." This day – right now... as you sit here this evening - you have a choice (Ezek. 18:21)! Will it cost anything to have a committed relationship with God? Yes, it will cost your life as you know it and everything you have; in exchange for life as He knows it and everything He has (Eph. 4:22-24)!

I am reminded of a simple chorus, "I gave Him my old, tattered garment; He gave me a robe of pure white." My brothers, you have been allowed to be in a program with a godly environment that most people in addictive situations will never experience. It is no accident that you are here. You have been brought to this place by God's design at this time of your life. Many people around you are pouring the love of God into your hearts. And with every opportunity, there always comes responsibility. What is your motivation for being in this program and this church? Is it because the court requires it? Is it merely at the request of your home pastor or a family member? Or do you desire to be a new person in Christ (2 Cor. 5:17)? How do you get along with the other men? How much do you value what is provided here? You may never get another opportunity as you have now. Will you one day be able to look back and thank God for His grace in bringing you here? Or will you spend your days going through the motions, saying what you know the church leaders want to hear? Are you living a lie? Is the thought of returning to your old lifestyle always in your mind? The choice is yours! Will your experience here be profitable long-term? Or will you leave without any real change of heart? Jesus suffered a horrible death so that we might live an extraordinary life here and in eternity. Love Him for that. Serve Him for that. By committing to the Word of God, we live in liberty that allows us to flourish while moving in the right direction. We gain freedom through commitment because we are no longer distracted by the unimportant and frivolous things in life. Now go and live the life God has freed you to live!"

As I spoke to the men, my objective was to get them to stop running from their past by chasing new things, new relationships, new activities, and new friends. I wanted them to begin running to something instead of running away from something. There is a vast difference between chasing things and running "with patience the race that is set before us, looking unto Jesus the author and finisher of our faith" (Heb. 12:1-2). The key is "looking to Jesus," for He sets the agenda for our freedom. The choice to obey is ours, and a response is always required when Jesus says, "Follow me." When the Israelites said, "All that the Lord hath said will we do" (Ex. 24), they created a relationship of abundant blessing and inheritance. People committed to a cause have learned that something more attractive will appear, yet they stay the course. Do not stop Kingdom work simply because there is a feeling of fatigue - or even pain. God provides endurance and strength (Col. 1:29). Remain devoted to God's will and purpose through prayer and the study of the Word. Our freedom in Christ is a result of continuing in obedience. Paul and Silas did not sing in prison to get free. They sang because they *were* free (Acts 16:16-40). Sometimes the opposition is evidence that we are doing things right (John 16:33). If we refuse to do anything until we are confident of comfortable success, we will never accomplish anything of importance. Very few things of eternal value are achieved without overcoming serious obstacles. Don't be discouraged by the opposition but take comfort in God's faithfulness (Ps. 27:1). He will not let us down! Jesus came to free humanity from sin, and when we surrender to His lordship, we are rescued from the slavery of Satan. There is a fundamental value in commitment to many things in life, and indeed, goal setting is essential. But it's only through total surrender and obedience to the Lord that we have the freedom to hope, love and trust.

A young man eager to grow in his Christian experience got a piece of paper and made a list of all the things he would do for God. He wrote down the things he would give up, the places he would go to serve, and the areas of ministry he would enter. He was excited. He took the list to the church and put it on the altar, thinking he would feel joy. But instead, he felt empty. So, he went home and started adding to his list. He wrote down more things he would do and wouldn't do. He took the long list and put it on the altar, but still, he felt no relief. He went to his pastor for help. The wise man of God said, "Take a blank sheet of paper. Sign your name at the bottom and put it on the altar." With this, a spirit of peace and freedom came to the young man's heart. Oh, may we surrender and commit everything to God! The Bible says, "Commit thy way (that is, all the affairs and business of life) unto the Lord; trust also in him; and he shall bring it to pass" (Ps. 37:5). Look closely at what God said: If we "commit and trust," He will "bring it to pass." What will He bring to pass? The plans He has for us (Jer. 29:11), the blessings of righteous living (Matt. 6:33), the assurance of eternity in heaven (1 Thess. 4:13-18). The most fulfilled life is one that is devoted to honoring God. Oh yes, there is incredible freedom in commitment!

Don't Lose Heart

Life is a battle. Therefore, the Christian life is a battle. The Bible speaks of believers as soldiers (Eph. 6:12-13) who are obedient and committed to God's will. Serving God means acknowledging His Lordship in our lives, demonstrated by a commitment to help others as Jesus did (John 13:34). There He was, offering His Kingdom in exchange for their pain. Serving means reaching lost souls with the gospel of Christ (Matt. 28:19-20). It means facing adversity with hope (Ps. 46:10). It means making God visible in everything we think, say, and do by our obedience to the Bible (2 John 1:6). There will be times that, as you hold to the morality of Scripture, you will feel the assault of the world (Eph. 6:12). You will grow weary of the Christian journey. You will wonder if anyone cares (2 Cor. 4). But quitting is not an option. God never said the trip would be easy, but he did say that the arrival would be worthwhile. As an ocean buoy rings only during storms, the beating of the waves and wind will bring out the music within us. Trials reveal character. Do not quit.

John Wittier wrote, "When things go wrong, as they sometimes will; when the road you're trudging seems all uphill; when funds are low, and the debts are high, and you want to smile, but you have to sigh; when care is pressing you down a bit, rest if you must, but don't you quit." The temptation to give up is usually experienced during a difficult season. But if there is one thing the apostle Paul seemed to repeat repeatedly, it was don't quit! To the Galatians (6:9), he said, "And let us not be weary in well doing: for in due season we shall reap, if we faint not." This verse has a straightforward command and an incredible promise. We will have a reward if we do not become complacent in the work of the Lord. Paul uses the term "persevere," "press on," or "strive" many times in his writings to the New Testament churches. He linked perseverance to character and hope. When we lose heart, our days seem empty, and we lose hope. When we lose hope, we lose the ability to dream for the future. Therefore, quitting is not an option. Our "labor is not in vain in the Lord," and we have victory in Jesus Christ (1 Cor. 15:57-58). The key to endurance is remembering that we no longer exist to serve our agenda. We are the Lord's (1 Cor. 6:19-20), and the "well doing" part of Galatians 6:9 is returning God's love for us through worship and cheerful obedience!

We all live for something. It could be our family, our career, our friendships, our athletic or academic achievements – and so many other things. To say we are "living for" something is just another way of saying, "this is the motivation behind what I do." On June 5, 1998, Timothy Stackpole was injured in a five-alarm fire in Brooklyn. He spent over two months in the Burn Center with severe burns over forty percent of his body. He endured many surgeries and months of painful rehabilitation. He had two goals: to recover and spend as much time as he could with his family, and to return to full duty at a job he loved. He was a great firefighter. He was enthusiastic about his work and was soon promoted to captain. Three years later, at the age of forty-two, Timothy was one of the firefighters that ran into the second tower of the World Trade Center to try to save people on September 11, 2001. When he did, it collapsed and took his life. His wife Tara says, "Timmy had a huge heart. He shared his faith, compassion, and love with everyone he met. He was a loving husband and friend, an adored father, and a loving, devoted son and brother. He was a hero not only because of how he died but, more importantly, , because of how he lived." Timothy knew his calling; it was to save people. We must know our calling. God has called us to a life of service and ministry with eternal value. Don't forget your purpose. Do not give up on sinners. Whether they fully understand or not, they are dying without God (Rom. 6:23), desperate for someone to share the good news of Jesus Christ. This is God's agenda, and our privilege is to partner with Him in the power of the Holy Spirit.

The apostle Paul said, "I therefore, the prisoner of the Lord, beseech you that ye walk worthy of the vocation wherewith ye are called, with all lowliness and meekness, with longsuffering, forbearing one another in love" (Eph. 4:1-2). Why do some people abandon their calling to Kingdom work? Maybe the guilt and shame of the past weighed heavily on their mind. It could result from bad relationships with fellow believers or disagreements with church leadership. Then some people left the local church assembly, saying it was imperfect. I have news: There are no churches but imperfect ones. And the fact that Jesus started His church with bad people should make us marvel at God's incredible grace!

A faithful church attendee stopped going to church. The pastor found the man at home, alone, sitting by the blazing fire. Guessing the reason for the pastor's visit, the man welcomed him, led him to a comfortable chair near the fireplace, and waited. The pastor made himself at home but said nothing. In silence, the pastor took the fire tongs, carefully picked up a brightly burning ember, and placed it all alone on one side of the hearth. Then he sat back in his chair, still silent. The host watched all this in quiet contemplation. As the one lone ember's flame flickered and diminished, there was a momentary glow, and then its fire was no more. Soon, it was cold and dead. Neither man had spoken since the initial greeting. The pastor glanced at his watch and realized it was time to leave. He slowly stood up, picked up the cold, dead ember, and placed it back in the middle of the fire. Immediately, it began to glow once more with the light and warmth of the burning coals around it. As the pastor reached the door to leave, his host said, with a tear running down his cheek, "Thank you so much for your visit and especially for the sermon. I'll be back in church next time the doors are open."

We can become discouraged for many reasons. But I believe one's departure from following Christ is most often tied to the experience of pain or death. The typical "Why?" questions surrounding these events have caused good people to reject the sacrificial road that Jesus walked. "Why this? You are not who You say you are. I can tell by what's happening to me." Yes, our Lord wants to bear our burdens (Ps. 18:6). But questioning the sovereignty of God with a rebellious, untrusting heart will take us to ruin (Isa. 45:9-12, Rom. 9:20). Many will say they cannot accomplish what the Bible says. We a called to honor the Lord with fruit (John 15:8), not insult Him with excuses. Indeed, life is hard, and there will be reasons for disappointment. But not one is reason enough to walk out on the Savior! Some individuals must understand that no matter what we face, we have a bright and everlasting eternity. D.L. Moody said, "If I had ten thousand lives, Jesus Christ should have every one of them." In Hebrews 12:3, we are told to "consider him that endured such contradiction of sinners against himself, lest ye be wearied and faint in your minds." Satan is our enemy, and there is nothing more damaging to his evil influence than Spirit-filled people who love God.

Living for Jesus is a choice. We made the decision when we knelt at the Cross. We are saved by grace through faith (Rom. 6), striving to live as Jesus did (1 Cor. 11:1). Pleasing the Lord is our highest aim (Col. 1:10), and growing weary should not change any of this. In Luke 9:23, Jesus said, "If any man will come after me, let him deny himself, and take up his cross daily, and follow me." It's important to acknowledge the unfortunate fact that the enthusiasm of Christianity can wear off, mainly if we are not "abiding in Christ" (John 15:5). In Revelation 2:1-7 Jesus commended the believers in Ephesus for their labor, patience, and endurance. But he faulted them for having lost their "first love." Love is the difference between religious people and relational people. It is our testimony in the world (John 13:35). Discouragement and weariness can rob us of our joy, and the danger of not taking our burden to the Lord is that we will eventually become disillusioned with the Christian journey altogether. We have a powerful promise that "we will reap" if we do not faint. Think about the fruit of the harvest: dear people rescued from slavery to sin and set free in Christ, and then believers are strengthened in their faith! Did not God call you to do work for Him? Go to Him in prayer. Read His Word. Seek the wise counsel of a trusted friend if you must, but do not quit!

We are all called to follow Christ with equal depth and commitment, serving the people God has put in our lives. Helen Steiner Rice authored a poem she calls God's Assurance Gives Us Endurance: "My blessings are so many; my troubles are so few; how can I be discouraged when I know that I have You? And I have the sweet assurance that there's nothing I need fear if I but keep remembering I am Yours and You are near. Help me to endure the storms that keep raging deep inside me; and make me more aware each day that no evil can betide me. If I remain undaunted though the billows sweep and roll, knowing I have Your assurance; there's a haven for my soul. For anything and everything can somehow be endured, if Your presence is beside me and lovingly assured." When you feel like quitting, consider why you began walking with the Lord. Think about God's love. Take another look at the Cross!

God's Wonderful Family

Before the foundation of the world, God chose to have a family for Himself. In Ephesians 1:4-5 we are told that the adoption of children was God's idea. It was a predetermined plan established in His eternal grace. Therefore, this relationship whereby we are entitled to inheritance is not fragile or uncertain. As believers, our position as sons and daughters is firm, unshakable, and eternal. We are "sealed with the holy Spirit of promise, which is the earnest of our inheritance" (Eph. 1:13-14). The Holy Spirit guarantees our yet-to-be-received eternity in heaven with the Lord (2 Cor. 1:22). Our new birth into God's family is based on His free and sovereign grace, made possible through the blood of Jesus Christ (1 Cor. 15:1-5). It is a marvelous salvation available to all people everywhere! In 1 John 4:15, we read, "Whosoever shall confess that Jesus is the Son of God, God dwelleth in him, and he in God." The apostle John declares, "But as many as received him, to them gave he power to become the sons of God, even to them that believe on his name" (John 1:12). The reality that God saved me from the condemnation of sin and the penalty of everlasting torment is beyond my comprehension. Nevertheless, I have been redeemed by His blood. And for this, I will live with a heart of gratitude and thanksgiving! The Lord is good. His faithful love endures forever, and He is the God of my salvation (1 Chron. 16:34).

The Merriam-Webster Dictionary describes a family this way: "A group of people of common ancestry; deriving from a common stock; united with certain convictions or a common affiliation; related by common characteristics or fellowship." When we consider this description from a Biblical point of view, it translates as the family of God. We are His children. 1 John 3:1 says, "Behold, what manner of love the Father hath bestowed upon us, that we should be called the sons of God." We are a family of believers. Galatians 6:10 tells us, "As we have therefore opportunity, let us do good unto all men, especially unto them who are of the household of faith." We are members of a heavenly household. Ephesians 2:19-20 declares, "Now therefore ye are no more strangers and foreigners, but fellow citizens with the saints, and of the household of God; and are built upon the foundation of the apostles and prophets, Jesus Christ himself being the chief cornerstone." We not only belong to our earthly families, but we belong to a heavenly family. As much as Jesus is the son of Mary and Joseph, he is, even more, the Son of God. The "household of faith" is a phrase that is used in Scripture to refer to those who have been born again by the power of the Holy Ghost to become a new creation in Christ (2 Cor. 5:17).

It is wonderful to fellowship with the Creator of the universe through prayer and Scripture reading. And what a blessing it is to share a common salvation with those who have also confessed faith in Jesus Christ. As born-again believers (1 Pet. 1:3), we have access to God. We are no longer separated from Him (Eph. 2:15). Our Father invites us to "come boldly unto the throne of grace, that we may obtain mercy, and find grace to help in time of need" (Heb. 4:16). As a child of God, we have a purpose. We have a reason to live. We have the imperishable, unfading, eternal inheritance of heaven. And while on earth, we are called to use our resources to love, encourage, honor, and carry the burdens of our siblings. Jesus said, "This is my commandment, that ye love one another, as I have loved you" (John 15:12). In God's family, there is a sense of belonging. In His family, we are accepted for who we are; we are loved, cherished, and celebrated. In this "household of faith" (Gal. 6:10), we find greater love and acceptance than we have ever known. It is wondrous that a common belief identifies us and a shared affection unites us!

God's Church is a group of related people who do life together. The Church in the Book of Acts met in temple courts and homes. They were devoted to deep and abiding relationships. They were focused on obedience to the teachings of Jesus and the apostles. As part of God's family, we are called to serve others as Christ did us (Matt. 20:28). We bring a diversity of talents and abilities to the household. When everyone is working in harmony under the direction of the Holy Spirit, the family will accomplish the will of the Father. We speak truth, forgiveness, and reconciliation with a new identity in Christ. We love and forgive as He loves and forgives us. Rather than pursuing our gain, we desire to see every family member "grow in grace, and in the knowledge of our Lord and Savior Jesus Christ" (2 Pet. 3:18). These are marks of a true believer. The Church is a wonderful body of believers, blessed by God with peace and grace. In this family, we are drawn together to inspire, strengthen and encourage our brothers and sisters in the Lord. It is a privilege to be a child of God most High (Ps. 57:2)!

Now, we all understand that no family is perfect. After the dedication of his baby brother in Church, little Johnny sobbed all the way home in the car's back seat. His father asked him three times what was wrong. Finally, the boy replied, "That pastor said he wanted us brought up in a Christian family, but I want to stay with you guys!" Amusing? Yes. But thought-provoking as well. Why? Because we need to recognize that there will be times of conflict when people are involved. An unforgiving spirit is a favorite strategy of the devil to cause strife within the body of believers (Mark 11:25). Blame-shifting and disrespect will also damage our relationships. Staying silent when appropriate is often challenging, but it's essential (Prov. 17:27). And submission is in direct opposition to our inherent desire to rule and have our way. We defend our rights, champion our causes, defend our opinions, and assert our agendas whenever possible. We must crucify our flesh (Gal. 5:24, Rom. 6:11). According to Galatians 3:28, we are all one in Christ. Certainly, we will have differences. But they do not have to separate us. God desires that we would grow and mature through our relationships with one another. Healthy families communicate, interact, and share. We want the world around us to see God's love operating in this family, for it is through our testimony – individually and collectively – that we exalt the name of God to a lost world. Therefore, let's strengthen our family ties and lead people to Jesus!

Gloria Gaither tells the story behind the hymn "The Family of God," which involves a young family in their congregation, Ron and Darlene Garner. Gloria says, "While Ron was working with combustible material, there was an explosion. He managed to crash through the large double doors before the building blew apart and went up in flames, but he was severely burned over most of his body. Ron was alive but was not expected to make it through the night. Within minutes a chain of telephone calls alerted the family of God, and the whole Church began to pray for Ron. Easter morning, the sun rose on a sanctuary filled with a bleary-eyed congregation. The pastor came in with a report from the hospital. The doctor says he has a chance. Tears of praise and joy began to flow. On our way home from church, that morning, Bill and I told each other, 'They would do that for us, too! Just because we were a part of the family of God.' As I started dinner, Bill sat down at the piano. It wasn't long before the magnetism of the chorus Bill was singing drew me from the kitchen to the piano, and we finished the song that was to feed us better than any other food: 'I'm so glad I'm a part of the family of God - I've been washed in the fountain, cleansed by His blood! Joint heirs with Jesus as we travel this sod, for I'm part of the family, the family of God.'

I love the people of God. I have written elsewhere that it is my joy to fellowship with those who have deliberately chosen to follow Jesus and serve others. We sit together because of Him. We rejoice together because of His glory. We worship together because He is worthy. And, in a larger sense, we are a part of the family of Bible-believing Christians wherever they are found. Spirit-filled community is so important. We all struggle with the same problems and weaknesses. But God has established a family of believers who will support each other in all things. Together, we find safety and security. The Church is not a religious system, organization, or denomination. It is a group of individuals who have placed their faith in Jesus Christ for salvation. An unknown author wrote this poem: "God made us a family, a special caring part - of all that's near and very dear, and closet to the heart. Together on life's journey, each day a memory... thank you, God, for making us a loving family." Christian friend, be encouraged today and rejoice if you are part of God's wonderful family!

BIBLICAL JUSTICE

The following words were spoken by the Old Testament prophet Micah, "He hath shewed thee, O man, what is good; and what doth the Lord require of thee, but to do justly, and to love mercy, and to walk humbly with thy God?" In the timeframe of this text, the people of the nation of Judah were being led into the vilest forms of idolatry in a downward trend away from God and justice. And now, through the prophet Micah, God summons His people to court, calling them to return to Him. Indeed, all of us would say that we desire justice. But what is it, and how should it be applied? Biblical justice is not only for certain people or groups of people. It is not about political strategy or social leveraging. It is about truth. It's about relieving the oppressed with mercy and humility and doing it God's way. Biblical justice is "the faithful application of the law of God," which involves some fundamental truths: First, God is the habitation of justice; it is His nature (Jer. 50:7). He establishes what is right, and He maintains it through His actions. The Psalmist said, "Righteous art thou, O Lord, and upright are thy judgments" (Ps. 119:137). Throughout the Bible, the adjective 'just' is not the definition of someone who is merely fair toward others, but like Noah (Gen. 6:9), it describes one who practices righteousness. For example, Deuteronomy 24 contains instructions to pay just wages, to pass equal judgment for both the citizen and the foreigner, and to leave food in the field for the poor to gather. We who are filled with the Holy Spirit should be no less fair and charitable in our dealings with others. There is no room for blame-shifting in the sight of God. The expression of Biblical justice is impartially rendering judgment, righting wrongs, and meting out punishment for breaking the law.

The books of Psalms and Proverbs give instructions to care for the needy and speak up for oppressed people. Psalm 41:1 says, "Blessed is he that considereth the poor; for the Lord will deliver him in time of trouble." Psalm 82:3 tells us to defend the poor and fatherless and to do justice to the afflicted and needy. Proverbs 29:7 says that godly people will see the needs of others and do what they can to help. The wicked will ignore the condition altogether. Godliness includes protecting those who would otherwise be more likely to be disadvantaged because they have fewer resources to defend themselves. Biblical justice is based on God's character, not on the winds of society. This is where we often get it wrong. Justice is not a cultural issue. It is following the principles of righteousness found in God's Word. Jesus is the supreme expression of God's heart for the outcast. He continually reached out to those shunned by society, including the leper, the lame, and the broken. In a day when the world looked down on women, He included them (Luke 8:1-4). In a culture where Samarians were despised, Jesus went out of His way to give the gospel to the Samaritan woman at the well (John 8:3-11). Nobody has modeled biblical justice and God's heart of compassion like Christ.

Today, some people we admire sacrifice themselves to care for the disadvantaged. Christians worldwide continue caring for orphans, establishing hospitals, and opening schools for those in dire need. Where the gospel of Christ has gone forth, acts of mercy and compassion have always been a result. We should be on the front lines of compassionate care in our neighborhoods and communities. It would seem that all justice is created equal because unequal justice would be an impossible oxymoron. But terms can be slippery, and this is where social justice poses its challenges. No one would say they advocate for injustice. But in our culture, the term 'social justice' typically has a different meaning than the words suggest. In our society, crusaders for social justice seek to correct not merely the sins of man but the 'oversights of God' or 'the accidents of history.' They are seeking a universe designed for their vision of equality. How do they do this? By focusing on the process rather than the outcome. Certainly, a method to ensure equality is essential. But changing the definition of justice to mean a guaranteed result is dangerous. Why? Because the secular concept of social justice tends to place people into various victim categories. These categories include everything from skin color to ethnicity to education to gender to political views to food choices. This creates a feeling of despair that leads to rioting, looting, and other violent demonstrations of anger. Of course, these outbursts offer no real solutions to the problem. They only blind people to thoughtful and effective ways to change their situation.

The truth is that every injustice is the result of sin (Rom. 5:12). When we kneel at the foot of the cross, we understand that, to God, there is no difference in any person's worth (Rom. 10:12). And while secular crusaders speak of inclusion, they often refuse to include Bible-believing Christians in the conversation. Granted, not all who champion the cause of so-called social justice have the desire to push an anti-God agenda. But many with this agenda have used the terminology of justice to add credibility to ideas that would otherwise be rejected outright. For the most part, social justice is a politically charged rallying cry for many on the left side of the political spectrum. In reality, socialist programs do not work. They tend to create more problems than they solve. For example, public tax revenue to supplement the unemployed often has the effect of recipients becoming dependent on the government handout rather than trying to improve their situation. In every place where socialism has been tested on a national scale, it has failed.

So, what is the Christian view of social justice? In Matthew 25:40, Jesus spoke of the "least of these." He knows that, due to the Fall, there will be widows, fatherless, and those who are transient. Therefore, He made provision for His followers - not a government - to care, but on a more individual basis. There is tension between a God-centered approach to social justice and a man-centered approach to social justice. The man-centered system sees the government as the savior, bringing a paradise through government policies. The God-centered approach sees Christ as Savior, bringing heaven to earth when He returns. At His return, Christ will restore all things and execute perfect justice (Rev. 21). Until then, Christians are called to express God's love and justice by showing kindness and mercy to those less fortunate (John 13:34-35).

To heal relations between Germany and England after World War II, a group of German students volunteered to help restore an English cathedral that German bombs had extensively damaged during the war. They could repair most of the damage, but they had great difficulty repairing a statue of Jesus where once His arms spread wide, a piece bore the inscription

"Come unto Me." They made every effort to restore the hands of Jesus, but it could not be done. After discussing the matter with church officials, a decision was made to leave the hands off the statue and change the inscription to read, "Christ has no hands but ours."

From a Scriptural point of view, justice means loving our neighbor as we love ourselves. It is rooted in the character and nature of God. Jesus tells us, "Blessed are the peacemakers: for they shall be called the children of God" (Matt. 5:9). As believers in Christ, we recognize that God's justice is more profound and purer than our own best understanding of what is right. We are called to love our neighbor as we would love ourselves. We speak the truth in love. We promote change with a deep awareness of our sinfulness and the sin of our society. We are called to do justice and live in love. Where there have been racial or ethnic divisions, God desires reconciliation and restoration, not blame and separation (Col. 3:10-12). Nothing less than the blood of Jesus can regenerate a heart. Biblical justice takes place when Christians, filled with the love of Christ, see and serve others as God commands. We lose a passion for leading souls to Christ if we see the world through opinions denying humanity's sinful heart. When we forget that man's primary need is the gospel, we find ourselves more at home with social activists than fellow ambassadors of Jesus. When it comes to the issue of justice, our goal must be to avoid all messages that contradict the Word of God. Remember, as it was in the dark days of Micah, we are to do justly, love mercy, and walk humbly with God.

Throughout the ages and around the world, certain groups of people have regarded others as being inferior or somehow not entitled to equal treatment. Every generation has faced this problem, and Christians are not exempt. Racism and injustice neutralize our ability to obey Christ's command to reach all people with the Gospel (Matt. 28:19). Jesus did not select some people to hear the Gospel and others to be left out. All of us are born sinners (Rom. 5:12). No group is free from the sinful nature common to all humanity. No group receives salvation because of its heritage. No one is too good to need Jesus, nor is anyone too evil to be saved. No problem is beyond His ability to help, nor is anyone so secure as to never need His help. The mission of the church is to preach the Gospel. When we stand before God's throne, we will be in a multitude of people from every background imaginable (Rev. 7:9). We are created in the image of God, and we have no legitimate basis for feeling superior or inferior to any other person or group of people. God is no respecter of persons (Rom. 2:1). Every one of us stands before God as equal in His eyes. The good Samaritan did not ask the man in need what he thought of his people. He just helped him (Luke 10). We have the responsibility and privilege to bear one another's burdens (Gal. 6:2). It's difficult to understand what people from another culture may have experienced. But we don't have to understand to care for them. We are brothers and sisters in Christ, and the ultimate answer to injustice is the Gospel and its resulting transformation (2 Cor. 5:17). We are better together. May God give us the wisdom to know the right thing and the courage to do it.

Overwhelmed and Alone

A well-known pianist and gospel singer says, "If you want to have an audience, sing to the hurting because there's one in every pew." Then she adds, "The God I know will stay when others go away." Verses of Scripture become especially rich when we read about circumstances similar to what we are experiencing. We try hard to identify with the biblical author, especially in times of difficulty. We want to learn about what the writer went through and how to prevail. Soon-to-be king David was in a particularly desperate situation in Psalm 142. He was alone. He felt as if his life was hanging by a thread. David cries to the Lord, and certainly, this is the right place to start. What was it that made his situation so dire? He felt alone. The people with whom he shared history were not with him. And because those he loved the most didn't take notice, he felt small, walled in, with nowhere to go. David was a suffering man with a broken heart.

More than anything in the world, we long not to be alone. People fear loneliness so much that they stay in abusive relationships. They marry people they do not love. They join gangs. They violate their sexual purity. They do anything not to be alone. We crave companionship at all costs. From the beginning, God has created all humanity to enjoy loving relationships. Catherine Booth, a vibrant woman who cofounded the Salvation Army with her husband, frequently visited prisons. Entering a prison one day, she noticed a woman at the end of the corridor violently resisting being put into a cell. Catherine immediately proceeded down the hall toward her. As she went, she thought, "What can I do? Maybe I'll give her a Bible… no, she's too upset to read right now. Perhaps she might need some money… no, money will not help her." Before Catherine had fully settled on what she was going to do, she found herself face-to-face with the matted-haired young woman. Instinctively she kissed her on the cheek and walked away. The next day Catherine returned, and the warden told her she had to visit that woman they had booked the previous day. The disturbed woman had been asking, "Who was it that kissed me? Who was it that kissed me?" Catherine found her and gently asked, "Why do you ask?" The woman hesitantly replied, "When I was a baby, my father left the family. We lived in a dank tenement basement, and my mother caught tuberculosis. When I was seven, my mother died. But before she died, she took me in her arms and kissed me. That was the last time before yesterday I knew anyone cared." Sometimes people are just one kiss away from God. None of us holds the key to ourselves. When Jesus is the heart of our relationships, He will expand our hearts to include others. He will give us relationships that will last.

Perhaps the pain of Psalm 142 resonates with you right now. I have also experienced a deep grief that never seems to disappear. Maybe some of the people you thought would encourage you are gone. Perhaps they stay away because they think you're too passionate about your walk with God. David's family felt that way (1 Sam. 17:28). I believe David's brothers felt convicted by his stand for God and drew back when he didn't tone it down. Could it be that your people are not coming alongside you like you thought they would? I understand. But this I know: God will intervene by bringing people - family and friends alike - into our lives who are a tremendous strength to us! Notice that David cried out to the Lord. By praying aloud, he was more aware that a conversation was taking place. He pleaded with the Lord, almost as if he were begging. You cannot miss the fervency of David's plea. Calamity has a way of bringing intensity to our prayers! When David prayed, he held nothing back. He was a man who understood his need for God's mercy and grace. He felt alone and forsaken. Yet his cry to God proves that even in pain, he still knew God had not left him.

Every other refuge had failed, but David found an ear for the voice of his cry in God. Where did his confidence come from? He found faith in the promises of God. His circumstances pointed in the direction of despair, but the promises of God pointed in another direction. He cried out to the One who created the heavens and the earth, the God who sustains all things, the One who makes promises and keeps them! David appealed to the Lord's mercy in his prayer. His confidence did not rest in his goodness or righteousness. He knew he needed mercy. He understood that if God were to deliver him, it would be, not because he deserved it, but because the Lord is gracious. Prayer is acknowledging our insufficiency and God's all-sufficiency. Our supplication is not to inform God of our situation but to prepare us to receive that He will give. Lastly, notice how David spoke the truth to his own heart. His emotions were leading him to despair. Human reasoning undermined his confidence, but he preached truth to his soul. He confessed openly that his spirit was faint within him.

We all find ourselves in a dark and desolate cave from time to time, overwhelmed, anxious, and afraid. Maybe you wonder if your faith is genuine. Indeed, the one who killed Goliath felt himself to be very weak. Despair is familiar to everyone, including the people of God. The question is, what will we do when we find ourselves in that place? First, we must understand Who it is that we are trusting. We cannot come to God with our hands full, as if we had something to offer Him. We come with hands empty, crying out for deliverance. Now I will confess; it's incredible how quickly the promises of God vanish from my mind when Satan hits me with one of his "sucker punches." If I am honest with you, it seems easier to encourage others about God's promises than to preach the truths to my soul. This is why I must seek the fellowship of brothers and sisters in Christ. Charles Spurgeon said, "Caves make good closets for prayer; their gloom and solitude are helpful to the exercise of devotion." He said, "Had David prayed as much in his palace as he did in his cave, he might never have fallen into the act which brought such misery upon his later days." I understand what the nineteenth-century preacher is saying. And caves are effective classrooms in the school of faith and prayer. But for me, this concept often looks better on paper than it works in real life. Mere words – even prayerful ones – will not always bring relief. Still, I know that the security of the godly is to dwell in the secret place of the most High (Ps. 91:1), for it offers the promise of God's protection amid hardship and peril. The Lord stretches His "shadow" or "protective shade" over the man or woman who sets up camp in His presence.

Heaven's peace will only come as we surrender every emotion to God, holding nothing back. This is a choice that is ours to make. It's a work of the heart, sometimes a process. Notice that toward the end of the psalm, David moves from a complaint to an expression of confident expectation. But it wasn't the sound of celebration that we see in other psalms (Ps. 118:10-17). The deliverance of Psalm 142 is subtle, but it's there. Do we have a refuge when the storms of life beat us down? And if so, what can we find there? The answer to the first question is, "Yes, God is our refuge" (Ps. 46). The answer to the second question is, "Safety, security, and ultimate rest."

For a war-torn soldier, it's a bunker or friendly territory. For a frightened child, it's the arms of a loving parent. Whatever the case, a refuge provides shelter and protection from danger. When we say, "God is my refuge," it should mean two things; first, that we abide in Him at all times; and second, that His presence reassures us in times of trouble. Psalm 91 beautifully illustrates the life of an individual who "dwells" in the secret place of the most High as one who "abides" under the shadow of the Almighty. The words dwell and abide point to the fact that we should not wander around on our strength and run to God when life gets hard. Indeed, Jesus says, "Come unto me, all ye that labor and are heavy laden" (Matt. 11:28), but the absolute joy of life is resting in the presence of the Lord every day. God's presence is not only the absence of danger but the spirit of blessing! Those who take refuge in Him find great peace regardless of any circumstance.

Fanny Crosby (1820-1915) was made blind when she was six weeks old by the carelessness of a physician who treated her for a slight inflammation of the eyes. She accepted Christ early in life, and she never had one regret that she could not use her eyes; for she said, "Contented I will be. How many blessings I enjoy that other people don't! To weep and sigh because I'm blind, I cannot, and I won't." In 1868 Fanny Crosby wrote a fantastic song, 'Safe In The Arms of Jesus.' When General Grant's funeral was being conducted in New York, and the city's bells were tolling, the band played softly: *Safe in the arms of Jesus, safe on His gentle breast, there by His love o'ershaded. sweetly my soul doth rest. Hark! 'tis a song of heaven borne in the sweetest voice, echoed by saints in spirit, making my heart rejoice. Safe in the arms of Jesus, safe on His gentle breast, O how my heart rejoices… sweetly my soul doth rest.*

Christian friend, whatever our circumstances, we have committed to follow Christ as Lord. Therefore, if our troubles do not cause us to go deeper in faith and prayer, we miss the lesson of David's cave that led him to praise and worship!

GRACE, GRATITUDE
AND GENEROSITY

Cheerful giving reveals a heart of gratitude. We know that generosity is suitable for everyone, not just Christians. But those who appreciate the grace of God understand the meaning of advancing His purpose in the world through their giving. The apostle Paul speaks of a grace received and a heart of thankfulness from which flows a commitment to give (2 Cor. 8). And in his pointing to the churches in Macedonia as an example of charity - even as they were themselves struggling under the affliction of extreme poverty - we should understand that giving to others will be the conclusion of Christlike love for them. The temple offering provided by the widow in Luke 21 also illustrates generosity - not in terms of quantity - but of sacrifice. Giving of ourselves is a work of God's grace in us. What, where, when, why, and how we give says something about our commitment to the Lord. Unwillingness to give freely of our time, talent and treasure speak volumes about our profession of love for the One who first loved us.

Generosity begins in the heart. It begins when we stop complaining over what we are giving up and start rejoicing in all we have gained in Jesus Christ (Matt. 19:29). A thankful person knows that God is the source of all things, and His blessings are to be shared (1 Chron. 29:14-17). From a practical standpoint, a quick review of our financial records will speak volumes. If we give grudgingly, our approach will be "I must do it." If we give dutifully, our approach will be "I need to do it." But if we give thankfully, our approach will be "I want to do it." The Bible says, "For God so loved the world that He gave…" (John 3:16). In simple terms, our relationship with God is made known by our willingness to live like Jesus did (Phil. 2:4-5).

If you think about it, isn't thankfulness and generosity a choice? Paul tells us the Macedonian Christians "first gave their own selves to the Lord" (1 Cor. 8:5). Years ago, a gentleman was baptized in northern England. He was a prominent man in the community, a man who was known for his great wealth. This man had also been known for having no interest in Jesus or the church. But someone had invited him to a Bible study, and as a result of his research, he had come to understand who Jesus was and why He came to die on the cross. In time, the man offered his life to Christ in response to God's grace. He appeared in dramatic contrast to the others waiting to be immersed on the evening he was baptized. Most wore jeans, a T-shirt, or other simple clothing. The wealthy man came dressed in an impeccable three-piece suit and a wonderful silk tie. He looked ready to present a business opportunity in London, which he was always prepared for. And in his testimony, he explained why he had dressed this way. He said he recognized that his suit, his tie, and the quality of his shoes represented all he once held dear and built his life upon; everything that gave status and significance to him when he walked into a meeting. And now he says, "I've decided to be baptized in all of this attire so that I might remind myself always from this day that Jesus Christ has all of me." William Booth was asked to explain the extraordinary usefulness that God had made of him in the founding and framing of the Salvation Army. Mr. Booth replied without any pride, "Jesus Christ has all of me." None of us will get beyond the starting block of godly living until we are convinced that God's grace is cause for giving.

God's favor is not granted to us because of anything we have done (Rom. 11:6). But this does not mean that good works are unrelated to a new life in Christ. Good deeds do not save us, but we are dedicated unto acts of kindness that will glorify God (Eph. 2:8-10). Living according to the teachings of Jesus is an expression of our thankfulness for God's wondrous grace (Phil. 2:13). When we live with an awareness of God's grace and forgiveness, we will use what we have in praise and worship. To the extent we appreciate the love of God, there will be joy in helping others. Developing a heart of gratitude often comes as the result of our struggles, for by it, we are more prone to recognize the troubles of those around us. Much of our character development happens during the storms of life and in the refining fire of difficult circumstances (1 Pet. 1:7). A dear woman writes, "My name is Wendy, and this is the backstory about One Exceptional Life and how it all began... Have you ever had a time when your life was turned completely upside down? That was me back in 2011 when what started as flu symptoms progressed to a life-threatening illness within three days. The doctors told my husband and kids that I had less than a one percent chance of survival and to plan for my passing. My husband replied, "you don't know my God and what He can do!" My family never lost faith. Word spread, and hundreds of people prayed. God saved my life, but I lost my limbs. After three weeks in a medically induced coma and three months in the hospital, I came home to a new way of living. My family loved, supported, and cared for me. But the life I previously had was over. I questioned for a long time, "what do I do now?" I knew God had a plan for me. But what was it? Why did this happen to me? I dug into God's Word, and I continually counted my blessings. But there was still doubt, hopelessness, depression, and frustration. One day I realized I was capable of so much more than I was giving myself credit for. That was the day my pity party ended, and my quest to help other women move past their challenges began. That was the day One Exceptional Life was born."

If we open our hearts, the grace, gratitude, and generosity cycle will start and finish with God. Paul said the Macedonian saints gave even beyond their ability (v3). They were willing to forego a legitimate want to supply a legitimate need; that is, they were happy to squeeze themselves so that others might not feel the pinch. And they did it without external prodding. Who among us is not a product of God's grace demonstrated through the contribution and influence of others? When Christ is our treasure, we will pledge our resources - our money, our time, our talents - to His purposes in the world (Col. 3:23-24). The eternal reward that awaits a child of God will far outweigh any inconvenience of this life (Rom. 8:18). When we consider the love of God and His grace toward us, the only appropriate response is to offer ourselves a living sacrifice to Him (Rom. 12:1). This is the only logical response to such a generous, merciful, and forgiving God!

So, what can we give that will most glorify God? There are several ways our service to the Lord will bring eternal reward. First, what we value determines what we do. We show our love by following God's commandments (John 14:15-21). Therefore, if we esteem God as the highest order of grace, our every thought and action will be that which converts to eternity. The things of this world will pass away (1 John 2:17). Only two things in this life are eternal: people and the Word of God. Therefore, I want to invest heavily in both. Money and possessions are fleeting, and they must be subservient to reaching souls with the gospel of Christ (Matt. 28:16-20). And yet, our finances can - and should - be used to honor God. We can also give the respect and credibility we gain from a professional lifestyle. This is often scorned in the Christian community. But I believe our testimony in the secular world will serve the purposes of God insofar as it draws others to Christ. The Bible tells us that Jesus "increased in wisdom and stature, and favor with God and man" (Luke 2:52). We can give wisdom. The essence of wisdom is to make Christ the center of our lives, not merely something to enjoy. Education and knowledge will also serve to promote the work of God. Several Bible passages highlight the importance of education. Psalm 119 is dedicated to contemplating God's law and wisdom. The prophet Daniel and his friends were skilled "in all learning and wisdom" (Dan. 1:17). Knowledge of the law was part of Paul's pedigree of accomplishments. But all of this is divinely useful only in the service of God (Phil. 3:5-8). The closest we can come to things of eternal value on earth is our influence in the world; that is, the people we reach for Christ (2 Cor. 3:2-3) and a sincere faith that inspires our brothers and sisters in the Lord (2 Tim. 1:5). Our godly witness is a legacy that will long endure beyond our passing.

One of the greatest misconceptions about giving is that what we part with to help the needy or spread the gospel disappears and is gone forever. We even buy into the devil's lie that giving will rob us of the good life. We could not be more wrong (Matt. 6:19-21). Martin Luther is credited with saying, "I have held many things in my hands, and I have lost them all. But whatever I have placed in God's hands, that I still possess." Rooted in our fallen human nature is a conflict between two value systems: the earthly and the eternal. Our natural inclination is to look to and be shaped by temporal things as if they were lasting. But that value system only delivers what it promises. It leads to futility and delusion. Jesus taught us not to store treasures that can be destroyed or stolen (Matt. 6:19-20). Only when we embrace the eternal value system will we find true fulfillment, reality, and wisdom. This does not mean we ignore temporal things, only that we leverage them in light of eternity. Psalm 90 is a prayer that God would teach us to number our days, that His glory would appear to our children, and that His beauty would be upon us to establish the work of our hands. When we consider the brevity of this life and the eternity of the life to come, we will not lose heart when temporal things fail us (2 Cor. 4:16). When we recognize that our days on earth are finite, we will have an appreciation for God's grace that leads to thankfulness and generosity (Ps. 90:12).

THE SANCTITY OF LIFE

Our worldview is influenced by the culture around us, the family we were raised with, the education we received, the dominant voices that have spoken into our lives, and our personal experiences. In our society, there is an ever-increasing tendency to define "quality of life" as a standard by which we – not God – determine when someone will be too burdensome to be born or if they are not dying according to our timetable. We live in a day where the moral climate has never been as evil as it is now. There is simply no way anyone can read the first two chapters of Genesis and not understand that humanity is both the crown of God's creation and the center of God's attention. And the Bible teaches that all innocent human life is to be cherished, protected, and defended. Everyone's viewpoint is limited and fallible. Only the Creator of life can provide a perfect, complete, and eternally consistent perspective on His creation. We live in a day when human life is no longer considered sacred. The devaluing of life is spreading not only through violence in the ghettos; but also through abortion on demand. On the other end of life, the push for euthanasia further erodes human life's sanctity. All of these problems stem from the erosion of the Bible as the standard for truth in our society. If you throw out the Bible and accept evolution, man is just an animal, and there is no basis for human morality other than cultural norms. Without the Bible, there is no basis for affirming that humans are created in the image of God and that human life is thus sacred. For the survival of our nation and culture, we desperately need to understand and proclaim the biblical truth regarding the sanctity of human life. C. Everett Koop, M.D., formerly the U. S. Surgeon General, states that during his 35-plus years of practicing medicine, "Never once did a case come across my practice where abortion was necessary to save a mother's life."

Abortion can be a complex topic to discuss, and tone matters. It is possible to hold a Biblical position and communicate it in truth and love (Eph. 4:15). We must remember that the person we speak to may be dealing with emotional trauma or regret. Or they might be troubled by a friend's termination of a pregnancy. God's grace is profound, and His forgiveness is greater than any remorse we may experience. Abortion is an issue that draws upon deep values and personal experiences. That's what makes it such a challenging topic. But sometimes, the most complex conversations are the ones we need most. When I consider that I may find myself discussing the issue of abortion with someone I care about deeply, I'm reminded of my similarities to the sins of David, Moses, the apostle Peter, and others, where I learned that, through repentance, God brings beauty and healing to the pain of wrong decisions (1 John 1:9). I am so thankful that forgiveness is one of the marvels of God's grace (Ps. 103:10-12). His cleansing healing power is cause for a grand celebration!

We have been deceived into believing that being "pro-life" is a political issue. We often see this battle as one between political parties, conservatives, and liberals. The sanctity of life is not a political issue; it is a moral issue! The decision to end an innocent life in the mother's womb is a choice between life and death. The term "pro-choice" is a politically correct way of saying it is okay to kill an unborn child. Abortion, euthanasia, suicide, or murder is the ultimate form of rebellion against God. We are formed in God's image (Gen. 1:26-27). This means we have a soul, a spirit, and the capacity for a relationship with God. Human life has sacred value. How can we use the word sacred? Because through the Holy Spirit, Paul emphasizes the origin of life, and he affirms that God "gives to all life, and breath, and all things" (Acts. 17:25). The soul within us is what sets us apart from the rest of Creation. We can mirror God's image in significant ways, demonstrating love, mercy, justice, and compassion. God places exceptional value on human life (Gen. 2:7), which we must also protect (Ex. 20:13). Our belief in the sanctity of life mustn't be built on statistics or science. It must be based on Scripture. How did we get to the point where we see life as expendable? The Bible provides the answer in John 3:19: "And this is the condemnation, that light is come into the world, and men loved darkness rather than light, because their deeds were evil." The prophet Jeremiah said, "The heart is deceitful above all things, and desperately wicked" (Jer. 17:9). The devaluing of life began after the Fall when Cain killed his brother Abel (Gen. 4:8). The human heart, without Christ, is depraved and willing to make self-centered choices – even if it means taking another life.

On December 18, 2003, a biology professor at Calvin College in Michigan reported using a plastic-encased, 3-month-old fetus in his human biology classes. A visit from a young woman showed him that the fetus was more than an educational tool. The student told him that a generation earlier, her mother had also been a student in one of his biology classes. Unknown to the professor, that former student (now mother) was three months pregnant on a day he had shown the class the fetus with its tiny fingers, facial features, eyes, and other human features. She had already visited a pregnancy center and was advised to have an abortion. In fact, she had an appointment scheduled for the following morning. But after the class, she realized she had more within her than a 'product of conception.' She canceled her scheduled abortion, continued her pregnancy, and delivered a healthy baby girl. The second-generation student informed the stunned professor, "I am that girl. Thank you for saving my life." The biology professor was amazed and speechless. He remembers in a halting voice telling the girl simply that she was beautiful. "Even now," he says, "I can barely tell the story without breaking up."

The Psalmist declared, "Know that the LORD he is God: it is he that hath made us, and not we ourselves (Ps. 100:3). The prophet Isaiah warns, "Woe unto him that striveth with his maker... shall the clay say to him that fashioneth it, What makest thou?" (Isa. 45:9). This issue of the sanctity of life is a spiritual - and a biblical - issue. Therefore, we must stand for life regardless of which way the political winds blow. Human life has a specific beginning (Jer. 1:5). Human life is sacred because we are made in the image of God (Gen. 1:27). Human life is sacred because we are elevated above the rest of creation (Matt. 10:31). Human life is sacred because God takes special care in creating each one of us (Ps. 139:13-14). Human life is sacred because we are eternal (Ps. 23:6). Human life is sacred because Christ was willing to pay an unspeakable price to redeem us from a sinful nature (Isa. 53:5). Human life is sacred because all of heaven celebrates when a sinner repents (Luke 15:10). Human life is sacred because we are made for God's glory (Isa. 43:7). It is sacred because God loves us beyond measure (John 3:16).

What can we do? We can pray. We can pray for mothers struggling with choices about their unborn children. We can pray for churches and Christian counselors interacting with mothers making these choices. We can pray for lawmakers to understand Scripture's clarity and act accordingly. We can speak. We can speak up when people voice their pro-abortion sentiments. We can help pregnant women and single moms through challenging times when they need a friend. We can foster and adopt, and if the Lord leads us into this ministry, He will enable us. We can educate. We can share biblical truths about the sanctity of life. We can vote. The biblical view on the sanctity of life makes it an issue worth determining our vote.

Every person, from conception to natural death, has immeasurable worth, including preborn children, older adults, those with special needs, and others marginalized by society. This is a privileged status reserved only for humanity (Ps. 139:14). Human dignity is bestowed upon us by God, and the cornerstone of this fundamental truth is to recognize the value of our own lives and the lives of others. We must declare to those around us the value of a life by speaking out for "those who cannot speak for themselves" (Prov. 31:8). Every unborn child deserves the chance to be born, live, and receive love. Every terminally ill patient should be comforted in their condition and allowed to pass from this life with as much grace as possible. Every person contemplating suicide deserves to be brought back to emotional health through the love of Jesus Christ. God can open eyes blinded to the sacredness of human life and forgive those who have taken it. Every human being, from conception through death, must be valued, respected, nurtured, and protected. The Bible describes a moral order to which all of us are accountable. At the end of life, we will stand before God to give account for our actions (2 Cor. 5:10). Indeed, we have a great responsibility to bring the light of God's Word to all conversations that bear on the sanctity of life (Rom. 13:10).

Overflowing Love, Abundant Life

Some of the most descriptive words used in the Bible are these: whole, new, complete, holy, beautiful, blessed, precious, sacred, and beloved. In Psalm 23:5, when the Psalmist said, "My cup runneth over," he was using the expression to help us understand the excellence of God's presence, provision, and power, all designed to overflow into the lives of others. The description of a cup running over teaches us that God is a generous provider (Prov. 3:10). Many will quote John 10:10 as support for the idea that Christianity leads to physical prosperity. The material blessings of this life are wonderful, and I thank God for every one of them. But the ultimate blessing is new life in Christ. Why? Because there is no condemnation to those who are walking after the Spirit (Rom. 8:1). An abundant life is, first and foremost, eternal life (John 17:3). The great life means gaining a heavenly perspective that leads to a growing trust and knowledge of God (Rom. 12:2, 2 Pet. 3:18). The abundant life is filled with love, joy, peace, longsuffering, gentleness, goodness, faith, meekness and self-control (Gal. 5:22–23).

The blessings of grace and forgiveness are for time and eternity, and we who believe in the death, burial, and resurrection of Jesus have found the well of water springing up into everlasting life (John 4:13-14). We receive a limitless supply of God's goodness by spending time with Jesus, and then we splash spiritual refreshments everywhere we go! With a full cup, we are free to love and care for those around us. God reveals Himself in the lives of faithful men and women. When Jehovah revealed Himself to Abraham in Genesis 17:1, He used the Hebrew name El Shaddai, which translates as "The All Sufficient One." When God, who is more than enough, told

Moses to "Stretch out thine hand" over the Red Sea, millions crossed to the other side on dry ground (Ex. 14). When the prayers of Elijah released fire from heaven, sinners believed and worshiped Almighty God (1 Kings 18). When the power of God came upon David and his mighty men, a great victory was won (2 Sam. 23). When worshipful singing was raised from earth to heaven, chains fell off, and prison doors were opened (Acts 16). Never doubt. Our God is more than sufficient - even in the most desperate circumstances!

As we grow older, we tend to relegate everything to the past. We say, "Oh, yesteryear was wonderful; God could do mighty things back in those days." Or we want to skip over the present and talk about what heaven will be. We say, "Someday, it will all be over. Here we wander like a beggar, but one of these days, we will leave this vale of tears." Oh no, friend! God is not just the God of yesterday. He is the God of now. He did not say, "I was El Shaddai" or, "Someday, I will be the God who is more than enough." No! He said, "I AM" - I am the Almighty God (Rev. 1:8). I am El Shaddai, the God who is more than enough yesterday, today, and forever more!

Salvation opens the door to a life in Christ that is rich and full. Our narrow imaginations will never limit the richness of heaven's glory! The apostle Paul tells us that because our God has all wisdom, power, and authority, He can do more than we can ask or think. God's love is inexhaustible, and his vision for our lives is always greater than our own. We will grow spiritually by spending time in prayer and searching the Scriptures. A group of tourists visiting a picturesque village walked by an older man sitting beside a fence. Condescendingly, one tourist asked him, "Were any great men born in this village?" The old man replied, "Nope, only babies." Every person who is a born-again believer starts life as a baby in Christ, and a baby Christian who has been saved for forty years is a tragedy. God intends for us to grow and mature into a positive influence in the lives of others. And until we learn to dig into God's Word for ourselves, this will not happen. I pray I will be so deeply rooted and established in Him that my faith cannot be shaken. I pray that the love of God would be my rock, foundation, rest, and refreshment, not because of what I have achieved, done, or believed, but because of His grace. I want to understand the breadth and length and height and depth of the love of God in Christ Jesus (Eph. 3:18-20). No matter how great our requests of God are, no matter how we envision what God can do, He can do so much more! So, with all confidence in this truth, I will lift my eyes to see the grand horizon of God's power so that He might be glorified in the world. In general terms, sufficiency means possessing something that is enough or the quality of being good enough for a particular purpose. But to speak of the sufficiency of God is to say that His provision can never be exhausted or run dry.

In Paul's second letter to the Corinthians (3:5), we read, "Not that we are sufficient of ourselves… but our sufficiency is of God." Let your inadequacy drive you to God. Spend time in prayer and pour out your heart to Him. Insufficiency reminds us to stop trying to do God's will in our own strength. If we continue down the path of self-indulgence, we will become overwhelmed and burdened. But when we admit our shortcomings to God, the burden is lifted, and we discover the contentment that comes from a dependent, trusting heart. The Lord is more than enough for every need, and His strength is perfect in our weakness (2 Cor. 12:9).

A young boy traveling by airplane to visit his grandparents sat beside a man who happened to be a college professor. The boy was reading a Sunday school take-home paper, and the professor thought he would have some fun with the lad. "Young man," said the professor, "if you can tell me something God can do, I will give you a big, shiny apple." The boy thought for a moment and replied, "Mister, if you can tell me something God cannot do, I'll give you a whole barrel of apples!"

The Bible paints a picture of a limitless supply of God's goodness, and He desires to do for us beyond our highest expectations. How wondrous is God's love!

For in Him we have:

Not just a counselor, but a *wonderful* counselor (Isa. 9:6)
Not just grace, but *sufficient* grace (2 Cor. 12:9)
Not just life, but *abundant* life (John 10:10)
Not just promises, but *precious* promises (2 Pet. 1:4)
Not just hope, but a *blessed* hope (Titus 2:13)
Not just peace, but *perfect* peace (Isa. 26:3)
Not just love, but *sacrificial* love (John 15:13)
Not just rest, but *quiet* rest (Psalm 116:7)

Not just a reward, but a *heavenly* reward (Matt. 5:12)

Not just joy, but *unspeakable* joy (Psalm 32:11)

Not just blessings, but *rich* blessings (Prov. 10:22)

Not just mercies, but *bountiful* mercies (Psalm 103:8)

Not just bread, but *daily* bread (Matt. 6:11)

Not just a calling, but a *high* calling (Phil. 3:14)

Not just wisdom, but *pure* wisdom (James 3:17)

Not just cheer, but *good* cheer (John 16:33)

Not just compassion, but *unfailing* compassion (Lam. 3:22)

Not just a crown, but a *glorious* crown (1 Pet. 5:4)

Not just deliverance, but *great* deliverance (1 Chron. 11:14)

Not just faith, but *sanctifying* faith (Acts 26:18)

Not just a foundation, but a *sure* foundation (2 Tim. 2:19)

Not just persuasion, but *full* persuasion (Rom. 4:21)

Not just a habitation, but a *peaceable* habitation (Isa. 32:18)

Not just a song, but a *new* song (Psalm 40:3)

Not just water, but *living* water (John 4:14)

Not just a home, but an *eternal* home (Heb. 11:16)

The Psalmist said, "O how great is thy goodness, which thou hast laid up for them that fear thee" (Ps. 31:19). If you want to see God for Who He is, here's a good starting point: "O give thanks unto the Lord; for he is good" (1 Chron. 16:34). "O taste and see that the Lord is good" (Ps. 34:8). "The Lord is good; his mercy is everlasting, and his truth endures to all generations" (Ps. 100:5). We will experience the abundant life as we follow God's ways, pursue holiness, and seek to be more like Him (Ps. 18:30). For what purpose? That the world may see the light of God. That He may be glorified through the testimony of His overflowing love in us (Matt. 5:16). We are told in 1 Peter 2:9 that we should show forth the praises of God to the world. Christian friend, we are blessed to bless others. It is through our witness that God becomes a light shining in the darkness; for in Him, there is hope for the hopeless, help for the helpless, peace for the troubled, and joy for the sorrowful. The love of Jesus is amazing and without end. Jesus is completely and utterly sufficient. Yet, He has chosen to be seen through the lens of our lives. And if we are willing to surrender, the overflow of His abundant grace will influence those around us!

THE WHOLE COUNSEL OF GOD

Recently I had a conversation with a Christian man who was disheartened over what was described as the incessant drumming of a denominational mantra at his church. We talked about the importance of teaching and preaching the entire Bible, not just a few favored topics punctuated by overused Bible verses. Without knowing his pastor's heart, I still thought of Acts 20:27, where the apostle Paul said, "For I have not shunned to declare unto you all the counsel of God." Paul shared the whole of what God reveals in His Word. And we must do the same, for it is the power of God unto salvation to everyone who believes (Rom. 1:16). We cannot choose among texts of Scripture, only those that merely produce an emotional response. All Scripture is inspired and profitable (2 Tim. 3:16). Every word of the Bible is purposeful; each one is there for a reason. Every thought is divinely empowered (2 Pet. 1:3-4). When Jesus taught, the people were "astonished at his doctrine, for he taught them as one having authority, and not as the scribes" (Matt. 7:28-29). Every phrase in Scripture leads to a course of action, and when spoken, it will not return void (Isa. 55:10-11). That is to say, as the rain produces an earthly harvest, God's Word always fulfills His will and purpose. By the revelation of biblical truths, we learn how to live. (2 Tim. 3:17). By way of Solomon's writing, God said, "Let thine heart keep my commandments… write them upon the table of thine heart." The wisdom of God is the refreshment that will sustain us (Prov. 3:1-8).

We do not bring our agenda to the pulpit. On every page of the Bible, from Genesis to Revelation, the overarching theme is Jesus Christ. Dive deep into Scripture because when you understand its timeline and context, you begin to see the story and the glory behind every passage. You will see that these are actual events happening to real people. When you develop a love for the Bible, you will see it in a new light. I cannot think of anything more worthy than understanding Scripture more fully. Pray for the Holy Spirit to illuminate what you read. Jesus said, "Follow me" (Mark 8:34), and the key to following Him is gaining a more precise knowledge of who He is. As we read Scripture, two defining characteristics of Jesus will stand out: faith and love. If we want to become like Him, faith and love must also become our defining characteristics. In Romans 10, we read that faith comes by hearing and hearing by the word of God. Our love for God will increase as we daily read of His love for us!

Jesus Christ is the central figure and theme of the Bible (Luke 24:27). The real message of the Bible is that God is restoring the world to His original design through Christ (Rev. 21-22). Paul testified to the grace of God practically and effectively. He proclaimed the kingdom of God with nothing left unsaid, yet he did not go beyond the Scriptures. Our words are only authoritative as they are evidenced to come from the biblical text, not of man, but of God. John Newton declared, "If I venture beyond the pole of the Bible, I am on enchanted ground and subject to illusions and distortions." The Pharisees were notorious for adding to, subtracting from, and twisting what God said. Jesus confronted them in Mark 7:9, 13, saying, "Ye reject the commandment of God, that ye may keep your own tradition... making the word of God of none effect through your tradition." Our society hates authority, and there is nothing as authoritative as the Bible. Some passages of Scripture are hard to understand, and some are hard to believe. And certainly, we are free to preach and teach from our favorite Scripture texts. But, regardless of how uncomfortable, we must also deal with the problematic verses and how they apply to our lives. Satan desires nothing more than to hinder God's work. And one of the best ways he can accomplish this is by restricting our knowledge of the Bible or altering our understanding of it. Christianity is an active faith (Mark 16:15). The way we show ourselves "approved unto God" (2 Tim. 2:15) is to be doers of His Word, not merely hearers (James 1:22). When we study, teach and preach all of God's word, we serve and worship Him more completely. How do we honor God? By loving the "lamp unto our feet and the light unto our path" (Ps. 119:105).

We should be developing a long-term understanding and love for the Bible. The prophet Jeremiah's ministry became so disheartening that he mourned the fact that he had ever been born. However, in his sadness, he said: "Thy word was unto me joy and rejoicing of mine heart" (Jer. 15:16). Jeremiah learned to love the Word of God and take great comfort in it. The primary job of a prophet was to speak God's word to God's people, and the knowledge of Scripture was necessary to accomplish his calling. The Psalmist David said, "How sweet are thy words unto my taste" (Ps. 119:103). I recently heard the story of a Sunday school teacher who asked her class if anyone knew what Palm Sunday was. To her dismay, after a few awkward moments, one child raised his hand, spread his fingers, and pointed to his palm. He wasn't joking. Make it your goal to love and treasure the Bible as God's holy and transforming message!

I will never grow spiritually, and I cannot help others without developing a greater understanding and appreciation for God's Word. Every word of the Bible is accurate. God breathes every word out for our sanctification. Today, more than ever, church attendees are abandoning sound doctrine for progressive Christianity and the prosperity gospel. In 2 Timothy 4:3, Paul warns the church as he urges Timothy to keep preaching sound doctrine. He knows that people will want sermons that charm rather than challenge, messages that entertain rather than edify. God is not concerned with scratching our itches but in transforming us into the image of His Son (Rom. 12:2, 2 Cor. 4:4). The Bible is the mind of God revealed, and if we would know God's mind, we must know what His Book says. The task of teaching all of Scripture will never be easy. But as we faithfully grow in knowledge, our joy will also increase as we see the One of whom the law, the prophets, and the Psalms testify. The Bible is a book like no other. It is a letter of love that tells us how we can be saved from the power and penalty of sin (Matt. 19). It is our instruction on how to have a personal relationship with Jesus (Rom. 3). It is our direction for this life and all eternity (Psalm 32). Charles Spurgeon said, "It is the whole business of the whole church to preach the gospel to the whole world." Consider the Word. It is a privilege to love, learn, and live the entire counsel of God!

The Spirit of Thanksgiving

In Psalm 95, we see a call to praise the Lord, "O come, let us sing unto the Lord; let us make a joyful noise to the rock of our salvation; Let us come before his presence with thanksgiving, and make a joyful noise unto him with psalms. For the Lord is a great God, and a great King above all gods. In his hand are the deep places of the earth: the strength of the hills is his also, The sea is his, and he made it; and his hands formed the dry land. O come, let us worship and bow down; let us kneel before the Lord our Maker."

Thanksgiving begins in our hearts. It begins when we start rejoicing for what we have gained by following Jesus Christ. Thankfulness is a choice made by people who understand that God is the source of all things. Living according to biblical principles is an expression of our gratitude for His wondrous grace (Phil. 2:13). When we appreciate the love of God, there will be joy in our hearts. Developing a spirit of gratitude often comes as a result of our struggles. For by it, we are more prone to recognize the troubles of those around us. With gratitude, we will forgo a legitimate want in our lives to supply a legitimate need in someone else's. That is, we will squeeze ourselves so others might not feel the pinch. And we will do it without prodding. Who among us is not a product of the contribution and influence of others? When Christ is our treasure, we will pledge our resources - our money, our time, our talents - to His purposes in the world (Col. 3:23-24). When we consider the love of God and His grace toward us, the only appropriate response is to offer ourselves a living sacrifice to Him (Rom. 12:1). Martin Luther said, "I have held many things in my hands, and I have lost them all. But whatever I have placed in God's hands, that I still possess." When we consider the shortness of this life and the eternity of the life to come, we will not lose heart when temporal things fail us (2 Cor. 4:16). When we recognize that our days on earth are limited, we will have an appreciation for God's grace that leads to thankfulness and generosity (Ps. 90:12).

From the beginning of time, Satan's goal was to make Adam and Eve discontent with their condition as if it were not so good as it might be — and should be (Gen. 3). No condition (not even Eden's beauty) will of itself bring contentment unless we are thankful. Through every trial, the apostle Paul experienced God in all wisdom and goodness. Why? His treasure was in heaven. To him, each test was a means of receiving new lessons from God. Paul was a man who, after experiencing trouble of every kind, could yet say, "I have learned in whatsoever state I am therewith to be content" (Phil. 3 and 4). Many Christians are unthankful - not because they aren't doing well, but because others are doing better. But if we believe that every circumstance is according to the providence of God, we will be content; and, therefore, thankful.

Consider this: How thankful would others be if they were in your position? Is your condition so bad that it might not be worse? Surely not. We are quick to look upward toward the few who seem to have greater advantages in life, and we covet their good fortune. But we seldom consider the many good people beneath us in earthly accommodation. When we consider the case of most people, we will have many reasons to be satisfied with our own. Thankfulness is a state of mind. It is not the gathering of assets. Nothing in this world can make a discontented person happy. Contentment can be found only in Jesus Christ. And when we are content in Christ, we become useful. When we try to change what God is doing because we think we can arrange things better, He cannot use us - and we will always make mistakes. Contentment does not always imply happiness. We are not obliged to say, "I like these circumstances," to be content with them. Thankfulness looks at what is left. It is not found in an exchange of places. A goldfish and a canary wanted to trade places, so they did. How long did their happiness last? God has given each of us a place suited to our nature. Thankfulness is something divine planted by the Spirit of God in our hearts. Satisfaction is in His promise, "I will never leave thee, nor forsake thee" (Heb. 13:5). A contented spirit is a quiet, cheerful, and thankful heart.

There is no end to the number of things to be thankful for. Gratitude is the recognition that life owes me nothing and that all the good I have is a gift. And we must make it known! Someone said, "Feeling gratitude and not expressing it is like wrapping a present and not giving it." The Bible has much to say about thankfulness. Far beyond any temporal blessings, we are to be thankful to God for His spiritual gifts. And the greatest of these is His grace that was provided for us at Calvary (2 Cor. 5:21). Complaining comes all too easy for us, and ungratefulness turns us into self-centered, dissatisfied people. But contentment and joy can be ours when we live with a spirit of appreciation. America's inspirational poet Helen Steiner Rice said, "Thank you God for everything, the big things and the small. For every good gift comes from God, the giver of them all." Jesus pointed out both the importance and the rarity of thanksgiving when only one of the ten lepers He had healed returned to thank Him (Luke 17:11–19). Friends, the eternal life that we have received through faith in Christ (Eph. 2:8–10) deserves an eternity of gratitude (John 3:15). The Bible is filled with prayers of thanksgiving (Psalm 9:1, Dan. 2:23, Eph. 5:19).

Giving thanks is a way of acknowledging God's faithfulness. The Psalmist David prayed, "Thine, O Lord, is the greatness, and the power, and the glory, and the victory, and the majesty; for all that is in the heaven and in the earth is thine... both riches and honor come of thee... Now therefore, our God, we thank thee, and praise thy glorious name" (1 Chron. 29:11–13). When we recognize that, apart from God, there is only death (John 10:10, Rom. 7:5), thankfulness will be a way of life. When we give thanks to God, we are praising Him for all He is, for all He has done, and for all He will do in the future. David said, "I will praise thee, O Lord, with my whole heart" (Psalm 9:1). Throughout the book of Psalms, he proclaims God as his strength, his refuge, hiding place, strong tower, and shelter in the storm (Psalm 91). We are told in Paul's letter to the Ephesians to speak to ourselves with psalms and hymns, singing and giving thanks unto God always and for all things (Eph. 5:19–20). Through thankfulness, our witness for Christ becomes effectual in the world (1 Peter 2:9). We whom the Blood of Jesus Christ has redeemed ought to declare God's faithfulness. Thanksgiving day is a time of rejoicing as we acknowledge the fulfilled promises of God and His abundant provision! Some of the most descriptive words used in the Bible are these: whole, new, complete, holy, beautiful, blessed, precious, sacred, and beloved. In Psalm 23:5, when the Psalmist said, "My cup runneth over," he was using the expression to help us understand the excellence of God's presence, provision, and power, all designed to overflow into the lives of others. We receive a limitless supply of God's goodness by spending time with Jesus, and then we splash a spiritual refreshment everywhere we go!

Indeed, life can be overwhelming. Chippie, the parakeet, never saw it coming. One second, he was peacefully perched in his cage. The next, he was sucked in, washed up, and blown over. The problems began when Chippie's owner decided to clean his cage with a vacuum cleaner. She removed the attachment from the end of the hose and stuck it in the cage. The phone rang, and she turned to pick it up. She'd barely said "hello" when "ssssopp!" Chippie got sucked in. The bird owner gasped, put down the phone, turned off the vacuum, and opened the bag. There was Chippie — still alive but stunned. Since the bird was covered with dust, she grabbed him and raced to the bathroom, turned on the faucet, and held Chippie under the running water. Then, realizing that Chippie was soaked and shivering, she did what any compassionate bird owner would do. . . she reached for the hairdryer and blasted the pet with hot air. Poor Chippie never knew what hit him. A few days after the trauma, the one who'd initially witnessed the event contacted Chippie's owner to see how the bird was doing. "Well," she replied, "Chippie doesn't sing much anymore — he just sits and stares." Ever felt that way? Sucked in, washed up, and blown over? Sure, you have! As we walk the Christian path, storms of life are inevitable. But trials are a test of our faith, and we who have known the Savior earlier in His kindness and love will also come to know Him in His wisdom and power.

In times of great disappointment, it may seem like God is asking too much of us. But even if we never obey this command perfectly in this life, we can develop an attitude of gratitude that will help us move toward the mark. Notice that the Bible says to give thanks in everything, not for everything. A little boy was asked to pray for dinner. Before he bowed his head to pray, he looked at the dish. Then, closing his eyes, he prayed, "Lord, I don't like the looks of it, but I'll thank you for it anyway." Thankfulness is not turning a blind eye to the difficulty. Nor does it mean we are resigned to accepting matters without praying and working for change. But when we understand that whatever comes into our lives is there by the will of God, giving thanks will make perfect sense.

After World War II, two families waited in line after a church service to greet the pastor. The church was preparing to build a building at that time. The first family in line said, "Pastor, as you know, our son was killed in the war, and we would like to give two hundred dollars as a memorial gift." The second family said, "Pastor, we were going to give two hundred dollars. But our son came home, so we'll give five hundred." Some of my greatest dissatisfactions occur when I focus on what I do not have. We will have a hard time appreciating God and other people when we feel entitled or envious. Ingratitude is most often associated with a low view of God's holiness and a high view of our worthiness. John Stott said, "Until you see the cross as that which is done *by* you, you will never appreciate that it is done *for* you."

Our Lord causes blessings to come progressively into our lives, perhaps a smile, a letter, a burst of music, a sermon, a book, or the kindness of a friend. He will impart wisdom and grace by arranging circumstances (Isa. 46:9–11, Deut. 32:39). He will change our hearts to conform to His plan (Rom. 6:1–14). He uses others to help develop spiritual growth and maturity in us (Eph. 4:11–13, Col. 3:16). Through prayer and the reading of Scripture, He gives purpose and direction. These are among the blessings of daily provision. Friend, if it concerns you, it matters to Him. And He hears and answers us in the best possible way. Ask the Holy Spirit to help you to look honestly at your actions this day and how you have responded in different situations. Review the events of the day. Think about opportunities you were given to grow in faith, hope, and love. Give thanks to God for his gifts and share them with others. Maybe you received divine wisdom today. Help someone in a crisis. Perhaps you were incredibly impressed with a passage of Scripture. Find someone who could use some encouragement in that area of life. Use what you have received for God's glory. Ask God to help you as you look forward to a new day tomorrow. Resolve to trust in His loving guidance. God loves us and wants us to make our requests known - with thankfulness (Phil. 4:6).

The Psalmist said, "I love the Lord because he has heard my voice. I will walk before the Lord in the land of the living. What shall I render unto the Lord for all His benefits towards me? I will pay my vows unto the

Lord now in the presence of all his people. I will offer Him the sacrifice of thanksgiving" (Psalm 116). Our hearts ache under the pressures of this life, but it is only because we were made for another world. Let faith guide you. God's ultimate provision has been given in the death of Jesus Christ. And, for those who believe, the best is yet to come (Titus 3:5–7). Oh, friend, God is so good to us that we must be thankful!

The first six verses of Psalm 19 read that all creation glorifies the Creator. There are no specific words, but creation has a voice of praise. And yet humanity is God's only creation for which Christ died. There is a beautiful yet humbling message here. Of all on earth, we who have been redeemed have the most occasion for gratitude. We are best qualified to appreciate the goodness of the Lord, for we have been reconciled to God through the precious blood of Jesus Christ (Col. 1:20). We who have cried unto the Lord in our trouble have been saved from the power and penalty of Satan. Jesus has satisfied our soul's longing (Isa. 29:8), and we have been delivered out of our distresses. Christ has made a way into that haven, a city of Light where we will eternally dwell with Him. We will enter that desired haven, an eternal home beyond all storms or tempests. Let us declare His works with thanksgiving and praise. Let us lift His name on high in the congregation of the people, not merely in private, but in public (v32). Indeed, our God is worthy of our worship!

The Bible says, "Let the redeemed of the Lord say so." We are told to proclaim the greatest story we can tell – the story of God's redemption! God broke our chains and led us into freedom. We are no longer slaves to sin and death. We are free to love, serve and share our hope (Rom. 6:18-22). We were delivered from our destruction and raised to new life in Christ (Col. 3:1-3). Five-year-old Hannah told her mother one day, "Mama, I think God moved out of my heart." With curiosity and concern, her mom asked her daughter where she thought the Lord may have gone. Hannah replied, "I think He moved to my mouth cuz all I want to do is tell people about Jesus." Gratitude is the first part of our response to God's goodness. All that we have comes from Him – our life, health, family and friends, opportunities for success, and most of all, salvation. And because our stories are not about the greatness of our change but the glory of the One who did the changing, we share them. We reflect on the goodness of God in our own Bible study and our conversations with each other. We speak of Him in the gathered assembly and private conversation. We never grow weary of telling of the mercy and grace of God. We tell how God saved us; and that He will save anyone who believes in Jesus Christ (Rom. 10:9). Let the redeemed of the Lord say so (Ps. 107:2)! Where should the redeemed say it? Mark 16:15, "Go ye into all the world, and preach the gospel to every creature." When should it be said? Psalm 34:1 says, "I will bless the Lord at all times: his praise shall continually be in my mouth." Why should the redeemed say so? Revelation 4:1, "Thou art worthy, O Lord, to receive glory, honor, and power." We "say so" because our Lord commanded us to do so (Matt. 28:19-20). We have a testimony to tell, and the world needs to hear what we say. He frees us from sin. He gives us freedom of spirit. He heals our sickness and delivers us through His sacrifice. He calms our storms and brings us to a place of rest. He is never far from us, and our salvation experience is that which we must tell wherever we go. Jesus Christ is the heart of every blessing, the hope of every sorrow. I am so thankful that someone took the time and effort to declare God's message of redemption to me. And may I likewise proclaim the forgiveness of sins through Christ's death at Calvary (1 Cor. 15:1-4). This is the grace wherein we stand (Rom. 5:1-2). Therefore, let the redeemed of the Lord say so!

Nothing can disappoint us in this life when the thankfulness of being with Jesus burns brightly in our hearts. While writing this devotional, I was impressed to write something to a friend who endured tremendous loss. I told her, "For every child of God, there has been – or there will be – an experience that will change Romans 8:28 from a memorization quote to a belief system. Your prayer will move from 'God heal me' to 'God use me for your glory and help me cope.' And then you will discover that thankfulness can indeed coexist with uncertainty, pain, and confusion." We thank God because He is worthy of praise (Ps. 18:3). He is perfect in truth, holiness, love, power, and wisdom. We praise Him for the beauty of His creation, grace, mercy, and forgiveness. Whether child or adult, the most powerful witness of God's grace is for someone to see the outpouring of a grateful heart. Thankfulness is contagious! The Psalmist said, "O magnify the Lord with me, and let us exalt his name together" (Ps. 34:3). Praising God is an expression, an outward manifestation of thanks, happiness, and awe. Glorifying God is expressed by a lifestyle. We praise God for what He has done. We worship Him for who He is!

THE HEART OF OUR MESSAGE

The central message of the Bible is Jesus Christ, and His Gospel is a matter of eternal consequences for the soul's destiny. It is the message that salvation can only be found at the cross of Calvary! This is the focal point of God's Word. Religion and Jesus are not the same. Religion promotes behavior (Matt. 23). Jesus encourages belonging (1 John 3:1-2). Religion condemns people who sin. Jesus Christ forgives people who sin (Rom. 8:1). When Christ lives in us, we are led by the Holy Spirit toward obedience. But perfect obedience is not the goal of a Christian. It is to belong to God. We look first to Jesus. And, seeing biblical instruction in the context of our love for Him, we trust God to transform our hearts. Paul's message is clear. True Christianity is based on faith, motivated by love, and characterized by joy. When Jesus becomes the heart of our message, people are compelled to respond to His gospel of glad tidings. Lives are changed because they are attracted to Him. Speaking of His death, Jesus said, "And I, if I be lifted up from the earth, will draw all men unto me" (John 12:32-33). When the people of Israel suffered from a self-inflicted plague, they could only be saved by looking at a bronze serpent lifted high on a pole (Num. 21). This Old Testament experience foreshadowed the eventual salvation received by those who look to the New Testament Messiah hanging on the cross of Calvary. Jesus said to Nicodemus, "And as Moses lifted up the serpent in the wilderness, even so, must the Son of man be lifted up" (John 3:14). Indeed, not everyone will respond to the gospel of Jesus Christ (John 6:44). Yet, the ministry of every believer is to point others to the truth that God saves us from the power and penalty of sin. Only the cleansing blood of Jesus can remove the venomous curse of Satan (Gen. 3), for which there is no natural cure (Heb. 9).

Too often, our culture and our personal religious preferences are interwoven into the simple message of the Bible. We want others to wear our logo and speak our lingo. We tend to value activity over relationship. But with hearts focused on Christ, philosophy and religion become immaterial. One hour in the presence of God will teach us more about Him than months of educational study. The words of Jesus, "If I be lifted," is the answer for a troubled soul. This verse of Scripture and others reveal the necessity of the Light in a dark world. He alone is the Door. He is the Bread of life and the Way to everlasting life in heaven. The Cross is the attraction of Christianity. Why? Because the death, burial, and resurrection of Christ are the most beautiful manifestations of love the world has ever known! Through Him, we are delivered from the guilt of past sin and its power over the present and future (John 10:28-30). He is the supremely all-sufficient One, the first and the last. Jesus Christ is indeed the image of Almighty God (Col. 1:16-17). The joy of the Bible is understanding and worshiping the Author. The request of many who gathered to celebrate the Jewish Festival of Passover was, "Sir, we would see Jesus" (John 12:20-36). Seeing Him, we are convicted of sin, for His love, grace, and power have no limitation.

We are told that standing behind the pulpit of the historic Church of the Open Door in downtown Los Angeles and looking out on the massive crowd gives the speaker a feeling of importance. But the sermon to be delivered comes into narrow focus when the minister looks down at a little plaque fixed to the pulpit with the words of John 12:21, "Sir, we would see Jesus." Our objective is not to win arguments about Jesus but to win people for Jesus. Opinions do not transform lives. Jesus does. The message of John the Baptist was, "Behold the Lamb of God" (John 1:29). When we focus on the Cross, the trappings of Christianity and religion grow dim. When we see Jesus in His beauty, things that once consumed our time and energy will give way to being in His presence. The whole story shifts when Jesus is the subject of our conversation. The wise men who traveled to Bethlehem saw a great light. The star was historical, and it was their privilege to see it. But it was not enough. They wanted to experience the One whom the light represented; the One who had come into the world to redeem all humanity. May we be inspired by more than intellectual curiosity or blessing. May we experience the presence of God made real by the precious blood of Jesus Christ! In Colossians 4:4, the apostle Paul asks people to pray that he proclaims the gospel of Christ in truth and with grace. Then he tells us to make the most of every opportunity to point people to Biblical truth. To the Corinthians, Paul came not with "excellency of speech or of wisdom" but with a resolve to preach "Jesus Christ, and him crucified" (1 Cor. 2:1-2). He made this message the central point and essence of all his knowledge. Why? Because he counted all things of no effect, save only the "excellency of the knowledge of Christ Jesus my Lord" (Phil. 3:8). Paul had no one else to promote, no doctrine to protect, no protocol to preserve.

It is the nature of humanity to be religious. But there is a vast difference between being religious and being a Christian in the true sense of the word. A Christian follows Christ. In Matthew 15: 18, Jesus tells of those who pay homage to God with their words, but their hearts are far from Him. In 2 Timothy 3:5, Paul warns of those who have the appearance of Christianity but deny God's power. To follow Christ is to have an inward love and devotion that bears outward fruits of righteousness (Gal. 5:22-23). Salvation is a matter of a heart that loves because it is loved, a soul whose treasure is Jesus Christ and him crucified. The entirety of the Gospel is the Person and the work of Christ. Salvation is the person of the Holy Spirit who enters and takes complete control. Salvation is God's grace. It is the gift of freedom from our sins that Jesus made possible by taking the punishment for our sins on the cross. In 1 John 1:9, the promise is, "If we confess our sins, he is faithful and just to forgive us our sins, and to cleanse us from all unrighteousness." This promise gives us freedom and hope for the future.

Jesus is the source of deliverance and salvation, for "there is none other name under heaven given among men, whereby we must be saved" (Acts 4:12). And as we become more like Christ, God works through us to share His love and grace with the world. Adrian Rogers says, "When you have said Jesus, you have said it all." People who encounter the risen Christ are transformed. Their outlook on life is altered forever. Through faith, they do not hesitate to face hardship, persecution, and even death. The power of Christ knows no boundary of time or space. Only the blood of Christ can free the soul of man from the bondage of sin and the wrath of God (Heb. 9:13-13, Eph. 1:7). Therefore, Jesus Christ must be the heart of our message to the world!

LET THE REDEEMED SAY SO

With blessing comes responsibility. And with great blessing comes great responsibility. As more of God's goodness is revealed to us, we should realize how greatly indebted we are to Him. The design of Psalm 107 is the repetition of the words, "Oh that men would praise the Lord for his goodness." The purpose of Psalm 107 is to praise Him for what He has done. By their sinful rebellion, the Israelites wandered in the wilderness, hungry and thirsty, with no city in which to dwell. Yet, when they humbly asked for the Lord's mercy, He led them to safety (v4-9). Those who sat in darkness and the shadow of death, having been cast down and punished for their sins, were delivered by the miraculous hand of God (v10-16). Those who were overcome by transgression and iniquity cried to the Lord, who saved them from their distress. The Bible says they were healed and delivered from destruction (v17-22). For those who encountered storms and tempests, whose souls were melted because of trouble, their sea was calmed, and they were brought into their desired haven (v23-32). The Lord prepared for His people rivers in the wilderness; water-springs from dry ground. He made possible the sowing of fields and the planting of vineyards. He blessed them and brought low their oppression, affliction, and sorrow (v33-42). In all of this, we see God's lovingkindness (v43). What a great song of salvation! We whom the Spirit leads are God's children (Rom. 8:14). We are the sheep of His pasture (Ps. 100:3). How can we who have been born again (John 3:1-7) "redeemed from the hand of the enemy" (v2) neglect to "praise the Lord for his goodness and his wonderful works?" He "satisfies the longing soul and fills the hungry soul with goodness" (v9), and His mercy endures forever. God's undying love for His people is celebrated in this psalm and many other Scripture verses.

Through the prophet Isaiah, God said we are created for His glory (Isa. 43:7). Depending on the context in which it is used, "glory" can be used in several ways. Primarily it is associated with ascribing splendor and majesty to God. When used as a verb, "glory" means to put confidence in and boast about or praise something. This word is also used to express importance, honor, and majesty. The first six verses of Psalm 19 read that all creation glorifies the Creator. There are no specific words, but the design has a voice of praise. And yet humanity is God's only creation for which Christ died. There is a beautiful yet humbling message here. Of all on earth, we who have been redeemed have the most occasion for praise. We are best qualified to appreciate the goodness of the Lord, for we have been reconciled to God through the precious blood of Jesus Christ (Col. 1:20). We who have cried unto the Lord in our trouble have been saved from the power and penalty of Satan. Jesus has satisfied our soul's longing (Isa. 29:8), and we have been delivered out of our distresses. Christ has made a way into that heavenly place, a city of Light where we will eternally dwell with Him. We will enter that desired haven beyond all storms or tempests; an eternal home. Let us declare His works with thanksgiving and praise. Let us lift His name on high in the congregation of the people, not merely in private, but in public (v32). Indeed, our God is worthy of our worship!

John Wesley was robbed as he was returning from a service one night. As the bandit was leaving, Wesley called out, "Stop! I have something more to give you." The surprised robber paused. "My friend," said Wesley, "you may live to regret this sort of life. If you ever do, here is something to remember: the blood of Jesus Christ cleanses us from all sin!" The thief hurried away, and Wesley prayed that his words would bear fruit. Years later, Wesley greeted people after a Sunday service when a stranger approached him. It surprised Wesley to learn that this visitor, now a Christian and a successful businessman, was the one who had robbed him years before! "I owe it all to you," said the transformed man. "Oh no, my friend," Wesley exclaimed, "not to me, but to the precious blood of Christ that cleanses us from all sin!"

The Bible says, "The effectual fervent prayer of a righteous man availeth much" (James 5:16). May the redeemed of the Lord forever tell the world about a Savior so glorious, a ransom so tremendous, and a deliverance so complete!

Children love a happy story. They always beg for more, whether it is a fictional tale or events from their parent's life. This love for the story does not die with age. Billions of dollars go into movie production so we can sit and watch a story unfold before our eyes. Celebrities are commended for revealing their courageous stories of personal successes, and previously unknown people rise to viral recognition by sharing their stories. The church is tasked with our orders regarding an even more incredible account. The inspired Word of God is complete, but the work He does in our lives continues. He is still redeeming and building His church in a thousand different ways. Therefore, we are told to proclaim the most remarkable story we can tell – the story of God's redemption! God broke our chains and led us into freedom. We are no longer slaves to sin and death. We are free to love, serve and share our hope (Rom. 6:18-22). We were delivered from our destruction and raised to new life in Christ (Col. 3:1-3).

Five-year-old Hannah told her mother one day, "Mama, I think God moved out of my heart." With curiosity and concern, her mom asked her daughter where she thought the Lord may have gone. Hannah replied, "I think He moved to my mouth cuz all I want to do is tell people about Jesus." Gratitude is the first part of our response to God's goodness. All that we have comes from Him – our life, health, family and friends, opportunities for success, and most of all, salvation. Why is it so hard to thank God with a grateful heart? It is because we often focus on what we do not have rather than on what we have. The goodness of the Lord should lead us to repentance (Rom. 2:4). God's mercy in dealing with humanity is not a sign of His indifference to sin. It is meant to inspire us to thankfulness, faith, and repentance. Psalm 107 ends with a simple directive: "Whoso is wise, and will observe these things, even they shall understand the lovingkindness of the Lord." What do the wise do? We find joy in telling of God's work in the world. We remind ourselves of His great blessings. And because our stories are not about the greatness of our change but the glory of the One who did the changing, we share them. We reflect on the goodness of God in our own Bible study and our conversations with each other. We speak of Him in the gathered assembly and private chat. We never grow weary of telling of the mercy and grace of God. We reveal how God saved us; and that He will save anyone who believes in Jesus Christ (Rom. 10:9).

Let the redeemed of the Lord say so! Where should the redeemed say it? Mark 16:15, "Go ye into all the world, and preach the gospel to every creature." When should it be said? Psalm 34:1 says, "I will bless the Lord at all times: his praise shall continually be in my mouth." Why should the redeemed say so? In Revelation 4:1, "Thou art worthy, O Lord, to receive glory, honor, and power." We "say so" because our Lord commanded us to do so (Matt. 28:19-20). We have a testimony to tell, and the world needs to hear what we say. Let us put our lamp where it belongs – on the lampstand (Matt. 5:15). Look for opportunities to "say so" to your brothers and sisters in Christ - and all who will hear. It was only seven weeks after the apostle Peter's tragic failure (Luke 22:54-62) and restoration (John 21:15-25) that the combination of his testimony and Scripture was used by the Holy Spirit to bring three thousand people into the Kingdom of God in one day (Acts 2). Forgiveness and redemption are from God!

Fritz Kreisler (1875-1962), the world-famous violinist, earned a fortune with his concerts and compositions, but he generously gave most of it away. So, when he discovered an exquisite violin on one of his trips, he could not buy it. Later, having raised enough money to meet the asking price, he returned to the seller, hoping to purchase the beautiful instrument. But to his great dismay, it had been sold to a collector. Kreisler went to the new owner's home and offered to buy the violin. The collector said it had become his prized possession and would not sell it. Keenly disappointed, Kreisler was about to leave when he had an idea. "Could I play the instrument once more before it is condemned to silence?" he asked. Permission was granted, and the great virtuoso filled the room with such heart-moving music that the collector's emotions were deeply stirred. "I have no right to keep that to myself," he exclaimed. "It is yours, Mr. Kreisler. Take it into the world, and let people hear it." The Gospel of Jesus Christ is 'music' to be heard. It is the message of salvation that must be shared with everyone everywhere. We cannot allow a philosophy of political correctness or the fear of ridicule to silence or tempt us to hide our convictions. Every benefit and bounty we enjoy is given to us by God (James 1:17). He frees us from sin. He gives us freedom of spirit. He heals our sickness and delivers us through His sacrifice. He calms our storms and brings us to a place of rest. He is never far from us, and our salvation experience is that which we must tell wherever we go. Jesus Christ is the heart of every blessing, the hope of every sorrow. I am so thankful that someone took the time and effort to declare God's message of redemption to me. And may I likewise proclaim the forgiveness of sins through Christ's death at Calvary (1 Cor. 15:1-4). This is the grace wherein we stand (Rom. 5:1-2). Therefore, let the redeemed of the Lord say so!

Live Beyond Condemnation

A most effective trick of Satan is to ascribe the guilt of past mistakes to a Christian trying to live an overcoming life. The devil would have you believe you are unforgivable and that you are not worth the death of Jesus Christ. The Bible is clear - Satan is a liar (John 8:44), he is the accuser of God's people, and he is defeated (Rev. 12:10). But sometimes, we feel trapped, alone, ashamed, and unworthy of perfect love. Though we are saved, reliving our past sins and failures is an easy thing to do. We tend to allow our failings to steal the center stage in our hearts by either reliving the guilt or trying to compensate for it through self-made confidence. Neither of these is the will of God. Sometimes, the pain comes to us at the most vulnerable times of life. These are the deepest wounds that leave ugly scars to remind us. Even when we say it no longer matters… even when we say it's okay… even when we do our best to move on with our lives, the past hurts.

Sometimes the pain from what we have done creeps up on us when we least expect it. Other times, it is just there in the back of our minds, taunting us, reminding us that we are no good deep down inside. Our past sins can leave lingering consequences that we deal with even years later. What would it look like for you to wholly give your past to God and trust His work in you, to reflect on His sanctifying work instead of your shortcomings? This can be done by acknowledging human frailty, repenting the sin, and leaving it at Calvary (Acts 3:19). God will do great things to the extent we allow Him to work in us. Nothing can lift our hearts like reading verses of Scripture like this one, "Brethren, I count not myself to have apprehended: but this one thing I do, forgetting those things which are behind, and reaching forth unto those things which are before, I press toward the mark for the prize of the high calling of God in Christ Jesus" (Phil. 3:13–14). Do not let your dreams for a future in Christ die because of your actions.

Guilt is the dread of the past, a pain in our hearts because we committed an offense or failed to do something right. It is a phantom pain similar to what people experience after a part of the body has been removed. For a born-again child of God, guilt is that which does not exist anymore continuing to scream for attention. Of all people, the Psalmist David had good reason for feeling guilty. Scholars believe David wrote Psalm 32 after he cried to God for forgiveness for his double sin of murder and adultery. David's guilt was immense. He says, "Mine iniquities are gone over mine head: as a heavy burden they are too heavy for me" (Ps. 38:4). But when David acknowledged his sin; when he confronted his guilt; when he confessed his guilt; then his release from guilt was sweet (Ps. 32).

Hurts and mistakes of the past can haunt us. We work overtime trying to prove to God that we are genuinely repentant, or we erect barriers against His loving grace. It's easy to stall in the wrong spot of regrettable memories, but do not park there. Our failures will never frustrate the purposes of God. With a heart of thankfulness for salvation, give your burdens to God — then move on. You are not the sum of your past mistakes. Satan wants us to live in the guilt and negativity of what was. If he can keep us looking back, we will make little progress in the future God has for us. Read the Bible for understanding and inspiration. Pray for wisdom. We cannot change the past, but we can change its meaning. What we have experienced can inspire us to move forward. Most of us remember Peter for denying Christ three times during the night of Jesus' trial (Matt. 26). But following his resurrection, Jesus took special care to assure Peter that he was forgiven (John 21). At Pentecost, the Holy Spirit filled the apostles. Peter was so overcome that he began to preach to the crowd (Acts 2). The Bible tells us that 3,000 people were converted that day. Our destiny is not found in the rearview mirror. Let's be grateful for the present and welcome a bright future with our Lord (Eph. 4:23–24). Jesus Christ specializes in new beginnings!

The apostle Paul was speaking to believers when he revealed a struggle that exists in mind, an inner conflict that rages in the hearts of Christians (Rom. 5–7). This is why he is saying to us, "There is therefore now no condemnation to them which are in Christ Jesus who walk not after the flesh but after the Spirit. For the law of the Spirit of life in Christ Jesus hath made me free from the law of sin and death" (Rom. 8:1–2). Why did Paul's audience — and why do we — need to hear this? Because before "now" we were all condemned. And, although today we "delight in the law of God after the inward man," we still war against the law of our minds (Rom. 7:22–23). It is the work of Satan to use the shame of our past to make us feel unworthy to approach the throne of God. And, though Jesus Christ took upon Himself the punishment for our sin at Calvary, too many Christians live with remorse, troubled by conscience. But when we release the regret of past failures to God, we can experience a fantastic victory in Christ. Get a vision that goes beyond anything you have experienced. Expect the goodness of the Lord based on the promises found in His Word. "Whosoever believes that Jesus is the Christ is born of God… for whatsoever is born of God overcomes the world: and this is the victory that overcomes the world, even our faith" (1 John 5).

A believer's triumph is living beyond condemnation. If the blood of Jesus Christ has cleansed you, you are redeemed and forever secure (Heb. 10:9–18). Do not try to compensate for your mistakes with self-made confidence. God wants your pain. But He also wants your pride. And when He has both, He will plan for you a wonderful future. Choose to trust in the power of His saving grace. Cast your burdens on Him (Psalm 55:22, Matt. 11:28–29) and travel light! The psalmist David was by no means a perfect man. His failures were as legendary as his accomplishments. He was a man who struggled with discouragement and depression. But he was a man of faith and wisdom who longed to be in God's presence (Psalm 63). He knew that God's grace and mercy were with us all the days of our lives (Psalm 23:6). Trust your faith, not your feelings. Measure your value through God's eyes, not your own. "For God sent not his Son into the world to condemn the world; but that the world through him might be saved. He that believeth on him is not condemned" (John 3:17–18). The hope of a born-again believer is anchored in God's proven, unchanging, perfect, and absolute forgiveness!

Printed in the United States
by Baker & Taylor Publisher Services